SOUTH EAST ENGLAND

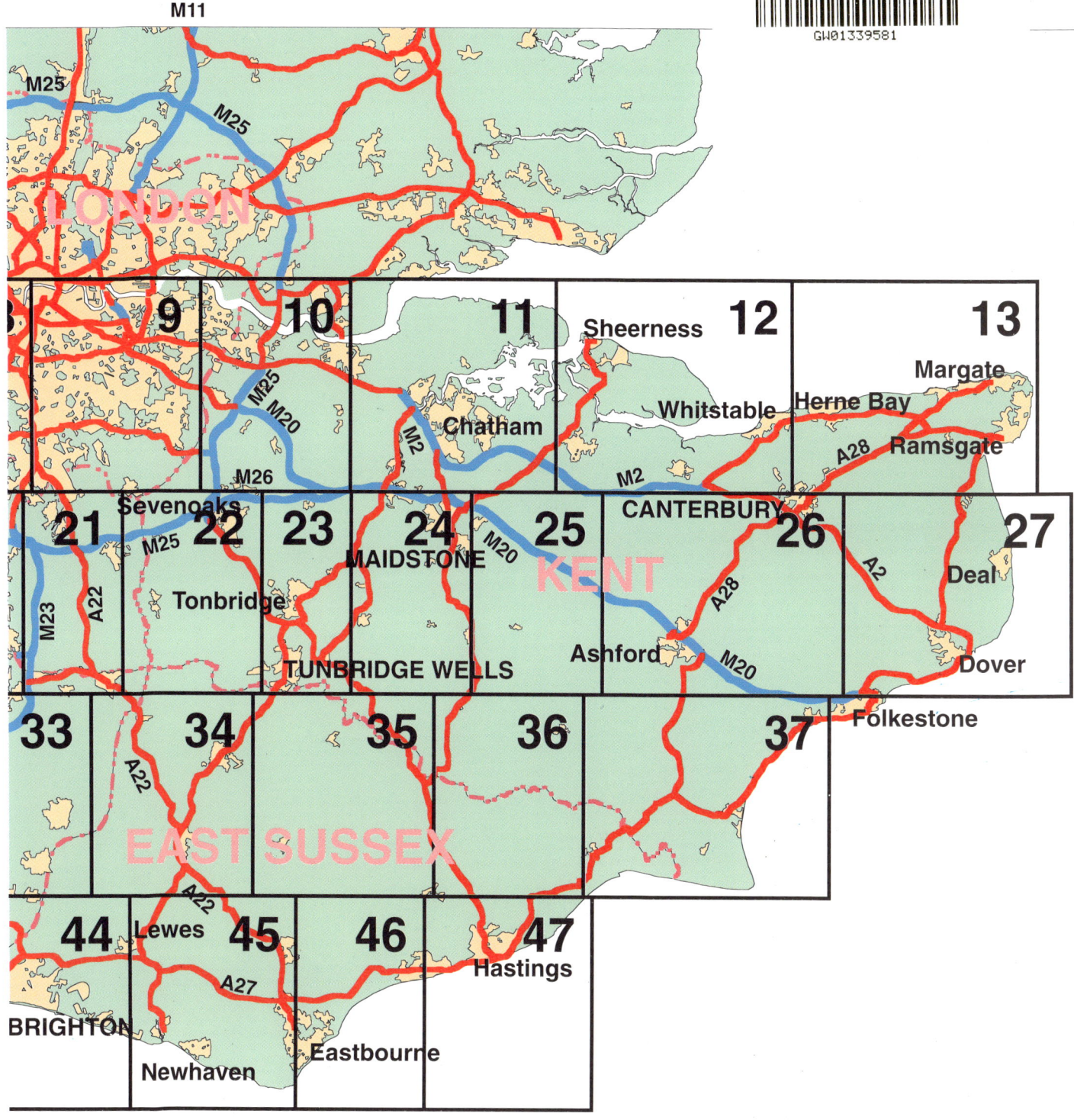

ROAD ATLAS FOR GARDENERS

© Beverly Cutress & Wimpey Knott 1997. All rights reserved.

Material in this book is copyright but may be used by a purchaser for his/her own reference. It may not be used as a basis for selling direct mail services to others, nor may copies of the whole or part be made for any purpose whatsoever by any form of copying process, including data processing systems, without the prior written consent and agreement of the copyright owners. The owners of the copyright have the exclusive right to make copies. No part of this book may be used for compiling another list, map or directory. Information may not be copied from this copyright work and sent out, for confirmation or correction.

Warning: the doing of an unauthorised act in relation to a copyright work may result in both a civil claim for damages and criminal prosecution.

The cartographic data used in this book were supplied by the Cartographic Department of The Automobile Association by means of datasets extracted from their database.

© The Automobile Association.   All Rights Reserved.

The AA makes no guarantee or warranty with regards to the accuracy of data supplied and accepts no liability for loss or damage incurred as a result of any reliance on the data.

SCALE 1 : 100,000

Published by
The Factory Shop Guide
in collaboration with Beverly Cutress & Wimpey Knott who have personally researched and compiled this atlas.
1 Rosebery Mews, Rosebery Road
London   SW2 4DQ
Phone: 0181 678 0593
Fax: 0181 674 1594

This atlas is based on an original idea by Paul Temple. Special thanks are due to Rolf Stricker for his vast technical expertise and to Sue Knott for her invaluable help with research and compilation.
Cover based on original design by Kate Bowen.

ISBN 0 948965 68 1

How this Atlas works

Each entry is clearly identified with its own unique black lozenge number which is shown on the map, in the text and in the index.

map page 38 → **38/4** ← entry number 4

South East England is an area crowded with places of interest for gardeners and garden-lovers. Our aim has been to produce clear and simple maps of this area so that you can easily and quickly find each place. At the same time we also wanted to make it easy to use the maps for touring.

The key to the success of the atlas is that each entry is on the same double page as the map and there is no need to turn the page. This limits the space for entries but where space allows we have included extra information that we and the owners think is important.

Where descriptions are included, we have tried to make them both factual and objective, however brief. We have not felt it right to discriminate, offer opinions or make any judgements which might be coloured by our personal preferences. If groups use particular phrases to describe their businesses we include these in quotation marks.

Opening hours

Opening dates and times have been quoted to us by the people concerned. However nurseries in particular can be a little flexible with their opening hours. In winter, if the ground is snow-covered or too wet to work, they may decide to close at lunch time, or even for a couple of days to take a well-earned break.

In spring and early summer they and garden and plant centres may stay open later in the evening.

Some plants and crafts people exhibit at national flower and garden shows and, of necessity, their nurseries and workshops may be closed at these times.

Summer opening usually starts either when the clocks go forward or at Easter. Winter closing for gardens and nurseries is usually at dusk, after the clocks have gone back.

We cannot recommend strongly enough that you should telephone first if you are travelling from a distance or making a special journey.

Access and facilities for disabled people and wheelchairs

Every place mentioned in this atlas accepts guide and hearing dogs. An increasing number of gardens and garden centres have reasonable or good facilities for disabled visitors. Some have wheelchairs to lend to visitors and a few large gardens have electric chairs: please phone in advance to find out if one is likely to be available.

Toilets and other facilities for disabled people are not often available at nurseries. Wherever we asked, we were told that help would be given gladly, either to lift wheelchairs over steps or to take plants to cars to show customers what was on sale.

Every one of the places featured here has been visited personally by the authors – a lengthy but enjoyable task – but there must be others we have missed. If so, we hope that they will forgive us and let us know so that we may include them in the next edition.

We have done our best to ensure that all information in this Road Atlas for Gardeners is correct. However, as we deal with thousands of details in both entries and maps, it is possible that errors have slipped in. Please let us know of any slip you notice. As every reasonable care has been taken in the preparation of this book, we can accept no responsibility for errors, omissions, or damage, however caused.

ALL ABOUT THIS ATLAS

This atlas is specially designed to show the way to over 800 places in South East England that are of interest to gardeners and garden-lovers and are open to the public.

- It is unique!
- It is comprehensive!
- It leads you directly to over 800 places.
- It complements all the garden guides, gardening books, handbooks, newsletters and tourist leaflets.
- It is designed as a valuable reference book.
- It is an easy-to-use atlas, to keep in your car.
- It will make it easy for you to
  – visit special places you have heard or read about;
  – plan a tour or a day out;
  – make the most of your holiday or any spare time in an unfamiliar place.

Specialist & General Nurseries, Garden and Plant Centres

These are grouped together because their names can be misleading. Most nurseries grow their own plants from seeds and cuttings or buy stock to grow-on, whereas most garden centres buy plants ready to sell (sometimes grown by their own wholesale nurseries). Perhaps some nurseries should be called garden centres and vice versa!

We have also found that some specialist nurseries hold a wide range of general stock and some general nurseries grow rare and unusual plants.

Some nurseries have international reputations and win prestigious medals. Others are small and supply their local community. All offer expert advice.

Small garden centres often carry a surprisingly wide range of popular stock on small sites. Medium sized garden centres are able to carry a much wider range of stock including gifts, books and bulky items such as garden furniture, paving and sheds. Large garden centres are becoming more like department stores with restaurants and a wide range of items unconnected with gardening.

If you are searching for particular plants, do phone first to see who has stock. We only have space to give a very brief listing of a few items each place sells – we might well have put 'etc' or 'lots more' at the end of each entry.

All the places mentioned in the atlas are ready to sell direct to the public. Somewhere in South East England you will find what you are searching for.

Water Garden Specialists

These are often on the same sites as garden centres, but are separate businesses. They usually sell the fish, plants, ponds, liners and equipment needed by beginners and experts alike. Some are famous and attract custom from all over Europe; others are small. But all are staffed by experts who are able to offer advice.

Artefact Suppliers

These are the people who specialise in making or stocking the hardware you need in your garden: wrought ironwork, garden furniture, pots, statuary, fountains, paving and walling. They include some fine English craftspeople, and many of the companies are well known exhibitors at national flower and garden shows. All those included in the atlas sell direct to the public.

Pick-Your-Own Farms (PYO)

These have been included on the assumption that gardeners like to buy fresh produce when they have insufficient time, or space in their gardens, to grow their own. Some farmers cultivate just one field of strawberries whereas others grow many varieties of crops. The fields are only open, of course, when the produce is in season but wet weather can cause their temporary closure. Some pick-your-own farms also have farm shops. These are generally open throughout the year and sell a range of other fruit and vegetables as well as their own produce. A few also sell locally produced and speciality foods for the gourmet.

Gardens

South East England has many of the finest gardens in the world. We have been able to include nearly 120 that you can visit either throughout the year or on a substantial number of days during their season.

Some are to be enjoyed for their historic or literary associations, their formality, informality or modernity. Others have unequalled collections of plants, shrubs or trees and yet others will provide spiritual refreshment and inspiration.

Some gardens hold special events such as plant fairs, flower festivals (*see page 51 for information about the 1998 European Gardens Festival*), concerts or firework displays. These events often involve additional charges and advance booking. Sometimes they call for changes in opening hours and occasionally the complete closure of the gardens for a day or two. Opening days and times can also vary between seasons so we suggest you phone the gardens first if you are travelling far.

Where entry charges are shown, they apply only to the gardens and not to any houses. Where an entry charge is not quoted, you should allow between £2 and £5 per adult.

We show the way to National Trust (NT) gardens. Their opening times and charges can be both complicated and variable! We give their telephone numbers and full details can be found in the members' handbook or in leaflets.

Many people open their private gardens under the auspices of The National Gardens Scheme Charitable Trust. Most of these gardens are open to the public on only a few specific dates and are therefore not included in this atlas.

Please use this atlas to explore, and make your own interesting and worthwhile discoveries.

BERKSHIRE

MAP 1

MAP 0

SPECIALIST & GENERAL NURSERIES, GARDEN AND PLANT CENTRES

1/1 ARBORTECTURE AT GARDEN ART
Barrs Yard
1 Bath Road
Hungerford
Berkshire
RG17 0HE
01488 681881

Plant centre in garden setting. Topiary, specimen trees, shrubs and unusual architectural perennials. Search service.
Open: All year except Xmas to New Year; 7 days a week, Mon–Sat 9–6 (often later in summer), Sunday 10–4.
Wheelchairs: Reasonable access.
Toilets: No.
Dogs: No.   **Credit cards:** No.

1/2 COUNTRY GARDENS HUNGERFORD
44 Bath Road
Hungerford   RG17 0HE
01488 682916

Country Gardens

'Good value garden centre with very wide plant selection. Free local delivery. Conservatories. Coffee shop.'
Open: All year; Mon–Sat 9–6, Sunday, 10.30–4.30. Extended spring hours – phone for information.
Wheelchairs: Easy access.
Toilets: Yes.
Dogs: On lead.   **Credit cards:** Yes.

1/3 FOXGROVE PLANTS

1/4 YEW TREE FARM GARDEN CENTRE

1/5 PENWOOD NURSERIES

SPECIALIST & GENERAL NURSERIES, GARDEN AND PLANT CENTRES

0/1 KENNEDYS GARDEN CENTRE
Cedar Cottage, Crown Lane
Farnham Royal, Slough
Berkshire   SL2 3SG
01753 645627

Garden centre with a wide range of gardening products. Giftware, pet shop, fencing and aquatics. Café.
Open: All year except Xmas/Boxing Days; 7 days a week, Mon–Sat 9–5.30 (winter), 9–6.30 (summer), Sunday 10.30–4.30.
Wheelchairs: Easy access.
Toilets: Yes.
Dogs: Guide dogs only.
Credit cards: Yes.

NURSERY AND GARDEN

1/6 HOLLINGTON HERB GARDEN

The Walled
Garden
Woolton Hill
Newbury
Berkshire
RG20 9XT
01635 253908

The old walled garden at Hollington makes an ideal setting for this famous **herb garden** *and nursery.*
Open: March–Sept; Mon–Sat, 10–5.30, Sunday & Bank Holidays 11–5. Phone for hours in winter.
Costs: Garden £1, nursery free.
Wheelchairs: Grass & gravel but flat.
Toilets: Yes.
Dogs: No.   **Credit cards:** Yes.

0/2 HAYDEN NURSERIES
The Walled Garden
Culham Court, Aston
01491 410709
Mature shrubs and trees.

0/3 MOOR GROWERS
North Town Moor
Maidenhead, Berkshire
SL6 7JR   01628 34275
Bedding, plants and baskets.

PICK-YOUR-OWN FARM

0/4 LOWER MOUNT FARM

PICK-YOUR-OWN FARMS

1/7 HIGHCLOSE PYO & FARM SHOP
Bath Road, Hungerford
Berkshire   RG17 0SP
PYO: 01488 686211

Pick-your-own soft fruit and vegetables. Farm shop selling quality local produce.
Open: All year except 25 Dec–8 Jan; April–Oct 9–7.30, Nov–March 10–4.
Wheelchairs: Easy access.
Toilets: Yes.
Dogs: No.   **Credit cards:** Yes.

1/8 HAMSTEAD GROWERS
Hamstead Marshall, Newbury
RG20 0JG   01635 254091
PYO, bedding and farm shop.

GARDEN

1/9 HIGHCLERE CASTLE

0

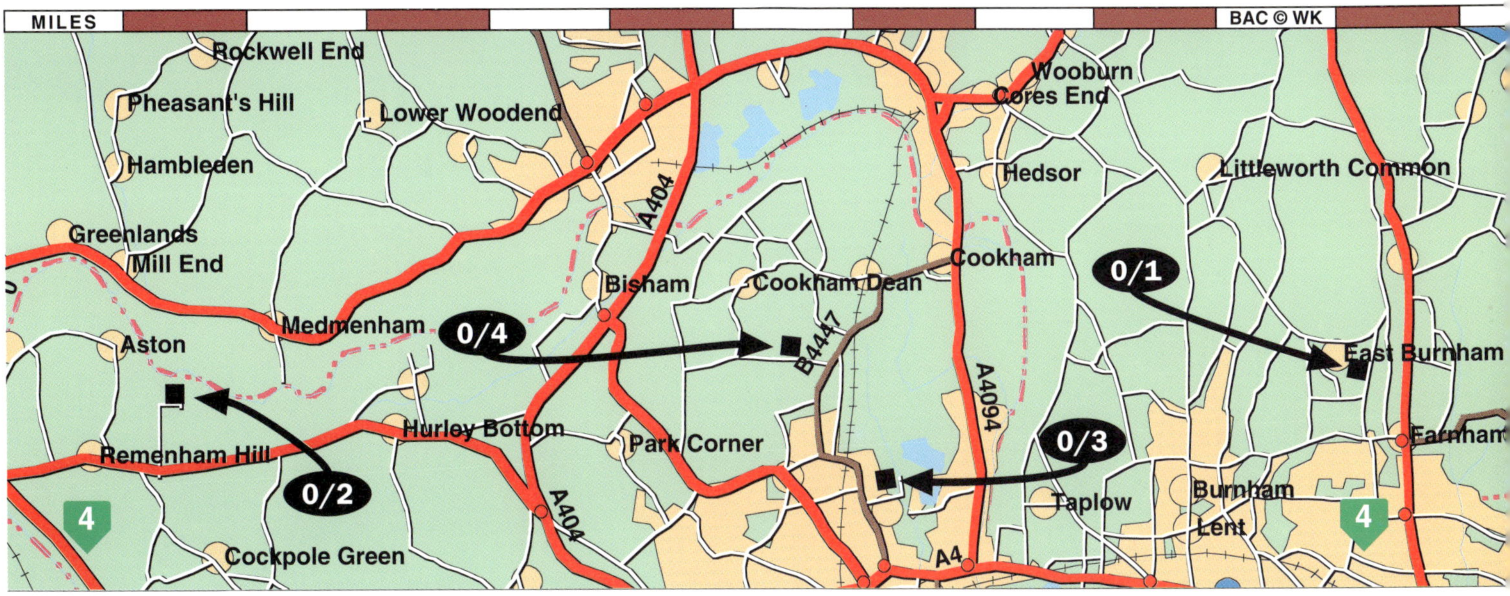

MILES
BAC © WK
Rockwell End
Pheasant's Hill
Lower Woodend
Hambleden
Greenlands
Mill End
Aston
Medmenham
Remenham Hill
Hurley Bottom
Cockpole Green
Bisham
Cookham Dean
Park Corner
A404
B4447
Cookham
Wooburn
Cores End
Hedsor
A4094
Taplow
A4
Littleworth Common
East Burnham
Farnham
Burnham
Lent
0/1
0/2
0/3
0/4
4
4

1

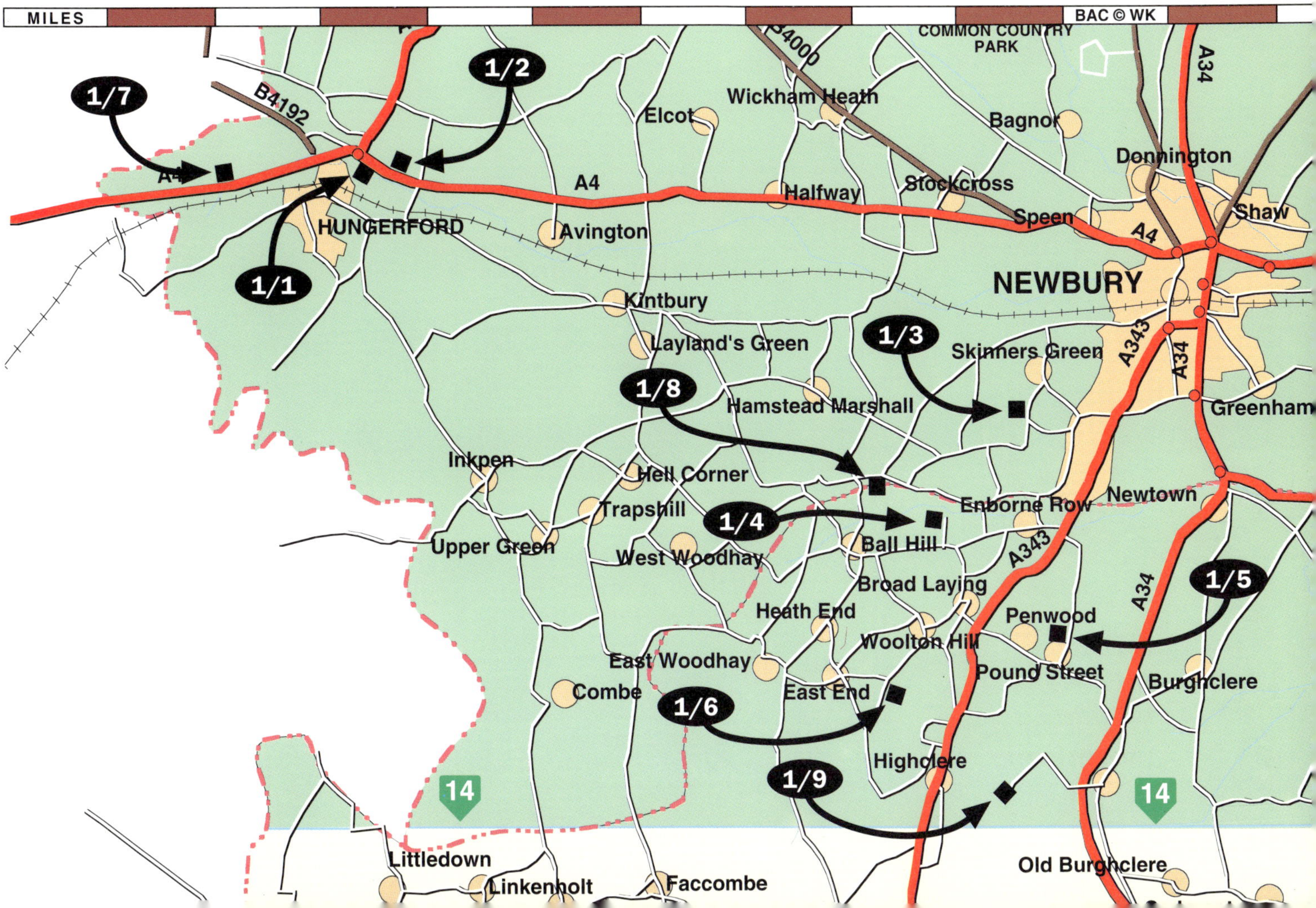

MILES
BAC © WK
COMMON COUNTRY PARK
1/1
1/2
1/3
1/4
1/5
1/6
1/7
1/8
1/9
B4192
A4
HUNGERFORD
Elcot
B4000
Wickham Heath
Bagnor
Donnington
Shaw
Halfway
Stockcross
Speen
A4
Avington
NEWBURY
Kintbury
Layland's Green
Skinners Green
A343
A34
Hamstead Marshall
Greenham
Inkpen
Hell Corner
Trapshill
Upper Green
West Woodhay
Ball Hill
Enborne Row
Newtown
Broad Laying
Heath End
Penwood
Woolton Hill
Pound Street
Burghclere
East Woodhay
Combe
East End
Highclere
Littledown
Linkenholt
Faccombe
Old Burghclere
14
14

BERKSHIRE

SPECIALIST & GENERAL NURSERIES, GARDEN & PLANT CENTRES

2/1 WOODSIDE FARM NURSERY
Priors Court Road, Hermitage
RG18 9TG   01635 201561
Growers of a wide range of plants.

2/2 HILLIER GARDEN CENTRE
Priors Court Road, Hermitage
RG16 9TG   01635 200442
'The heart of good gardening.'

WATER GARDEN SPECIALIST

2/3 AQUASCAPE
Hillier Garden Centre
Priors Court Road
Hermitage
Berkshire
RG16 9TG
01635 202300

Quality tropical coldwater fish and aquatic dry goods. Highly recommended by 'Practical Fishkeeping' magazine.
Open: All year except Xmas & Boxing Days; 7 days a week, 9.30–5.30.
Wheelchairs: Good access; disabled WC.
Toilets: Yes.
Dogs: Yes.   **Credit cards:** Yes.

NURSERIES & PLANT CENTRES

2/4 COUNTRY GARDENS THATCHAM
Garden Centre Roundabout, Bath Road
RG18 3AN   01635 871760

Country Gardens

'Good value garden centre with very wide plant selection. Free local delivery. Garden buildings, paving. Coffee shop.'
Open: All year; Mon–Sat 9–6, Sunday 10.30–4.30. Extended spring hours – phone for information.
Wheelchairs: Easy access.
Toilets: Yes.
Dogs: On lead.   **Credit cards:** Yes.

2/5 BOWDENSIDE FARM NURSERIES

2/6 GLENVALE NURSERIES
Hungerford Lane
Bradfield South End
Reading, Berkshire   RG7 6JH
0118 974 4006

Specialist growers of large zonal and ivy leaved **geraniums.** *Herbaceous plants, shrubs, fruit and ornamental trees. Florist.*
Open: 7 days a week; summer: Mon–Sat 9–5.30, Sunday 10–5; winter: Mon–Sat 9–5, Sunday 10–4.
Wheelchairs: Paved, ramps & gravel.
Toilets: Yes.
Dogs: On lead.   **Credit cards:** Yes.

2/7 WHITE TOWER NURSERY
Aldermaston Village
Reading, Berkshire RG7 4LD
0118 971 2123

Family nursery growing herbaceous, tender & hardy plants, shrubs, winter & summer baskets. **Bonsai,** *up to 2.5m. Floral work.*
Open: All year except Xmas & Boxing Days; 7 days a week, 9–6 or dusk if earlier. (May close for occasional exhibitions.)
Wheelchairs: Difficult – gravel.
Toilets: No.
Dogs: On lead.   **Credit cards:** Yes.

2/8 LAKESIDE GARDEN CENTRE

2/9 COTTISMORE GARDEN CENTRE

Newbury Road, Kingsclere
Newbury, Berkshire
RG20 4SY   01635 297979

Home grown plants, shrubs & trees. Paving, fencing & landscaping materials. Water & 'pallet' garden displays. Gifts. Tea shop.
Open: All year except Xmas & Boxing Days; 7 days a week, weekdays 9–5.30, Sunday 10.30–4.30.
Wheelchairs: Easy access.
Toilets: Ask if desperate.
Dogs: On lead.   **Credit cards:** Yes.

PICK-YOUR-OWN FARM

2/10 BUCKHOLDHILL FARM
Pangbourne, Reading
Berkshire   RG8 8QE
0118 974 4221

PYO soft fruit & vegetables. Farm shop with fresh fruit & vegetables, etc. Picked fruit orders taken & deliveries made. (Farm animals on view.)
Open: June–August, 7 days a week, 9–6.
Wheelchairs: Level ground, no steps.
Toilets: Ask if desperate.
Dogs: On lead.   **Credit cards:** No.

GARDENS

2/11 WYLD COURT RAINFOREST

Hamstead
Norreys
Newbury
Berkshire
RG18 0TN
01635 200221

A tropical rainforest created under glass with many rare plants and wildlife. Three different sub-climates. Plant sales.
Open: All year except Xmas & Boxing Days; 7 days a week, Mar–Oct 10–5.30, Nov–Mar 10–4.30.
Costs: £3.50, children £2, concessions £3.
Toilets: Yes.
Dogs: No.   **Credit cards:** Yes.

2/12 BASILDON PARK (NT)
0118 984 3040
Small formal garden; parkland.

Wyld Court Rainforest

2

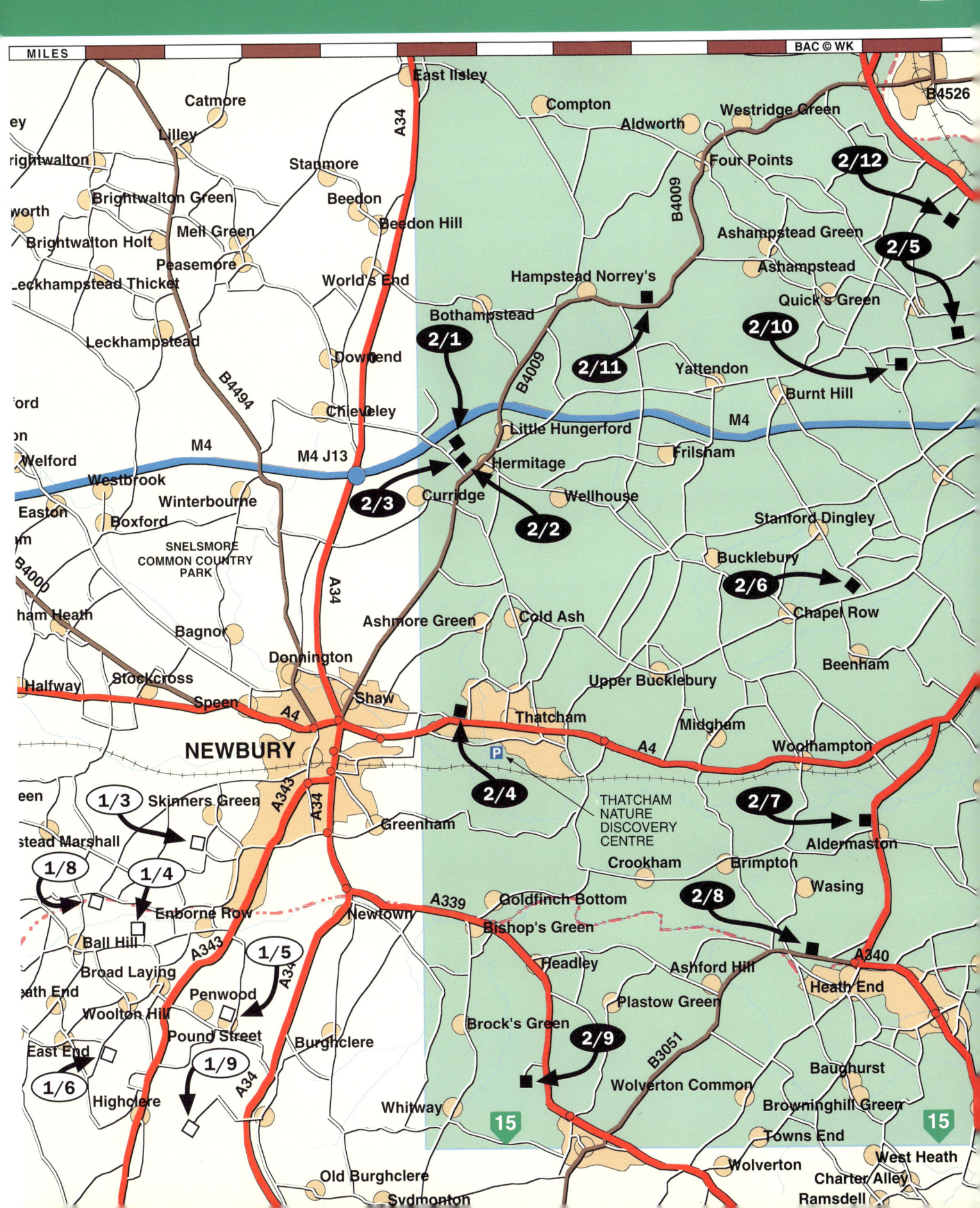

BERKSHIRE

SPECIALIST & GENERAL NURSERIES, GARDEN AND PLANT CENTRES

3/1 ENGLEFIELD GARDEN CENTRE
The Street, Englefield
Theale, Berkshire   RG7 5ES
0118 930 4898
*Alpines, herbs, **hanging baskets**, shrubs, bedding, cut flowers, indoor plants. Mostly own-grown in a delightful country setting.*
Open: Open all year; 6 days a week, 9–5 (CLOSED SUNDAY).
Wheelchairs: Good access.
Toilets: Yes.
Dogs: Yes.   **Credit cards:** Yes.

3/2 CHANDLERS FARM NURSERY

3/3 RURAL CRAFTS

3/4 D & S NURSERY & GARDEN CENTRE
Reading Road, Winnersh
Wokingham, Berkshire
RG11 5HE   0118 977 2141
Grower of large selection of bedding, shrubs and unusual patio, conservatory and basket plants. Terracotta, thai pottery, statuary.
Open: All year except 25 Dec–1 Jan; Mon–Sat 8.30–5.30, Sun 8.30–5.
Wheelchairs: Easy level access.
Toilets: Yes.
Dogs: On lead.   **Credit cards:** Yes.

3/5 GROVELANDS GARDEN CENTRE & FARM SHOP
166 Hyde End Road
Shinfield, Reading, Berkshire
RG2 9ER   0118 988 4822
Retail nursery specialising in indoor & outdoor plants. Aquatic centre & florist. Home cooked food in the farm shop.
Open: All year except Xmas & Boxing Days, Easter Sunday; Mon–Sat 9–5.30, Sunday 10.45–4.45.
Wheelchairs: Available on loan.
Toilets: Yes.
Dogs: On lead.   **Credit cards:** Yes.

3/6 LAURELS PLANT CENTRE
29 Ryeish Green
Three Mile Cross
Reading
RG7 1EP   0118 988 3792
*A family nursery growing **bedding** and patio plants, geraniums, fuchsias, planted tubs, hanging baskets, trees and shrubs.*
Open: 1 March–30 Apr & 12 Sept–24 Dec: 4 days a week, Fri, Sat, Sun & Mon, 9–6 or dusk if earlier; 1 May–20 July: 7 days a week, 9–6.
Wheelchairs: Reasonable access.
Toilets: Yes.
Dogs: On lead.   **Credit cards:** No.

3/7 BROOKSIDE NURSERY
Church Road, Swallowfield
Reading, Berkshire   RG7 1TH
0118 988 4122
*Over 1000 varieties of **fuchsias**, hanging baskets and patio plants; 250 varieties of geraniums.*
Open: March–August: 7 days a week, Mon–Sat 9–5, Sunday 10–4. (CLOSED SEPT–FEB).
Wheelchairs: Reasonable access.
Toilets: Yes.
Dogs: No.   **Credit cards:** No.

3/8 PUDDING LANE NURSERY
Reading Road, Arborfield
Reading, Berkshire   RG2 9HP
0118 976 1048
A family nursery in a landscaped garden, growing a wide range of shrubs, conifers, trees, heathers, perennials & bedding plants.
Open: All year except 25 Dec for two weeks; 7 days a week, Mon–Sat 9–5.30, Sunday 10–5.
Wheelchairs: Reasonable access.
Toilets: No.
Dogs: On lead.   **Credit cards:** Yes.

3/9 HENRY STREET GARDEN CENTRE

3/10 GREENACRES NURSERY

3/11 WHITEWATER NURSERY

WATER GARDEN SPECIALISTS

3/12 WORLD OF WATER
Hyde End Road, Shinfield
Reading   RG2 9ER
0118 988 5492
Water garden specialist.

PICK-YOUR-OWN FARM

3/13 MORTIMER HILL FRUIT FARM
The Street, Mortimer
Reading, Berkshire   RG7 3PG
0118 933 3157 (PYO message)
Full range of soft fruits & some vegetables, incl. broad and runner beans. Picnic and play areas. Refreshments. Plant centre.
Open: May–Oct: 7 days a week at strawberry time, otherwise 4 days a week (phone for days), 10–5.
Wheelchairs: Yes.
Toilets: Yes.
Dogs: No.   **Credit cards:** No.

GARDENS

3/14 BEALE PARK

3/15 ENGLEFIELD HOUSE GARDEN
Theale, Reading, Berkshire
RG7 5EN   0118 930 2221
Hillside, woodland, water and formal garden of historic house. Wide variety of trees, shrubs and herbaceous plants. Children's garden.
Open: April–July; 4 days a week – Mon–Thur, 10–6. Remainder of year MONDAY ONLY.
Costs: £2, children free.
Wheelchairs: Good access.
Toilets: Ask if desperate.
Dogs: No.   **Credit cards:** No.

3/16 STRATFIELD SAYE HOUSE

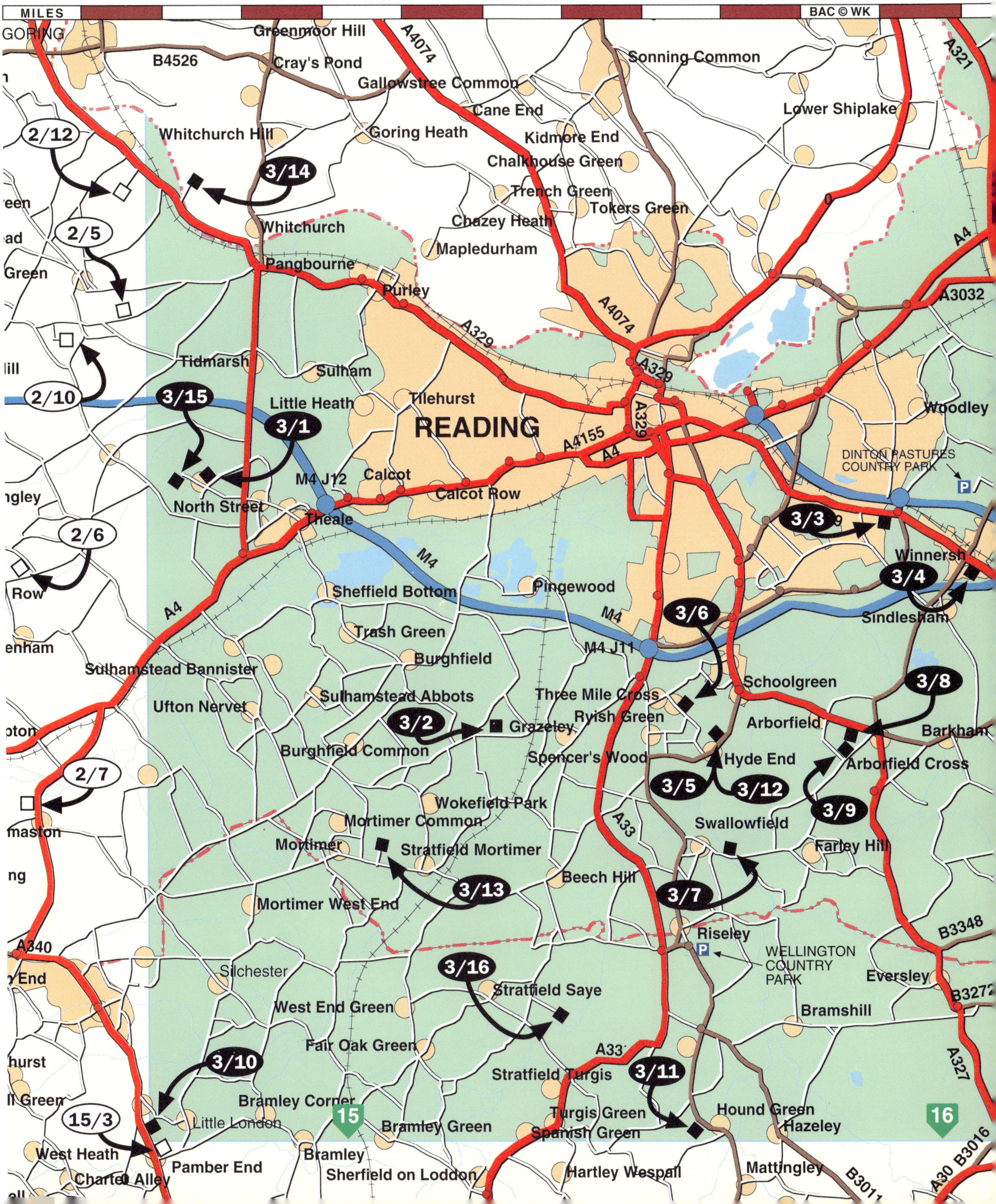
MILES
BAC © WK
GORING
Greenmoor Hill
B4526
Cray's Pond
A4074
Gallowstree Common
Sonning Common
A321
Cane End
Lower Shiplake
Goring Heath
Kidmore End
Whitchurch Hill
Chalkhouse Green
2/12
3/14
Trench Green
Tokers Green
Chazey Heath
2/5
Whitchurch
Mapledurham
A4
Pangbourne
Purley
A4074
A3032
A329
2/10
Tidmarsh
Sulham
A329
3/15
Little Heath
Tilehurst
Woodley
READING
A329
3/1
A4155
A4
DINTON PASTURES COUNTRY PARK
M4 J12
Calcot
Calcot Row
North Street
Theale
3/3
2/6
M4
Winnersh
Row
3/4
Sheffield Bottom
Pingewood
A4
M4
3/6
Sindlesham
Trash Green
M4 J11
Burghfield
Sulhamstead Bannister
Schoolgreen
3/8
Sulhamstead Abbots
Three Mile Cross
Ufton Nervet
Ryish Green
Arborfield
3/2
Grazeley
Barkham
Burghfield Common
Spencer's Wood
Hyde End
Arborfield Cross
2/7
3/5
3/12
3/9
Wokefield Park
A33
Swallowfield
Mortimer Common
Mortimer
Stratfield Mortimer
Farley Hill
Beech Hill
3/13
3/7
Mortimer West End
B3348
Riseley
A340
WELLINGTON COUNTRY PARK
Silchester
Eversley
3/16
Stratfield Saye
West End Green
Bramshill
Fair Oak Green
A33
A327
3/10
Stratfield Turgis
3/11
Bramley Corner
15/3
Little London
15
Turgis Green
Hound Green
16
Bramley Green
Spanish Green
Hazeley
West Heath
Bramley
Pamber End
Charter Alley
Sherfield on Loddon
Hartley Wespall
Mattingley
B3011
A30 B3016

BERKSHIRE

SPECIALIST & GENERAL NURSERIES, GARDEN AND PLANT CENTRES

4/1 KENNEDYS GARDEN CENTRE
Floral Mile, Hare Hatch
Twyford, Reading, Berkshire
RG10 9SW   0118 940 3933
Large centre, vast range of plants & garden products. Sheds, conservatories, greenhouses, stoneware, pet and farm shops, landscaping.
Open: All year but Xmas/Boxing Days; 7 days a week, Mon–Sat 9-5.30 (winter), 9–6.30 (summer), Sun 10.30–4.30.
Wheelchairs: Easy access.
Toilets: Yes. **Dogs:** Guide dogs only.
Credit cards: Yes.

4/2 PRIMROSE NURSERY

4/3 MJS GARDEN CENTRE

WATER GARDEN SPECIALISTS

4/4 D.H. WATER GARDENS
MJS Garden Centre
Wildmoor Lane, Sherfield-on-Loddon   01256 882019
Everything for the water garden.

4/5 MOSS END WATER GARDENS
Moss End Garden Centre,
Warfield   01344 300520
Everything for the water garden.

NURSERIES AND CENTRES

4/6 H.W. HYDE & SON
The Nursery, New Road
Ruscombe, Berkshire
RG10 9LN   0118 934 0011
Working nursery, est.1926. Good selection incl. unusual bedding, fuchsias (500+ varieties). Cut flowers, floristry, plants. Xmas bowls.
Open: All year: 6 days a week (CLOSED SUNDAY & BANK HOLS), 9–12.30 & 1.30–4.30.
Wheelchairs: No, but help available.
Toilets: No.
Dogs: No.   **Credit cards:** No.

4/7 BARN FARM NURSERIES

4/8 WYEVALE GARDEN CENTRE

4/9 RYEHURST COTTAGE GARDEN NURSERY

4/10 MOSS END GARDEN CENTRE

4/11 OAKTREE NURSERIES
Brock Hill, Bracknell Road
Warfield, Berkshire
RG42 6JX   01344 890667
A family-run nursery growing almost a million plants a year. Conifers, shrubs, trees, all bedding and basket plants. Compost and sundries.
Open: All year except Xmas & Boxing Days; 7 days a week, 8–5.
Wheelchairs: Mostly good access.
Toilets: Yes.
Dogs: On lead.   **Credit cards:** Yes.

4/12 SQUIRE'S GARDEN CENTRE

4/13 COUNTRY GARDENS WINDSOR
Dedworth Road
Windsor SL4 4LH
01753 841791
'Good value garden centre with very wide plant selection. Free local delivery. Garden buildings. Coffee shop.'
Open: All year; Mon–Sat 9–6, Sunday 10.30–4.30. Extended spring hours – phone for information.
Wheelchairs: Easy access.
Toilets: Yes.
Dogs: On lead.   **Credit cards:** Yes.

4/14 BOYER'S GARDEN SUPPLIES

4/15 NONSUCH NURSERIES
Church Road, Winkfield
Berkshire   SL4 4SF
01344 883213
*Growers of **fuchsias**, shrubs, bedding plants, hanging baskets, pot plants. October–Xmas: cut chrysanthemums. Garden sundries.*
Open: All year except Xmas, Boxing Days & Bank Holidays; 7 days a week, 8–6 or dusk if earlier.
Wheelchairs: Reasonable access.
Toilets: Yes.
Dogs: Yes.   **Credit cards:** No.

4/16 WOKINGHAM GARDEN CENTRE

4/17 WYEVALE GARDEN CENTRE

4/18 LINDUM NURSERIES

4/19 SOUTHVIEW NURSERIES

4/20 PETER TRENEAR NURSERIES
Chequers Lane, Eversley Cross
Hook RG27 0NX   0118 973 2300
Trees for bonsai and garden.

4/21 NOTCUTTS GARDEN CENTRE
Waterers Nurseries, London Road
Bagshot GU19 5DG   01276 472288
'For all that's best in gardening.'

4/22 COPPED HALL COTTAGE GARDENS

4/23 LONGACRES NURSERY

4/24 COUNTRY GARDENS WINDLESHAM
London Road
Windlesham   GU20 6LL
01344 21411
'Good value garden centre with very wide plant selection. Free local delivery. Garden buildings. Coffee shop.'
Open: All year; Mon–Sat 9–6, Sunday 10.30–4.30. Extended spring hours – phone for information.
Wheelchairs: Easy access.
Toilets: Yes.
Dogs: On lead.   **Credit cards:** Yes.

4/25 HILLIER GARDEN CENTRE
London Road, Windlesham
GU20 6LN   01344 23166
'The heart of good gardening.'

4/26 SUNNINGDALE WATER GARDEN
at Hillier Garden Centre, London Road, Windlesham 01344 25599
Fish, filtration and fountains.

PICK-YOUR-OWN FARMS

4/27 HOW LANE FARM

4/28 GRAYS PYO FARM

4/29 HEATHLANDS FARM
Heathlands Road, Wokingham
RG40 3BG   0118 978 2777
All soft fruit and vegetables.

NURSERIES AND CENTRES

4/30 HARE HATCH

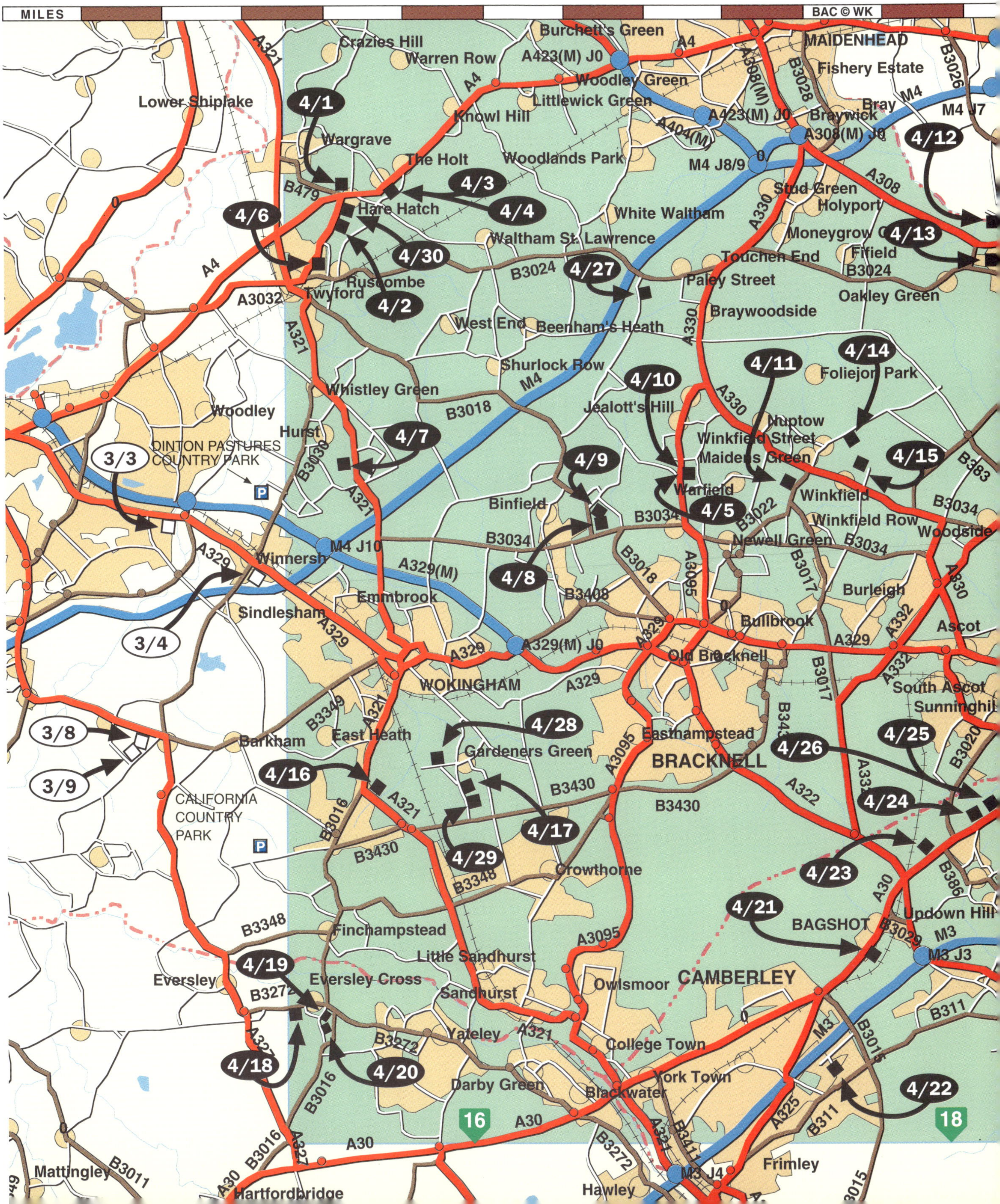
MILES
BAC © WK
Burchett's Green
A4
MAIDENHEAD
Crazies Hill
Warren Row
A423(M) J0
A308(M)
B3028
B3026
Fishery Estate
Woodley Green
A4
Lower Shiplake
A321
Littlewick Green
Bray
M4
M4 J7
4/1
Knowl Hill
A423(M) J0
Braywick
A404(M)
A308(M) J0
4/12
Wargrave
M4 J8/9
The Holt
Woodlands Park
0
B479
4/3
A308
Stud Green
Holyport
4/4
Hare Hatch
White Waltham
A330
4/6
Moneygrow G
4/13
4/30
Waltham St. Lawrence
Touchen End
Fifield
A4
B3024
4/27
B3024
Ruscombe
Paley Street
Oakley Green
A3032
Twyford
4/2
A330
Braywoodside
West End
Beenham's Heath
A321
4/14
4/11
Shurlock Row
Foliejon Park
M4
4/10
Whistley Green
A330
B3018
Jealott's Hill
Nuptow
Woodley
Winkfield Street
Hurst
4/7
Maidens Green
DINTON PASTURES
COUNTRY PARK
3/3
B3030
4/9
4/15
B383
Warfield
Winkfield
A321
Binfield
4/5
B3022
B3034
B3034
Winkfield Row
Woodside
M4 J10
B3034
Winnersh
A329
B3018
Newell Green
B3034
A329(M)
4/8
A3095
B3017
A330
Burleigh
Emmbrook
B3408
Sindlesham
0
Bullbrook
A332
Ascot
3/4
A329
A329(M) J0
A329
A329
Old Bracknell
A329
B3017
A332
WOKINGHAM
A329
South Ascot
Sunninghill
B3349
B343
A321
4/28
Easthampstead
4/25
3/8
Barkham
East Heath
4/26
B3020
Gardeners Green
A3095
BRACKNELL
A33
4/16
A322
4/24
3/9
B3430
CALIFORNIA
COUNTRY
PARK
A321
B3430
4/17
B3016
B3430
4/29
4/23
B3386
B3348
Crowthorne
A30
4/21
Updown Hill
B3348
BAGSHOT
B3029
M3
Finchampstead
A3095
M3 J3
Little Sandhurst
4/19
Eversley
Eversley Cross
Owlsmoor
CAMBERLEY
B3272
Sandhurst
B311
0
M3
B3015
B3272
Yateley
A321
College Town
A327
4/18
4/20
B3016
York Town
Darby Green
Blackwater
A325
4/22
16
A30
B3011
A321
18
B311
A30
B3272
Frimley
B3016
A327
Mattingley
B3011
A30
M3 J4
Hawley
Hartfordbridge
3015

BERKSHIRE, MIDDLESEX & SURREY

SPECIALIST & GENERAL NURSERIES, GARDEN AND PLANT CENTRES

5/1 BERKSHIRE GARDEN CENTRE

5/2 VERMEULEN'S GARDEN CENTRE
Horton Road, Stanwell Moor
Staines, Middlesex
TW19 6AE   01784 451737
Large garden centre with a wide selection of plants, rocks, fencing and aquatics. Coffee shop and craft centre.
Open: All year except Christmas and Boxing Days; 7 days a week, Mon–Sat 8.30–5.30, Sunday 9.30–5.30.
Wheelchairs: Easy access with wide pathways. **Toilets:** Yes.
Dogs: On lead. **Credit cards:** Yes.

5/3 COUNTRY GARDENS STAINES
42 Wraysbury Road
Wraysbury, Staines
TW19 6HA   01784 482146
Country Gardens
Good value garden centre with very wide plant selection. Free local delivery. Terracotta pots, compost, bulbs, furniture.'
Open: All year; Mon–Sat 9–6, Sunday 10.30–4.30. Extended spring hours – phone for information.
Wheelchairs: Easy access.
Toilets: Yes.
Dogs: On lead. **Credit cards:** Yes.

5/4 EGHAM GARDEN CENTRE
Vicarage Road, Egham
TW20 8NT   01784 433388
Expert advice. **Landscaping***.*

5/5 MAYFLOWER NURSERIES

5/6 NOTCUTTS GARDEN CENTRE
Staines Road, Laleham
TW18 2SF   01784 460832
'For all that's best in gardening.'

5/7 PANTILES NURSERIES

5/8 SQUIRE'S GARDEN CENTRE

5/9 THE OTTER NURSERY

5/10 BOURNE VALLEY GARDEN CENTRE

5/11 NURSERY COURT GARDENS

5/12 THE PLANT CENTRE
Mark Straver & Christopher Potts, Bagshot Road
Chobham, Woking, Surrey
GU24 8SJ   01276 855408
*An extensive range of plants, **shrubs** and all related gardening sundries. Expert advice always available.*
Open: All year except Xmas, Boxing & New Year's Days; 7 days a week, 8.30–6 (or till dusk in winter).
Wheelchairs: Good paved access.
Toilets: Yes.
Dogs: On lead. **Credit cards:** Yes.

5/13 LINCLUDEN NURSERY
Bisley Green, Bisley, Woking
Surrey   GU24 9EN
01483 797005
*Dwarf, slow-growing & unusual conifers. Large selection of **shrubs**, climbers etc. Chelsea Flower Show exhibitor.*
Open: All year except 20–30 May, 12–26 June, 22 Dec–5 Jan; 6 days a week, Mon–Sat 9.30–4.30. Open Sunday & Bank Holidays from Mar–Oct, 10–3.
Toilets: Yes.
Dogs: No. **Credit cards:** Yes.

5/14 BOTANY BARNS
Barrs Lane, Knap Hill
Woking   GU21 2JW
01483 481212
Plant orientated centre.

5/15 SQUIRE'S GARDEN CENTRE

5/16 CHOBHAM NURSERIES
Bagshot Road, Chobham
Surrey   GU24 8DE
01276 858252
*A well established nursery growing geraniums, 300 varieties of **fuchsias**, pot plants and cyclamen. Bedding plants. Cut chrysanthemums.*
Open: Mid-April–mid-June, 7 days a week, 9–5. Other months, phone to check opening times.
Wheelchairs: Reasonable access.
Toilets: Yes.
Dogs: On lead. **Credit cards:** No.

5/17 MIMBRIDGE GARDEN CENTRE
Station Road
Chobham, Woking
Surrey   GU24 8AS
01276 858237
Plants, peat and compost, topsoil (bagged & bulk), stoneware, sheds, fencing, sundries, garden furniture, barbecues. Café.
Open: Daily; 9–5.30, Sunday 11–5.
Wheelchairs: Good access.
Toilets: Yes.
Dogs: On lead. **Credit cards:** Yes.

5/18 RIVERSIDE NURSERIES
Philpot Lane, Chobham
Woking, Surrey   GU24 8HE
01276 857687
*A nursery specialising in bedding plants, summer and winter **hanging baskets**, winter pansies and bulbs.*
Open: All year except Xmas, Boxing & New Year's Days; 7 days a week, March–June & Sept–Nov, 9–5. (Other months closed Sunday.)
Wheelchairs: Easy paved access.
Toilets: No.
Dogs: Yes. **Credit cards:** No.

WATER GARDEN SPECIALISTS

5/19 WATERLIFE

5/20 WORLD OF WATER

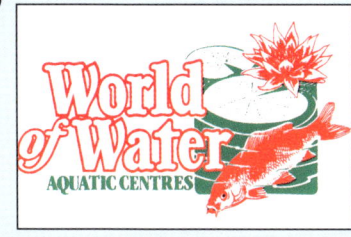

Holloway Hill, Chertsey
Surrey   KT16 0AE
01932 569690

Specialists in water gardens, fountains, filtration, fish, plants and everything for the garden pond.
Open: All year except Xmas, Boxing and New Year's Days; 7 days a week, 9–6. Nov–Jan, 6 days a week (CLOSED MONDAY).
Wheelchairs: Easy paved access.
Toilets: Yes.
Dogs: Yes.   **Credit cards:** Yes.

GARDENS

5/21 THE SAVILL GARDEN

Famous 35-acre woodland garden and temperate house.

SEE PAGE 48 FOR FULL DETAILS

5/22 VALLEY GARDENS
World-renowned woodland garden of 400 acres.
Cost: Free, but car park charge of £3.

5/23 VIRGINIA WATER
120-acre landscaped lake set in attractive woodland.
Cost: Free, but car park charge of £1.50.

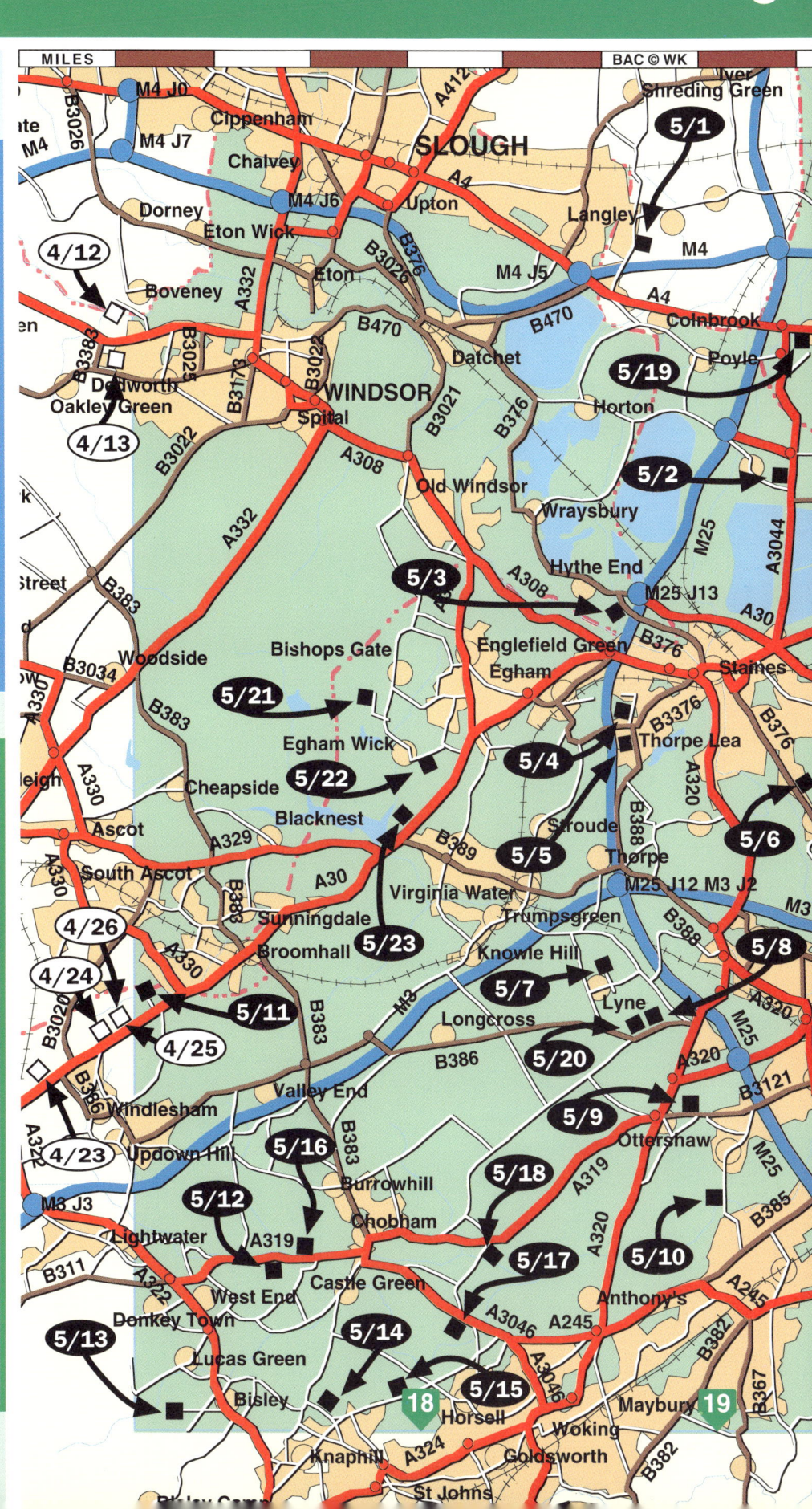

MIDDLESEX & SURREY

SPECIALIST & GENERAL NURSERIES, GARDEN AND PLANT CENTRES

6/1 JOHN TRAIN PLANTS

6/2 WYEVALE GARDEN CENTRE

6/3 HEATHROW GARDEN CENTRE
Sipson Road, Sipson
West Drayton, Middlesex
UB7 0HR   0181 897 8893
An extensive range of summer and winter bedding, herbaceous and alpine plants, shrubs, conifers and roses.
Open: All year except Xmas & Boxing Days; 7 days a week, Mon–Sat 8–6, Sunday 10.30–4.30.
Wheelchairs: Good access.
Toilets: Yes.
Dogs: On lead.   **Credit cards:** Yes.

WATER GARDEN SPECIALIST

6/4 AIRPORT AQUARIA

Heathrow Garden Centre
Sipson Road, West Drayton
Middlesex   UB7 0HR
0181 897 2563
A comprehensive selection of self-contained fountain and water features. 'The complete water gardening centre.'
Open: All year; 7 days a week, summer 9–6, winter 10–4.
Wheelchairs: Good access.
Toilets: No.
Dogs: Yes.   **Credit cards:** Yes.

SPECIALIST & GENERAL NURSERIES, GARDEN AND PLANT CENTRES

6/5 FRANK FAIRHEAD & SON

6/6 LAKESIDE GARDEN CENTRE

6/7 ADRIAN HALL

The Garden Centre, Feltham
Hill Road, Feltham, Middlesex
TW13 7NA   0181 890 5057
Est. over 30 years. A 4.5-acre specialist garden centre with vast garden construction materials department.
Open: All year; Mon–Sat 8–5.30 (Bank Hols 9–5), Sun 10–4.
Wheelchairs: Level site with good access. A wheelchair is available and there are disabled toilets. **Toilets:** Yes.
Dogs: On lead.   **Credit cards:** Yes.
SEE PAGE 50 FOR FULL DETAILS

6/8 FRANK FAIRHEAD & SON

6/9 LALEHAM NURSERIES

6/10 THE HIDDEN GARDEN

6/11 SQUIRE'S GARDEN CENTRE

6/12 JUNGLE GARDEN CENTRE

6/13 WOBURN HILL NURSERY

6/14 CROCKFORD PARK GARDEN CENTRE

6/15 SQUIRE'S GARDEN CENTRE

6/16 JAQUES CANN OF WEYBRIDGE
Seven Hills Road
Weybridge   KT12 4DD
01932 844575
Wide range of own-grown stock.

6/17 COBHAM PARK NURSERY
Plough Lane, Downside
Cobham, Surrey   KT11 3LU
01932 863933
Nursery in old walled garden, growing all own general stock, summer bedding and 400 varieties of herbaceous perennials.
Open: All year except Xmas Day; 6 days a week (CLOSED WEDNESDAY), 10–5.
Wheelchairs: Reasonably paved access.
Toilets: No.
Dogs: On lead.   **Credit cards:** No.

PICK-YOUR-OWN FARM

6/18 CROCKFORD BRIDGE FARM
New Haw Road, Addlestone
KT5 2BU   01932 847840
PYO and farm shop. Xmas trees.

PYO FARM & GARDEN CENTRE

6/19 GARSON FARM

Winterdown Road, West End
Esher, Surrey   KT10 8LS
Garden centre: 01372 460181
PYO: 01372 464389
A large range of fruit and vegetables to pick from May to October, and a large, modern garden centre.
Open: All year except Xmas & Boxing Days; 7 days a week, winter 9–5, summer 9–6, Sunday 11–5.
Wheelchairs: Good; disabled toilets.
Dogs: On lead, not in PYO fields.
Toilets: Yes.   **Credit cards:** Yes.

PICK-YOUR-OWN FARM

6/20 CHURCH FARM
Burhill Road, Hersham
Surrey   KT12 4BJ
01932 242212
PYO with a large range of fruit and vegetables. Farm shop.
Open: PYO May–Oct. Farm shop all year except Xmas & Boxing Days; 7 days a week, winter 9–5, summer 9–6, Sun 11–5.
Wheelchairs: Yes in shop.
Dogs: On lead; not at all in PYO fields.
Toilets: Yes.   **Credit cards:** Yes.

6

WATER GARDEN SPECIALISTS

6/21 AQUARIUM AND POND CENTRE

At the Garden Centre
Staines Road
Hounslow Heath
Middlesex
TW4 5DS
0181 569 5658

Quality tropical coldwater fish and aquatic dry goods. Highly recommended by 'Practical Fishkeeping' magazine.
Open: All year except Xmas & Boxing Days; 7 days a week, 9.30–5.30.
Wheelchairs: Good access. Disabled WC.
Toilets: Yes.
Dogs: Yes. **Credit cards:** Yes.

6/22 JUNGLE AQUATICS

Jungle Garden Centre
Fordbridge Road
Sunbury-on-Thames,
Middlesex
TW16 6AY
01932 787361

Quality tropical coldwater fish and aquatic dry goods. Highly recommended by 'Practical Fishkeeping' magazine.
Open: All year except Xmas & Boxing Days; 7 days a week, weekdays 9.30–5.30, Sunday 10.30–4.30.
Wheelchairs: Good access.
Toilets: Ask if desperate.
Dogs: On lead. **Credit cards:** Yes.

GARDENS

6/23 THE WALLED GARDEN
Small formal garden. Free.

6/24 PAINSHILL PARK
Between Streets, Cobham
For times please phone
01932 868113
18th century landscape garden.

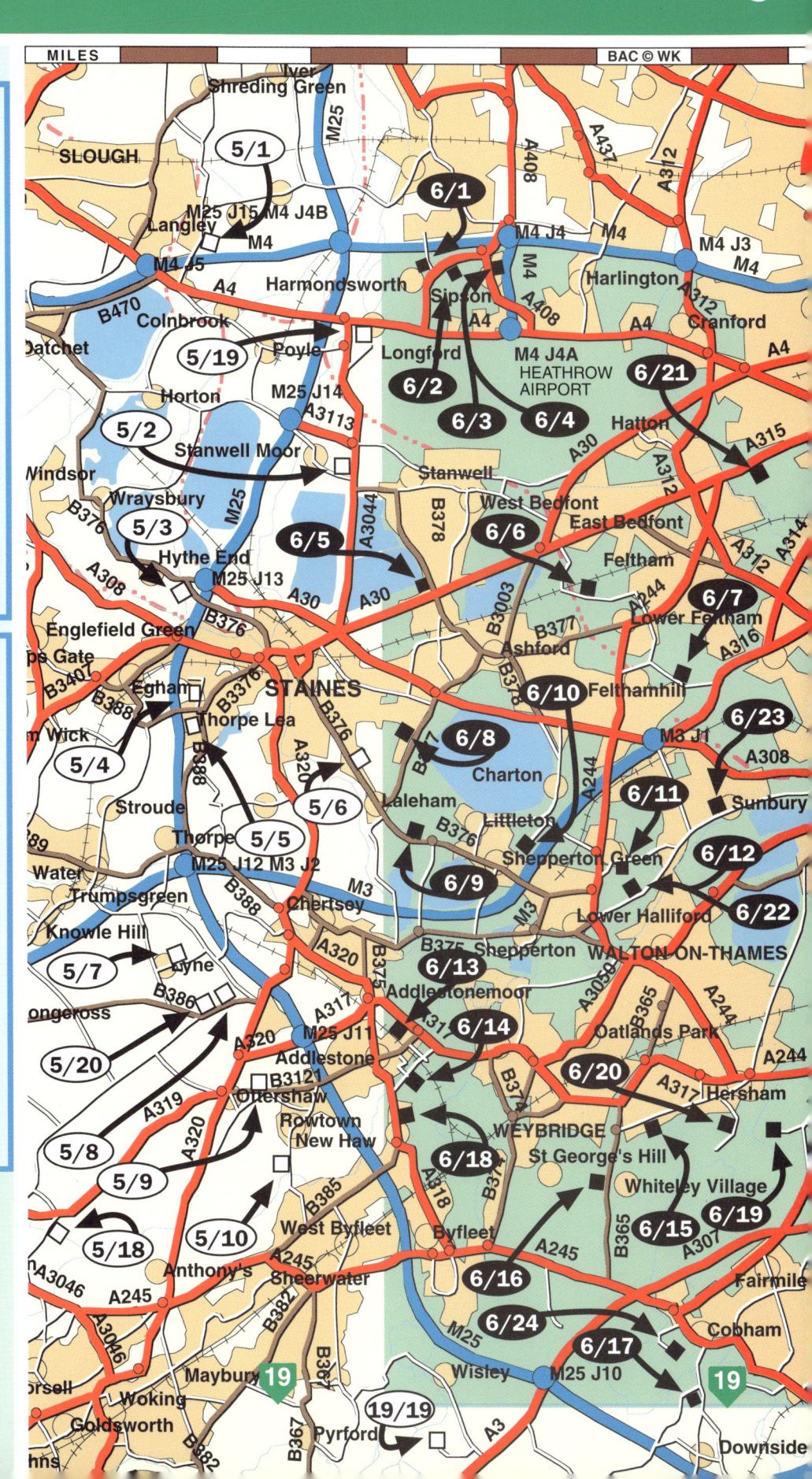

MIDDLESEX & SURREY

SPECIALIST & GENERAL NURSERIES, GARDEN AND PLANT CENTRES

7/1 PANNELLS GARDEN CENTRE

7/2 KENNEDYS GARDEN CENTRE
Oaken Lane, Claygate, Surrey
KT10 0RH   0181 398 0047
Garden centre with a wide range of plants and gardening products. Giftware, pet shop and conservatories.
Open: All year except Xmas & Boxing Days; 7 days a week, Mon–Sat 9–5.30 (winter), 9–6.30 (summer), Sunday 10.30–4.30.
Wheelchairs: Easy access.
Toilets: Yes.   **Credit cards:** Yes.
Dogs: Guide dogs only.

7/3 SYON PARK GARDEN CENTRE
Syon Park, Brentford
Middlesex   TW8 8JG
0181 568 0134
Large retail garden centre, landscape supplies, garden and design service.
Open: All year except Xmas & Boxing Days; Mon–Sat 9–5.30, Sunday 10.30–6 (shop 10.30–4.30).
Toilets: Yes.
Dogs: No.   **Credit cards:** Yes.

7/4 COUNTRY GARDENS OSTERLEY
Windmill Lane
Osterley, Middlesex
TW7 5PR   0181 847 2468
Country Gardens
'Good value garden centre with very wide plant selection. Free local delivery. Garden buildings, compost, seeds.'
Open: All year; Mon–Sat 9–6, Sunday 10.30–4.30. Extended spring hours – phone for information.
Wheelchairs: Easy access.
Toilets: Yes.
Dogs: On lead.   **Credit cards:** Yes.

7/5 SQUIRE'S GARDEN CENTRE

7/6 TEDDINGTON STATION GARDEN CENTRE
Station Road, Teddington
TW11 9AA   0181 943 5222
'Teddington's little secret!'

7/7 THE PALM CENTRE
2 miles from Kew at
563 Upper Richmond Road West
SW14 7ED   0181 876 3223
Indoor & garden **palms** & *exotics*.

7/8 ROCKINGHAMS GARDEN CENTRE

7/9 PETERSHAM NURSERIES
Petersham Road, Petersham
Richmond, Surrey TW10 7AG
0181 940 5230
Grower of quality bedding plants and large selection of shrubs and trees. Very close to Richmond Park.
Open: All year except Xmas, Boxing & New Year's Days; 7 days a week, Mon–Sat 9–5.30, Sun 10–4.
Wheelchairs: All plant areas are accessible.   **Toilets:** Yes.
Dogs: On lead.   **Credit cards:** Yes.

7/10 HILL PARK ROSES
Woodstock Lane North
Long Ditton, Surbiton, Surrey
KT6 5HN   0181 398 0022
Specialist nursery with **60,000 roses** *in bloom during summer. Bare root and container stock. Expert advice available.*
Open: All year except 24 Dec–2 Jan; 7 days a week, Mon–Fri 8–5.30, Sat 9–5, Sun 10–5.
Wheelchairs: Paved sales area.
Toilets: Yes.
Dogs: No.   **Credit cards:** No.

7/11 WOODSTOCK GARDEN CENTRE
Woodstock Lane North
Long Ditton   KT6 5HN
0181 398 6040
Large range of **shrubs**.

7/12 GARDEN CARE SUPPLIES

7/13 WILLOUGHBY'S NURSERIES

7/14 CHESSINGTON GARDEN CENTRE

7/15 BEECHCROFT NURSERY
127 Reigate Road, Ewell
Surrey   KT17 3DE
0181 393 4265
A nursery growing **conifers**, *alpines, heathers, perennials and summer and winter bedding.*
Open: All year except Xmas–New Year & Aug holidays; 7 days a week: Mon–Sat 10–5 (summer), 10–4 (winter); Sun 10–4 (all year).
Wheelchairs: Reasonable access.
Toilets: Ask if desperate.
Dogs: No.   **Credit cards:** Yes.

WATER GARDEN SPECIALIST

7/16 EGMONT WATER GARDEN CENTRE
132 Tolworth Rise South
Surbiton, Surrey   KT5 9NJ
0181 337 9605
Specialists in all aquatic life including equipment and accessories. Also a large range of stoneware, trees and shrubs.
Open: All year except Xmas & Boxing Days; March–Aug, 7 days a week; Sept–Feb, 6 days a week (CLOSED MONDAY), 10–5.
Wheelchairs: Easy paved access.
Toilets: Yes.
Dogs: No.   **Credit cards:** Yes.

GARDENS

7/17 OSTERLEY PARK (NT)
0181 560 3918
142-acre, 18th century park.

7/18 WOODLAND GARDENS, BUSHY PARK
Landscaped, woodland glades.

7/19 THE PALACE GARDENS, HAMPTON COURT
Tudor, Baroque and Victorian gardens, Privy Garden & maze.

7/20 ISABELLA PLANTATION, RICHMOND PARK
Rhododendrons and azaleas.

7/21 SYON PARK

Brentford, Middlesex
TW8 8JF   0181 560 0881

30 acres of gardens in Capability Brown parkland. Great Conservatory and rose garden.

Open: All year except Xmas & Boxing Days; 7 days a week, 10–6 or dusk.
Costs: £2.50, OAPs £2, families £5.
Wheelchairs: Access throughout the gardens. There are disabled WCs.
Toilets: Yes.
Dogs: No.   **Credit cards:** No.

7/22 HAM HOUSE (NT)
0181 940 1950
18-acre, 17th century garden.

7/23 CLAREMONT LANDSCAPE GARDEN (NT)
01372 469421
18th century landscaped garden.

7/24 ROYAL BOTANIC GARDENS, KEW

Kew, Richmond, Surrey
TW9 3AB   0181 940 1171

The world's leading botanic garden and plant research centre.

Open: All year except Xmas & New Year's Days; 7 days a week, 9.30–dusk.
Costs: £4.50, children £2.50, concessions £3, families £12.
Wheelchairs: Easy access to most areas. Wheelchairs are available and tours can be pre-booked in a special bus for the disabled.   **Toilets:** Yes.
Dogs: No.   **Credit cards:** Yes.

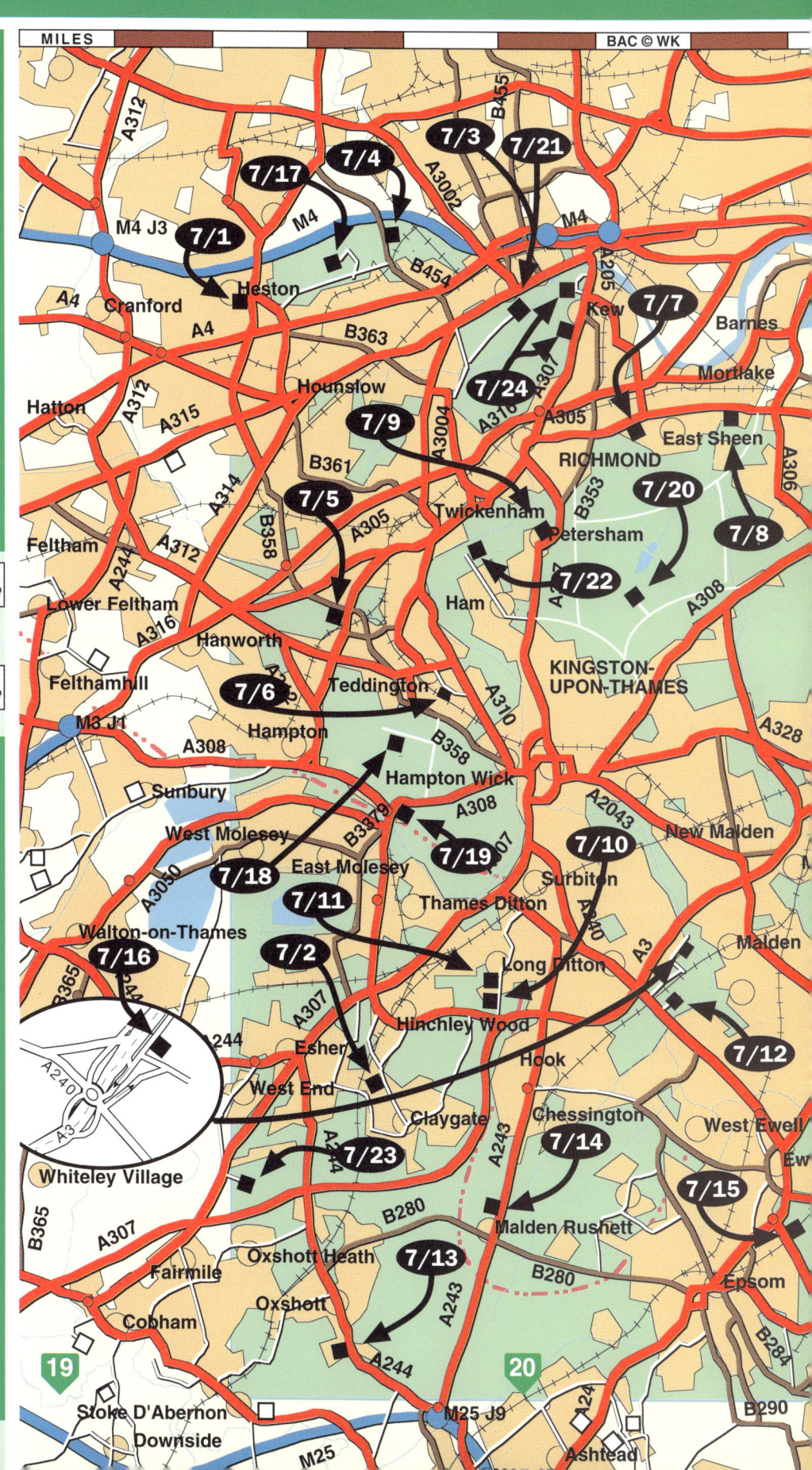

SURREY & LONDON

SPECIALIST & GENERAL NURSERIES, GARDEN AND PLANT CENTRES

8/1 ADRIAN HALL
Putney Garden Centre
Dryburgh Road
Putney
London   SW15 1BN
0181 789 9518
A wide selection of products and plants for the London garden. Pots, containers and trellis a speciality.
Open: All year; Mon–Sat 9–5.30, Sunday & Bank Holidays 10–4.
Toilets: Yes.
Dogs: On lead.   **Credit cards:** Yes.

8/2 WYEVALE GARDEN CENTRE

8/3 THOMMO'S FLOWERS
237 Sutton Common Road
Sutton, Surrey   SM3 9PZ
0181 288 1571
A retail nursery on one acre specialising in plants, with much own-grown produce. Cut flowers a speciality.
Open: All year except Xmas & Boxing Days; 7 days a week, Mon–Sat 8–6, Sunday 10–4.
Wheelchairs: Good access.
Toilets: Yes.
Dogs: On lead.   **Credit cards:** Yes.

8/4 MORDEN HALL GARDEN CENTRE

8/5 BRYAN'S GARDEN CENTRE

8/6 RUSKIN ROAD GARDEN CENTRE

8/7 LAWMANS GARDEN CENTRE

8/8 THE VERNON GERANIUM NURSERY
Cuddington Way, Cheam
Surrey   SM2 7JB
0181 393 7616
A wide variety of **pelargoniums** *available from the nursery or by mail order, plus fuchsias and patio plants. Open weeks, with tours: last two full weeks of July.*
Open: 1 Feb–end of open weeks in July; 7 days a week, Mon–Sat 9.30–5.30, Sun 10–4.
Wheelchairs: Reasonable access.
Toilets: Yes.
Dogs: On lead.   **Credit cards:** Yes.

8/9 ROCKHAM NURSERY

8/10 BRIAN HILEY
Telegraph Track
25 Little Woodcote Estate
Wallington   SM5 4AU
0181 647 9679
Specialist in **tender and unusual perennials, penstemons, Salvia canna and ornamental grasses.** *H.P.S. member.*
Open: Wed–Sat, 9–5.
Wheelchairs: Partial access.
Toilets: Ask if desperate.
Dogs: No.   **Credit cards:** No.

8/11 WOODCOTE GREEN NURSERY

8/12 G.J. BEADLE

8/13 W. BARTRAM & SON
0181 647 7649
Bedding plants, PYO, soft fruit and vegetables.

8/14 BARNES NURSERY
46 Woodmansterne Lane
Wallington, Surrey   SM6 0SW
0181 647 8213
A long established family nursery. Specialists in summer and winter **hanging baskets** *– new and refills.*
Open: All year except Xmas and Boxing Days; 7 days a week, 8.30–5.30 (later in summer).
Wheelchairs: The areas are paved.
Toilets: Ask if desperate.
Dogs: On lead.   **Credit cards:** Yes.

8/15 FLITTONS NURSERY AND PLANT CENTRE
51 Woodmansterne Lane
Wallington, Surrey   SM6 0SW
0181 647 5615
An old established family nursery specialising in **bedding plants and hanging baskets.** *(Also Teleflorist).*
Open: 365 days a year; 7 days a week, 9–5.
Wheelchairs: Easy paved access.
Toilets: No.
Dogs: On lead.   **Credit cards:** Yes.

8/16 S.G. CLARKE MARKET GARDEN & NURSERY
23 Croydon Lane, Banstead
Surrey   SM7 3BE
0181 643 3836
Bedding plants, shrubs, farm shop with fruit, vegetables and flowers. Christmas trees.
Open: Farm shop June–Xmas. Nursery stock April–Xmas; 7 days a week, 9–5.
Wheelchairs: Paved access.
Toilets: Ask if desperate.
Dogs: On lead.   **Credit cards:** No.

8/17 COULSDON GARDEN MARKET

8/18 MELBOURNE NURSERY

43 Woodmansterne Lane
Wallington, Surrey SM6 0SW
0181 647 2368

Family nursery growing bedding plants, flowers, pot plants. Also hanging baskets and planted containers.
Open: All year except Xmas Day; 6 days a week (CLOSED MONDAY) but open 7 days a week in the spring bedding season, 9–7 when busy.
Wheelchairs: Concrete and gravel paths. **Toilets:** No.
Dogs: On lead. **Credit cards:** No.

8/19 WONDER NURSERIES

69 Lower Pillory Downs
Little Woodcote, Carshalton
SM5 4DD   0181 668 3133

*An old established nursery specialising in fuchsias, geraniums, universal pansies and **bedding plants**.*
Open: All year except Xmas week; 7 days a week, 9–6 in summer, 9–4 in winter (when clocks change).
Wheelchairs: Paved access.
Toilets: Ask if desperate.
Dogs: On lead. **Credit cards:** No.

PICK-YOUR-OWN FARM

8/20 NORTH LOOE FRUIT FARM

GARDEN

8/21 MORDEN HALL PARK (NT)
0181 648 1845
'A green oasis in S.W. London.'

SURREY

SPECIALIST & GENERAL NURSERIES, GARDEN AND PLANT CENTRES

9/1 KENNEDYS GARDEN CENTRE
Waddon Way, Purley Way
Croydon, Surrey CR0 4HY
0181 688 5117
Large centre with wide range of plants and gardening products. Pet shop, swimming pool centre, conservatories, sheds, stoneware. Café.
Open: All year except Xmas & Boxing Days; 7 days a week, Mon–Sat 9–5.30 (winter), 9–6.30 (summer), Sunday 10.30–4.30.
Wheelchairs: Easy access.
Toilets: Yes. **Dogs:** Guide dogs only.
Credit cards: Yes.

9/2 COUNTRY GARDENS CROYDON
Country Gardens
Wickham Road, Shirley
Croydon, London
CR9 8AG 0181-654 3720
'Good value garden centre with very wide plant selection. Free local delivery. Terracotta pots, compost, seeds, buildings.'
Open: All year; Mon–Sat 9–6, Sunday 10.30–4.30. Extended spring hours – phone for information.
Wheelchairs: Easy access. **Toilets:** Yes.
Dogs: On lead. **Credit cards:** Yes.

9/3 MOTTINGHAM PLANT CENTRE (HADLOW COLLEGE) 
Mottingham Lane
Mottingham, London
SE12 9AW 0181 851 8793
RHS 'Award of Garden Merit' plants, many college grown & guaranteed one year. Bulbs, compost, books, sundries. Nature walk.
Open: Feb–July & Sept–Dec; 6 days a week (CLOSED MONDAY), Tues–Sat 9–5, Sun 10–5.
Wheelchairs: Easy access; disabled WC.
Toilets: Yes.
Dogs: On lead. **Credit cards:** Yes.

9/4 THE GARDEN MARKET

9/5 CASTLE NURSERY

9/6 MENDIP COTTAGE NURSERY
43 Copers Cope Road
Beckenham BR3 1NJ
0181–658 6094
Small, but large variety of stock.

9/7 EDEN PARK NURSERIES

9/8 WYEVALE GARDEN CENTRE

9/9 THOMPSON'S NURSERY

9/10 THOMPSON'S NURSERY

9/11 WEATHERLEY FENCING & GARDEN CENTRE
The Orchard
135 North Cray Road
Sidcup, Kent
DA14 5HE
0181 308 1316 
Family run garden and fencing centre. Good selection of shrubs, trees and alpines. Large selection of fencing and sheds. Sheds made to order.
Open: All year except Xmas & Boxing Days; 7 days a week.
Wheelchairs: Easy access.
Toilets: Yes.
Dogs: On lead. **Credit cards:** Yes.

9/12 RUXLEY NURSERIES

9/13 RUXLEY MANOR GARDEN CENTRE

9/14 COUNTRY GARDENS KNOCKHOLT
Country Gardens
Main Road, Knockholt
Sevenoaks, Kent
TN14 7LJ 01959–532 187
'Good value garden centre with very wide plant selection. Free local delivery. Large paving and walling centre. Coffee shop.'
Open: All year; Mon–Sat 9–6, Sunday 10.30–4.30. Extended spring hours – phone for information.
Wheelchairs: Easy access.
Toilets: Yes.
Dogs: On lead. **Credit cards:** Yes.

9/15 COOLINGS NURSERIES
Rushmore Hill, Knockholt
SEE PAGE 50 FOR FULL DETAILS

9/16 RANDLES HANGING BASKETS

WATER GARDEN SPECIALISTS

9/17 WORLD OF WATER

9/18 WORLD OF KOI
Oakley Road, Bromley
BR2 8BR 0181 4629479
All koi and pond supplies.

9/19 KOI WATER BARN
Lilly's Farm, Chelsfield Lane
Chelsfield Village
01689 878161
Koi and associated equipment.

ARTEFACT SUPPLIERS

9/20 DULWICH VILLAGE POTTERY
North Dulwich Station
SE21 7BX 0171 978 8310
'Outstanding collection of pots.'

9/21 I VASI TERRACOTTA
Adj. Bickley Station, Bickley
BR1 2EB 0181 295 4848
Pots/giftware. **Open:** Thur–Sat.

PICK-YOUR-OWN FARMS

9/22 HEATHFIELD FARM

9/23 HEWITT'S FARM

GARDENS

9/24 HEATHFIELD
Riesco Drive, Coombe Lane
18 acres around Georgian mansion.
Open: Daily, dawn–dusk.
Costs: Free.

9/25 COOMBE WOOD GARDENS
Conduit Lane, off Coombe Road
Ornamental gardens.
Open: Daily, dawn–dusk.
Costs: Free.

9/26 L.B. OF CROYDON CENTRAL NURSERY
0181 686 4433
Open: Viewing only (no plant sales) Tues, Wed & Thur 2–4.

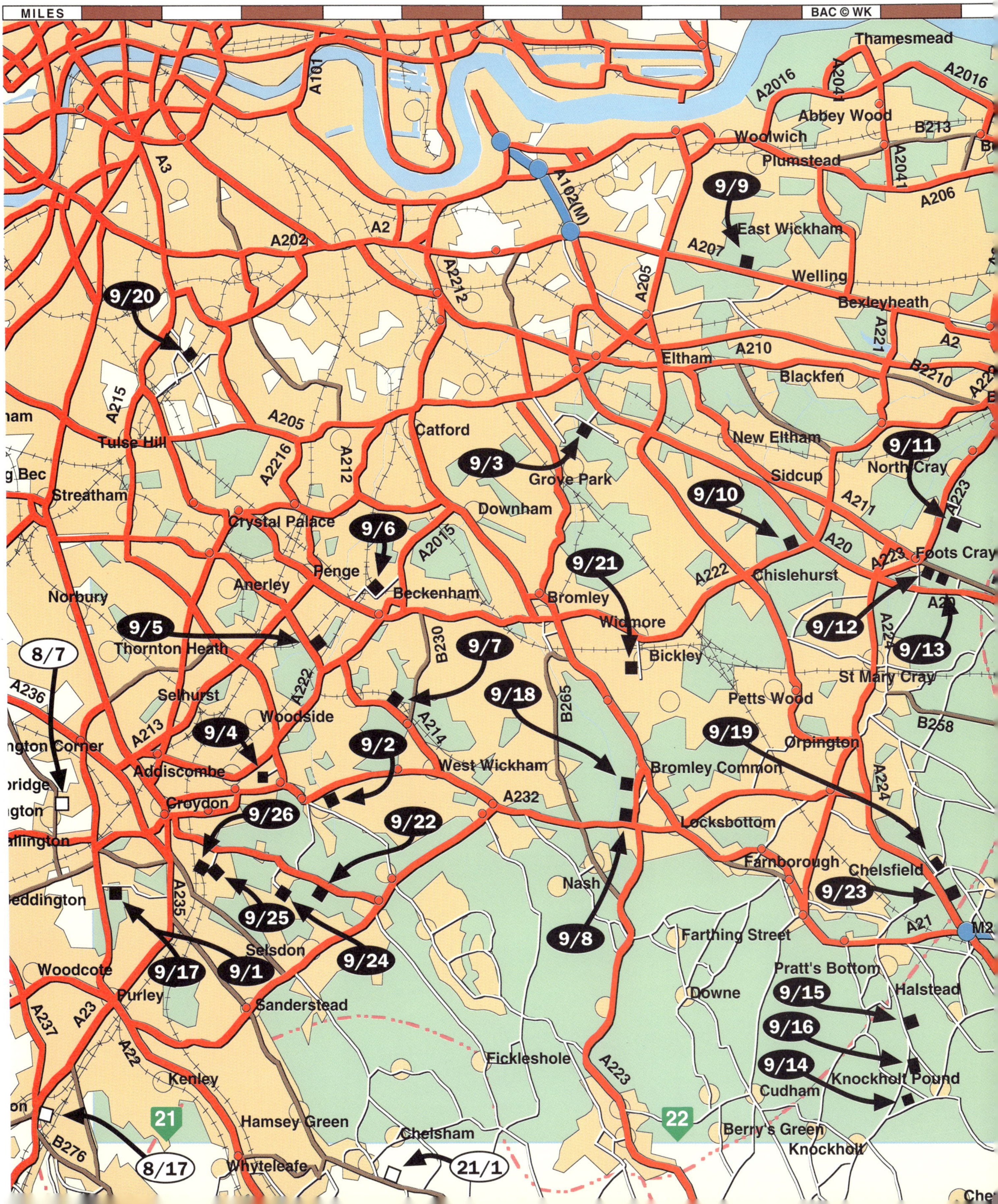
MILES
BAC © WK
Thamesmead
A2016
A2041
Abbey Wood
B213
Woolwich
Plumstead
A206
9/9
East Wickham
A207
Welling
Bexleyheath
A101
A3
A202
A2
A102(M)
A2212
A205
9/20
Eltham
A210
Blackfen
A221
B2210
A215
A205
Tulse Hill
Catford
9/3
Grove Park
New Eltham
Sidcup
9/11
North Cray
A223
Streatham
A2216
A212
Downham
9/10
A211
Crystal Palace
9/6
A2015
9/21
A20
Foots Cray
Chislehurst
A222
Anerley
Penge
Beckenham
Bromley
Norbury
Widmore
9/12
9/13
9/5
Thornton Heath
B230
9/7
Bickley
A224
St Mary Cray
8/7
A236
A222
Selhurst
9/18
B265
Petts Wood
Woodside
A214
B258
A213
9/4
9/2
9/19
Orpington
Addiscombe
West Wickham
Bromley Common
A232
Croydon
9/26
9/22
Locksbottom
Farnborough
Chelsfield
A235
Nash
9/23
A21
9/25
9/24
9/8
Farthing Street
M25
Selsdon
Woodcote
9/17
9/1
Pratt's Bottom
Halstead
Purley
Downe
9/15
A237
A23
Sanderstead
9/16
A22
Fickleshole
A223
9/14
Knockholt Pound
Kenley
Cudham
21
22
Hamsey Green
Berry's Green
Chelsham
Knockholt
B276
8/17
Whyteleafe
21/1

KENT

SPECIALIST & GENERAL NURSERIES, GARDEN AND PLANT CENTRES

10/1 STUART'S NURSERIES
North Cray Road, Sidcup
Kent   DA14 5EU
0181 300 1933
Wide range of shrubs, perennials, bedding plants, hanging baskets. Top quality turf. 'Stonemarket' stockists. Landscaping service.
Open: All year except Xmas Day–New Year; 7 days a week, 9–5 (but Sunday in winter 10–4).
Wheelchairs: Reasonable access.
Toilets: Ask if desperate.
Dogs: No.   **Credit cards:** Yes.

10/2 ST. MARY'S NURSERY
103 Birchwood Road,
Wilmington, Dartford, Kent
DA2 7HQ   01322 667883
*Established over 90 years – **bedding and fuchsia** specialists. Also shrubs, conifers, cut flowers and pot plants.*
Open: All year except Xmas & Boxing Days; 7 days a week, 8.30–5.30.
Wheelchairs: Easy access.
Toilets: Ask if desperate.
Dogs: On lead.   **Credit cards:** Yes.

10/3 HARRINGTON'S NURSERY
Silver Birches, Highlands Hill
Swanley, Kent   BR8 7NB
01322 663239
Established nursery specialising in all bedding plants, geraniums, standard fuchsias, basket plants. Hanging baskets.
Open: 7 days a week; Mon–Fri 9–5, Sat 9–1, Sun 9.30–12; 9–5 every day in spring.
Wheelchairs: Access to most areas.
Toilets: Yes.
Dogs: On lead.   **Credit cards:** No.

10/4 HAWLEY GARDEN CENTRE

10/5 EYNSFORD NURSERY
Riverside, Eynsford, Dartford
DA4 0AE   01322 864439
Pot plant *specialists.*

10/6 RIVERSIDE FUCHSIAS
Gravel Road, Sutton-at-Hone
Dartford, Kent   DA4 9HQ
01322 863891
*5000 varieties of **fuchsias & the National Collection**. 1000 varieties of **geraniums** incl. hardy varieties & erodiums. Penstemons.*
Open: All year except Xmas & Boxing Days; 6 days a week (CLOSED MONDAY), 9–5.
Wheelchairs: Good access, disabled WC.
Toilets: Yes.
Dogs: On lead.   **Credit cards:** Yes.

10/7 COBLANDS GARDEN CENTRE

10/8 SPRINGHEAD NURSERIES

10/9 WALNUT HILL NURSERY
Walnut Hill Road, Gravesend
Kent   DA13 9HL
01474 704859
A wide range of trees, shrubs, climbers, conifers and perennials, many in more mature sizes for instant effect.
Open: All year except Xmas–New Year; Mon–Fri only (CLOSED SATURDAY & SUNDAY), 8–5.
Wheelchairs: Easy access to most areas.   **Toilets:** Yes.
Dogs: No.   **Credit cards:** No.

10/10 SOUTH HOUSE GARDEN CENTRE & FLORIST
South House, Culverstone
Meopham, Kent   DA13 0QN
01732 822353
*An extensive range of **bedding plants**, shrubs & conifers. Perennials, heathers and house plants. Floristry section.*
Open: All year except 24 Dec–2 Jan; 7 days a week, Mon–Sat 9–5, Sunday 9.30–4.
Wheelchairs: Easy access.
Toilets: Ask if desperate.
Dogs: No.   **Credit cards:** Yes.

10/11 POLHILL GARDEN CENTRE

10/12 WOODLAND NURSERIES & GARDEN CENTRE

10/13 FALSTON NURSERIES
Newlands Lane, Culverstone
DA13 0RD   01732 822203
Plant, gift and floristry centre.

10/14 MILLBROOK GARDEN CENTRE
Station Road, Southfleet
Gravesend, Kent   DA13 9PA
01474 331135
Large modern centre with full range of plants, garden sundries and gifts. Award-winning landscapers. Restaurant.
Open: All year except Xmas, Boxing & New Year's Days; 7 days a week: Mon–Sat, winter 9–5, summer 9–6, Sunday 10–4.30.
Wheelchairs: Available.
Toilets: Yes.
Dogs: On lead.   **Credit cards:** Yes.

WATER GARDEN SPECIALIST

10/15 SWALLOW AQUATICS
Millbrook Garden Centre
Station Road, Southfleet
Gravesend, Kent   DA13 9PA
01474 561123
A very large selection of fish, ponds, aquaria and accessories.
Open: All year except Xmas, Boxing & New Year's Days; 7 days a week, Mon–Sat 9–5 (winter), 9–6 (summer), all Suns 10–4.30.
Wheelchairs: Accessible.
Toilets: Ask if desperate.
Dogs: On lead.   **Credit cards:** Yes.

PICK-YOUR-OWN FARMS

10/16 LOWER HOCKENDEN FARM PYO
Hockenden Lane, Swanley
Kent   BR8 7QH   01689 831945
Top fruit, soft fruit & vegetables.

10/17 SEPHAM FARM
Filston Lane, Shoreham
Sevenoaks, Kent
Wide range of soft fruit.

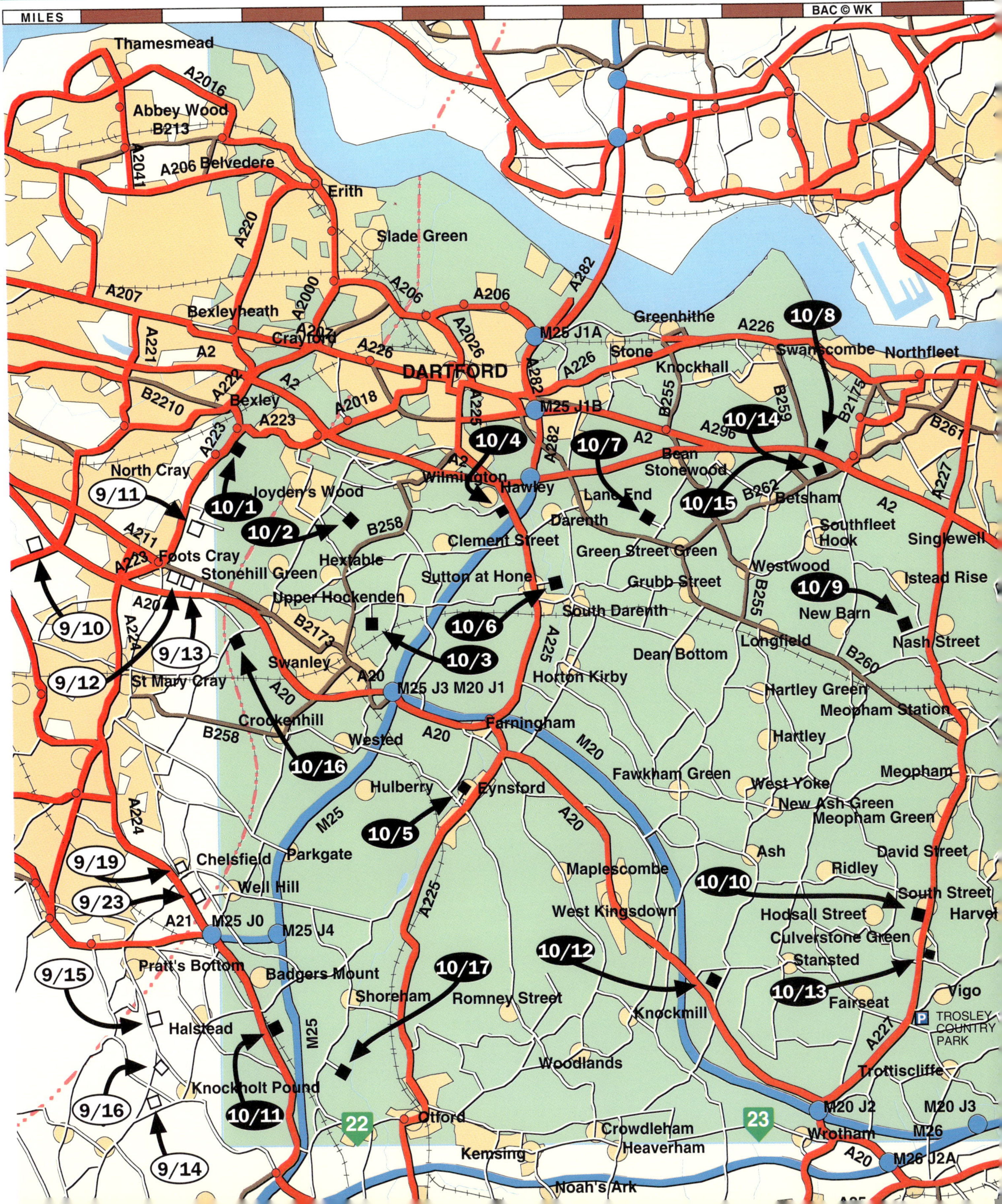

MILES
BAC © WK
Thamesmead
A2016
Abbey Wood
B213
A2041
A206
Belvedere
Erith
A220
Slade Green
A207
Bexleyheath
A2000
A206
A206
A282
A221
A2
A207
Crayford
A226
A2026
M25 J1A
Greenhithe
A226
Stone
10/8
Swanscombe
Northfleet
DARTFORD
Knockhall
A222
B2210
Bexley
A2
A2018
A225
A282
A226
M25 J1B
B255
B259
B2175
A223
A223
A282
10/4
10/7
A2
A296
10/14
B261
A2
Wilmington
Hawley
Bean
Stonewood
North Cray
Joyden's Wood
Lane End
10/15
B262
Betsham
A227
9/11
10/1
Darenth
A2
10/2
B258
Clement Street
Southfleet
Hook
Singlewell
A211
Foots Cray
A223
Hextable
Green Street Green
Stonehill Green
Westwood
Sutton at Hone
Grubb Street
10/9
Istead Rise
A20
Upper Hockenden
B255
New Barn
9/10
South Darenth
A224
B2173
10/6
Nash Street
9/13
Longfield
10/3
A225
Dean Bottom
Swanley
9/12
St Mary Cray
A20
M25 J3 M20 J1
B260
A20
Horton Kirby
Hartley Green
Meopham Station
Crockenhill
B258
Farningham
A20
M20
Wested
Hartley
10/16
Fawkham Green
Meopham
Hulberry
Eynsford
West Yoke
A224
M25
New Ash Green
A20
Meopham Green
10/5
9/19
Chelsfield
Parkgate
Ash
David Street
Maplescombe
Ridley
10/10
9/23
Well Hill
South Street
A225
West Kingsdown
Harvel
A21
M25 J0
Hodsall Street
M25 J4
Culverstone Green
10/12
9/15
Pratt's Bottom
10/17
Stansted
Badgers Mount
Shoreham
Romney Street
10/13
Fairseat
Vigo
Knockmill
TROSLEY
COUNTRY
PARK
Halstead
A227
M25
Woodlands
Trottiscliffe
9/16
Knockholt Pound
10/11
M20 J2
M20 J3
22
Otford
23
Crowdleham
M26
Heaverham
Wrotham
Kemsing
A20
M26 J2A
9/14
Noah's Ark

KENT

SPECIALIST & GENERAL NURSERIES, GARDEN AND PLANT CENTRES

11/1 HOMELEIGH NURSERY
Ratcliffe Highway, Hoo
Rochester   01634 250235
Garden centre and farm shop.

11/2 TORRENS GARDEN CENTRE

11/3 WYEVALE GARDEN CENTRE

11/4 BREDHURST NURSERY
Dunn Street, Bredhurst
Gillingham
Kent ME7 3ND
01634 377745
A family-run nursery selling a large selection of shrubs, conifers and bedding plants. Landscaping is a speciality.
Open: 7 days a week, 9–5.
Wheelchairs: Easy access.
Toilets: Yes.
Dogs: On lead.   **Credit cards:** Yes.

11/5 MERESBOROUGH NURSERY
Meresborough Road
Rainham, Kent ME8 8PP
01634 231639
Specialist growers of geraniums and fuchsias.
Open: First weekend in April–end June; 7 days a week 8–5. Cut chrysanthemum blooms: Sept–Xmas, Mon–Fri 8–5, Sat/Sun 9–12.
Wheelchairs: Easy access.
Toilets: Yes.
Dogs: Yes.   **Credit cards:** No.

11/6 BERENGRAVE NURSERIES

11/7 KNOWLER NURSERY
143 Berengrave Lane,
Rainham, Gillingham, Kent
01634 361631
Specialist fuchsia growers.

11/8 WAVERLEY NURSERIES
622 Lower Rainham Road
Rainham, Gillingham
Kent ME8 7TX
01634 232520
Old-established, small family nursery, growing perennials, bedding, rockery plants. A good selection of roses, shrubs & conifers.
Open: All year except Xmas–New Year; 7 days a week 9–5.30.
Wheelchairs: Easy access.
Toilets: No.
Dogs: No.   **Credit cards:** No.

11/9 GORE HOUSE NURSERIES
Newington, Sittingbourne
ME9 7PD   01795 842365
A range of hardy plants.

11/10 SHILLINGHURST NURSERY
Oad Street, Borden
Sittingbourne ME9 8LA
01795 842446
Shrubs, trees & general stock.

PICK-YOUR-OWN FARM & NURSERY

11/11 WESTMOOR FARM
Moor Street, Rainham
Gillingham, Kent ME8 8QF
01634 365135
A wide range of PYO fruit and vegetables. Also ready-picked in farm shop. Nursery growing bedding and hanging basket plants.
Open: Nursery & farm shop: all year; PYO: mid–June to end Oct; 7 days a week, 9–5.
Wheelchairs: Good access.
Toilets: Yes.
Dogs: No.   **Credit cards:** No.

PICK-YOUR-OWN FARM

11/12 GORE FARM PYO
Oak Lane, Upchurch
ME9 7BE   01634 388856
Seasonal PYO: daffodils – apples.

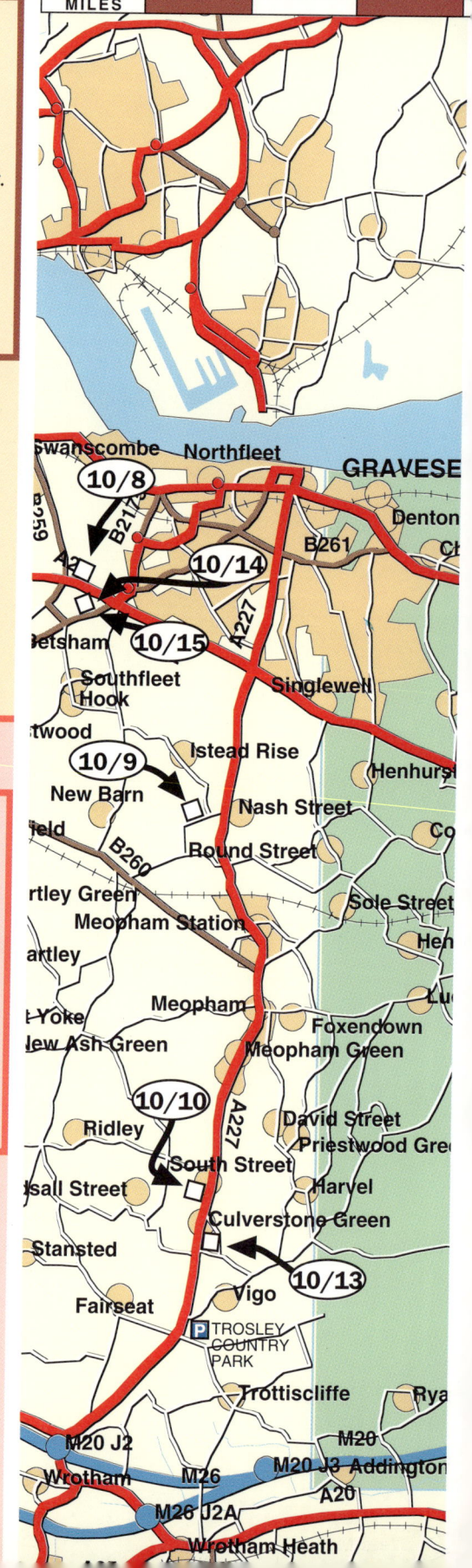

11

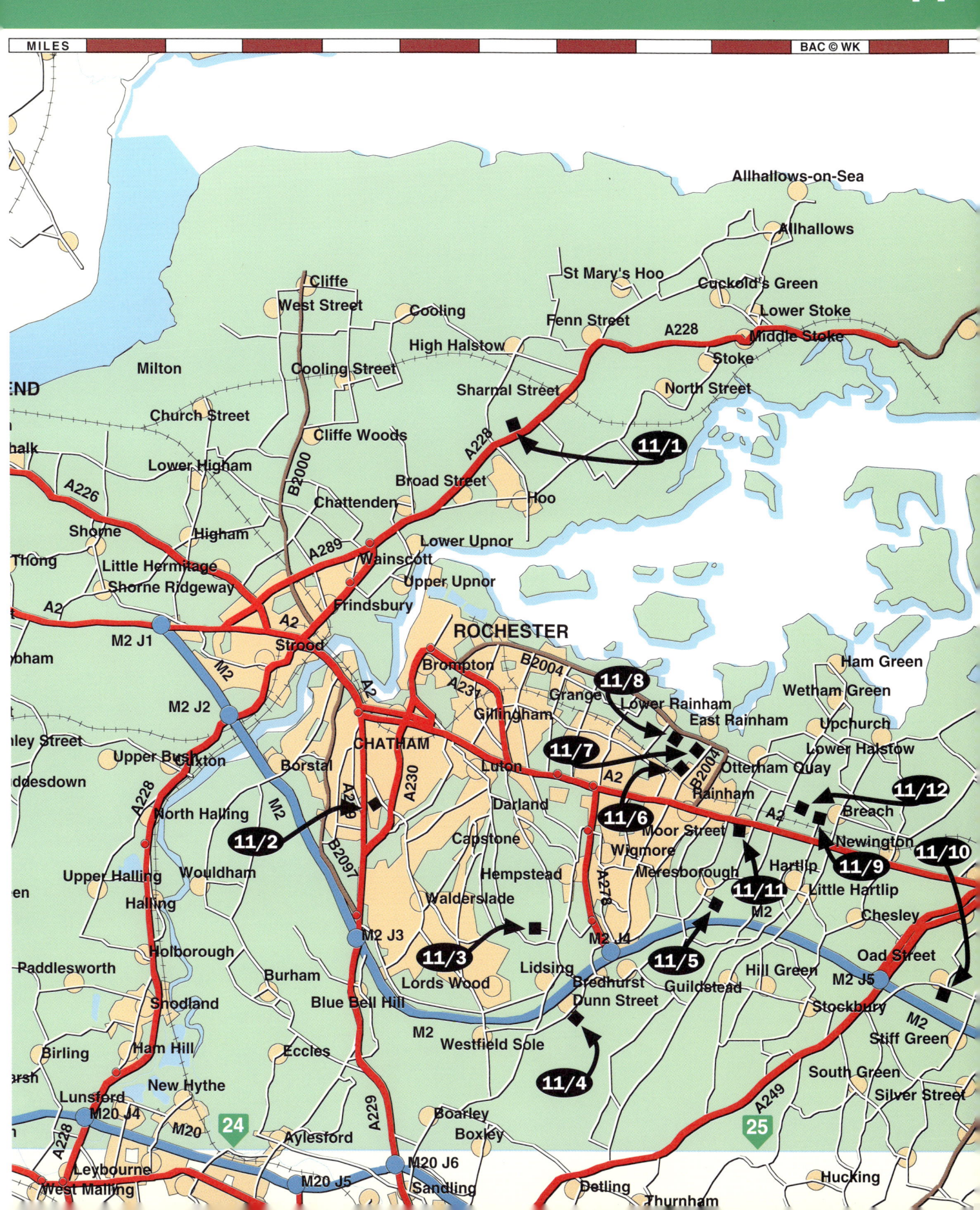

KENT

SPECIALIST & GENERAL NURSERIES, GARDEN AND PLANT CENTRES

12/1 COUNTRY GARDENS FAVERSHAM
Norton Crossroads
Norton, Faversham
ME9 9JY   01795 521549
'Good value garden centre with very wide plant selection. Free local delivery. Craft shops. Sheds. Coffee shop.'
Open: All year; Mon–Sat 9–6, Sunday 10.30–4.30. Extended spring hours – phone for information.
Wheelchairs: Easy access.
Toilets: Yes.
Dogs: On lead.   **Credit cards:** Yes.

12/2 COPTON ASH SPECIALIST GARDENS
01795 535919
Rare perennials, *fruit trees.*
Open: 2–6 (not Mon & Fri).

12/3 NABOTH'S NURSERY
'The sign of the scarecrows.'
Canterbury Road, Faversham
Shrubs, trees, plants, advice.

12/4 MACNADE GARDEN CENTRE

12/5 MEADOW GRANGE NURSERY
Honey Hill, Blean, Whitstable
Kent   CT5 3BP   01227 471205
A family nursery growing shrubs and trees, bedding plants and full range of patio plants. Farm shop and garden sundries.
Open: All year except Xmas & Boxing Days & Easter Sunday.
Mon–Sat 8.30–6, Sunday 10–4.
Wheelchairs: Easy access.
Toilets: Yes.
Dogs: Yes.   **Credit cards:** Yes.

PICK-YOUR-OWN FARMS

12/6 BREDGAR PYO & FARM SHOP
01622 884423
Raspberries and strawberries. Farm shop in Bredgar.

12/7 FOUR OAKS FIELD PYO

12/8 MACNADE PYO & FARM SHOP

ARTEFACT SUPPLIER

12/9 WHELAN'S
50/60 High Street
Blue Town, Sheerness
Kent   ME12 1RW
01795 663879
The UK's largest manufacturer of concrete garden ornaments – 1000 different items always in stock.
Open: All year except Xmas week; 7 days a week, Mon–Sat 9–6, Sunday 10.30–4.30.
Wheelchairs: Good access.
Toilets: Yes.
Dogs: Yes.   **Credit cards:** No.
SEE PAGE 49 FOR FULL DETAILS

GARDENS

12/10 BROGDALE HORTICULTURAL TRUST
Brogdale Road, Faversham
Kent   ME13 8XY
01795 535286
*The home of the **National Fruit Collection**, over 4000 varieties grown. Guided tours of 150-acre orchards. Plant centre and shop.*
Open: All year except Xmas & Boxing Days; 7 days a week, 9.30–5.30.
Costs: Guided tours £2.50, OAPs £2.
Wheelchairs: Ramps & disabled WC.
Toilets: Yes.
Dogs: No.   **Credit cards:** Yes.

12/11 MOUNT EPHRAIM GARDENS
01227 751496
Edwardian garden with views.
Open: Easter–mid Sept, 7 days 1–6.

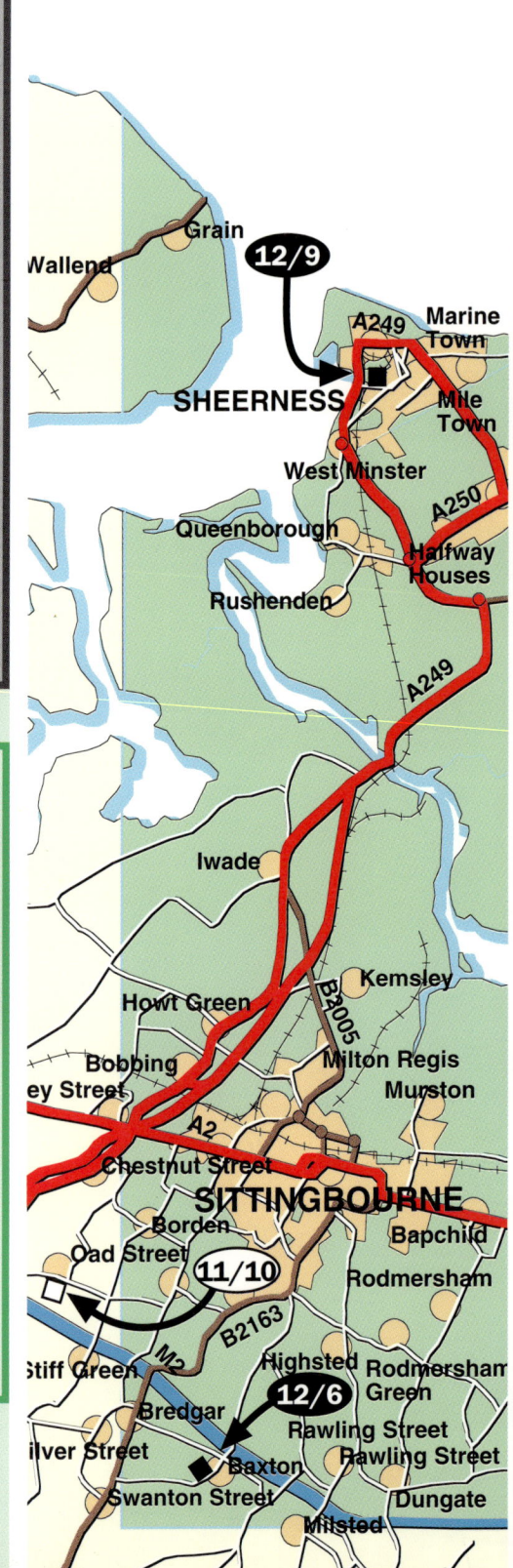

12

KENT

SPECIALIST & GENERAL NURSERIES, GARDEN AND PLANT CENTRES

13/1 JOHNSONS NURSERY

Thanet Way, Whitstable
Kent   CT5 3JD
01227 793763
Large selection of all types of roses. Shrubs, summer and winter bedding plants and general stock. Friendly service.
Open: All year except Xmas, Boxing & New Year's Days; 7 days a week, 9–6.
Wheelchairs: Good access.
Toilets: Yes.
Dogs: On lead.   **Credit cards:** Yes.

13/2 VINCENT NURSERIES

Eddington Lane
Herne Bay, Kent   CT6 5TS
01227 375806
A well established family nursery, with a comprehensive range of plants for the home and garden. Associated sundries.
Open: All year except Xmas & Boxing Days & Easter Sunday; 7 days a week, Mon–Sat 9–5, Sunday 10–4.
Wheelchairs: Easy access.
Toilets: Yes.
Dogs: No.   **Credit cards:** Yes.

13/3 FOXHILL NURSERY

13/4 KINGSGATE & KENVER NURSERIES

13/5 J. BRADSHAW & SON

Busheyfields Nursery
Herne Common, Herne Bay
Kent   CT6 7LJ
01227 375415
Climbing and wall plant *specialists, especially clematis and lonicera. Covered sales area, display field, specimen plants.*
Open: 1 March–31 October; Tues–Sat & Bank Holiday Mondays 10–5.
Wheelchairs: Limited access.
Toilets: Ask if desperate.
Dogs: No.   **Credit cards:** No.

13/6 EAST NORTHDOWN FARM

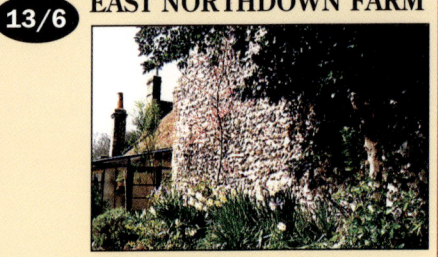

Margate, Kent   CT9 3TS
01843 862060
Nursery and farm shop specialising in **coast and chalk-loving plants**. *3-acre gardens. Tearoom, play area, farmyard animals & pets.*
Open: Nursery: daily 10–5.
Garden tea rooms: daily in July & August, Sat & Wed from Easter–September, 2–5.
Wheelchairs: Moderate access.
Toilets: Yes.
Dogs: On lead.   **Credit cards:** Yes.

13/7 COUNTRY GARDENS RAMSGATE

Hereson Road
Ramsgate, Kent
CT11 7ET   01843 592393

Country Gardens

'Good value garden centre with very wide plant selection. Free local delivery. Compost. Seeds. Coffee shop.'
Open: All year; Mon–Sat 9–6, Sunday 10.30–4.30. Extended spring hours – phone for information.
Wheelchairs: Easy access.
Toilets: Yes.
Dogs: On lead.   **Credit cards:** Yes.

MILES

13

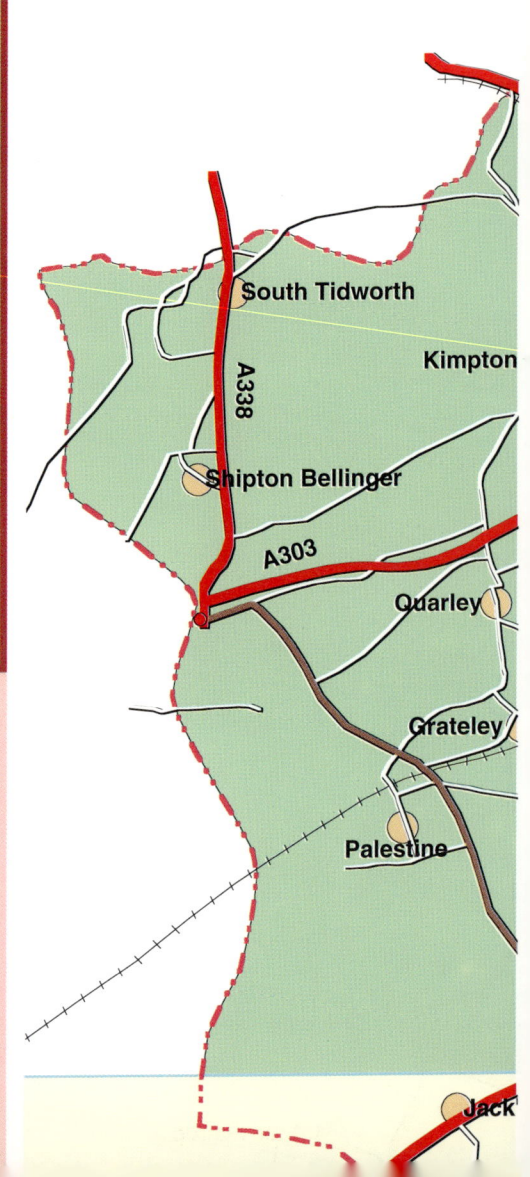

HAMPSHIRE

SPECIALIST & GENERAL NURSERIES, GARDEN AND PLANT CENTRES

14/1 COUNTRY GARDENS ANDOVER

Salisbury Road
Andover, Hampshire
SP11 7DN   01264 710551

'Good value garden centre with very wide plant selection. Free local delivery. Garden buildings, paving centre.'

Open: All year; Mon–Sat 9–6, Sunday 10.30–4.30. Extended spring hours – phone for information.
Wheelchairs: Easy access.
Toilets: Yes.
Dogs: On lead.   **Credit cards:** Yes.

NURSERY & GARDEN

14/2 LONGSTOCK PARK NURSERY

Longstock, Stockbridge
Hampshire   SO20 6EF
01264 810894

Specialist grower of home-propagated trees, shrubs and plants. Walled garden. Herbaceous border. Clematis/rose archway.

Open: All year; Mon–Sat 8.30–4.30, Sunday (APRIL–OCTOBER ONLY) 2–5.
Wheelchairs: Easy access.
Toilets: Yes.
Dogs: On lead.   **Credit cards:** Yes.

PICK-YOUR-OWN FARMS

14/3 WILLOW FARM PYO

14/4 BOURNE VALLEY PYO

14/5 WHERWELL FARM PYO

MILES
BAC © WK
1/9
Highclere
Whitway
1
Littledown
Faccombe
Old Burghclere
Linkenholt
Netherton
Ashmansworth
Vernham Street
Vernham Dean
Crux Easton
A343
A34
Upton
Woodcott
Ibthorpe
Litchfield
Dunley
Hurstbourne Tarrant
Binley
Tangley
Egbury
B3048
Stoke
14/4
Cole Henley
Wildhern
Swampton
St Mary Bourne
Hatherden
Upper Enham
Little London
Redenham
A342
Enham-Alamein
Smannell
Clanville
B3400
Appleshaw
B3048
WHITCHURCH
East Anton
Penton Mewsey
Tinker's Hill
Charlton
Penton Grafton
Picket Piece
Tufton
Weyhill
Hurstbourne Priors
Fyfield
A3093
B3400
Thruxton
A303
East Cholderton
East Aston
Longparish
Sarson
ANDOVER
14/3
Monxton
Amport
Anna Valley
Middleton
A303
Upper Clatford
Forton
Abbotts Ann
Cottage End
14/1
14/5
Goodworth Clatford
Bransbury
B3420
B3048
Bullington
Wherwell
Barton Stacey
A3057
Newton Stacey
Chilbolton
Hunton
Sutton Scotney
14/2
Fullerton
Wonston
Over Wallop
WATER GARDEN
A30
Middle Wallop
28
Leckford
29
Longstock
's Bush
Nether Wallop
A30
A272

HAMPSHIRE

SPECIALIST & GENERAL NURSERIES, GARDEN AND PLANT CENTRES

15/1 HARDY'S COTTAGE GARDEN PLANTS

Priory Lane, Freefolk
Whitchurch, Hampshire
RG28 7NJ   01256–896 533

Specialist growers of **herbaceous perennials**, *over 900 varieties, both old and new. Chelsea gold medalists in '94, '95 and '96.*
Open: 1 March–31 October; 7 days a week 9–5.30.
Wheelchairs: Yes.
Toilets: Yes.
Dogs: On lead.   **Credit cards:** Yes.

15/2 COUNTRY GARDENS BASINGSTOKE

Winchester Road
North Waltham
RG25 2DT   01256 397155

Country Gardens

'Good value garden centre with very wide plant selection. Free local delivery. Buildings, paving and walling centre.'
Open: All year; Mon–Sat 9–6, Sunday 10.30–4.30. Extended spring hours – phone for information.
Wheelchairs: Easy access.
Toilets: Yes.
Dogs: On lead.   **Credit cards:** Yes.

15/3 BEAUREPAIRE MARKET GARDEN

15/4 BAILEYS GARDEN CENTRE

15/5 MJS GARDEN CENTRE

15/6 ELM PARK GARDEN CENTRE

Aldermaston Road, Pamber
End, Tadley, Basingstoke
Hampshire   RG26 5QW
01256 850587

An established family-run garden centre and **rose nursery**. *Rose field open in summer. Wide range of plants & sundries.*
Open: All year except Xmas week; Mon–Sat 8.30–5, Sun 10–4.
Wheelchairs: Yes.
Toilets: Yes.
Dogs: On lead.   **Credit cards:** Yes.

15/7 HOOK GARDEN CENTRE & NURSERY

15/8 CONKERS GARDEN CENTRE

15/9 AVENUE NURSERIES GARDEN CENTRE

The Avenue
Lasham
Alton
Hampshire
GU34 5RX
01256 381648

Large garden centre with a wide selection of plants, gifts and aquatics. Sheds. Coffee shop.
Open: All year except Xmas & Boxing Days; 7 days a week 9–6, Sunday 10.30–4.30.
Wheelchairs: Easy access.
Toilets: Yes.
Dogs: On lead.   **Credit cards:** Yes.

15/10 VALLEY NURSERIES

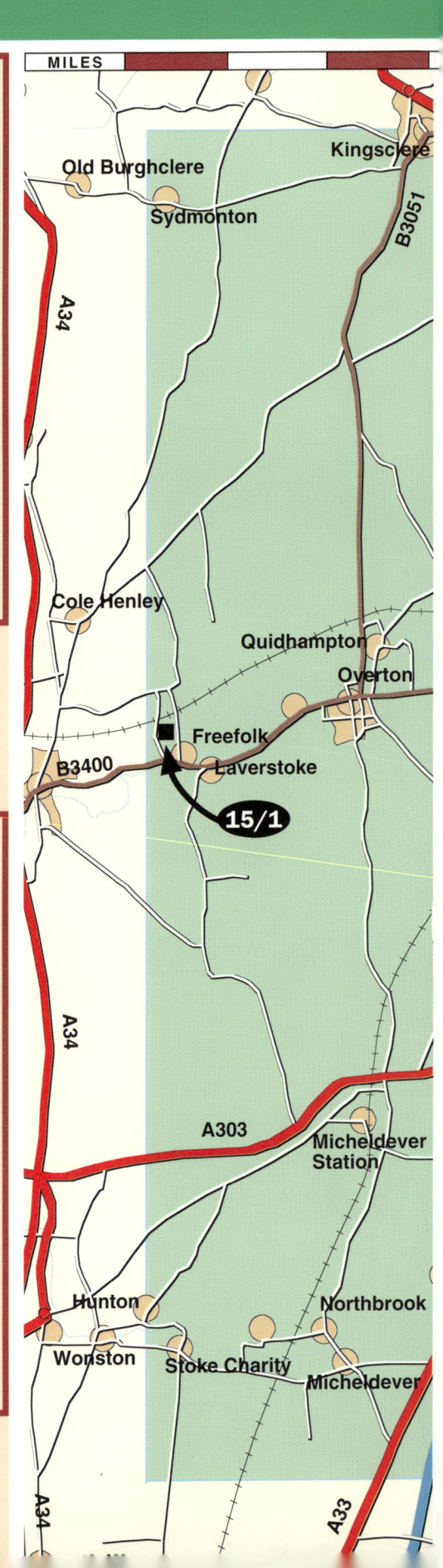

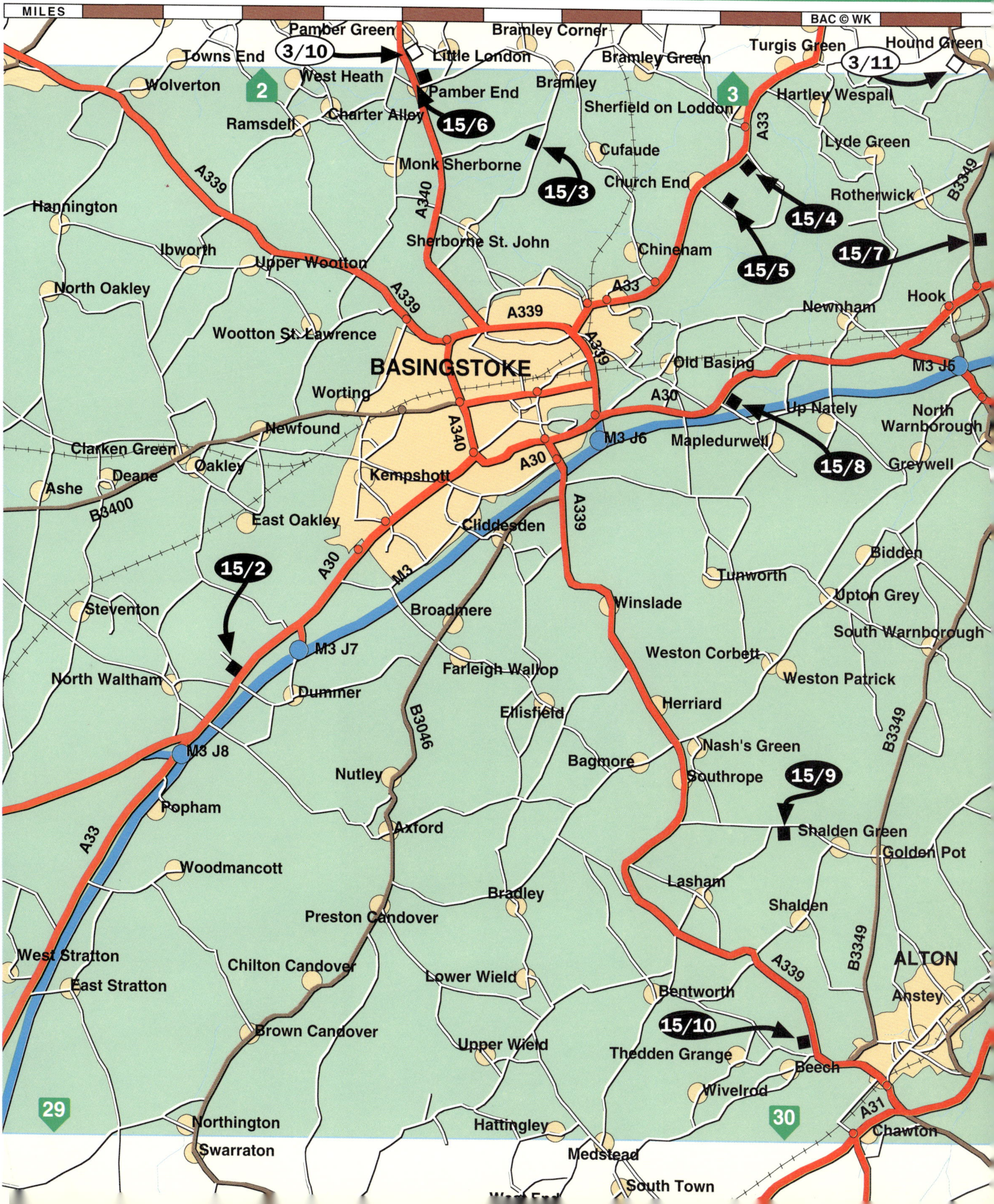
MILES
BAC © WK
Pamber Green
Bramley Corner
3/10
Little London
Towns End
Bramley Green
Turgis Green
Hound Green
3/11
West Heath
Wolverton
2
Pamber End
Bramley
3
Hartley Wespall
Sherfield on Loddon
Ramsdell
Charter Alley
15/6
A33
Lyde Green
Cufaude
Monk Sherborne
A339
15/3
Church End
B3349
Rotherwick
A340
15/4
Hannington
Sherborne St. John
15/7
Ibworth
Chineham
Upper Wootton
15/5
North Oakley
A339
A33
Hook
Newnham
A339
Wootton St. Lawrence
A339
BASINGSTOKE
Old Basing
M3 J5
Worting
A30
Up Nately
North Warnborough
A340
Newfound
M3 J6
Mapledurwell
Clarken Green
A30
15/8
Greywell
Deane
Oakley
Ashe
Kempshott
B3400
A339
East Oakley
Cliddesden
Bidden
15/2
Tunworth
A30
M3
Winslade
Upton Grey
Steventon
Broadmere
South Warnborough
M3 J7
Weston Corbett
Farleigh Wallop
Weston Patrick
North Waltham
Dummer
Ellisfield
Herriard
B3046
B3349
M3 J8
Nash's Green
Nutley
Bagmore
Southrope
15/9
Popham
Axford
Shalden Green
Golden Pot
A33
Woodmancott
Lasham
Bradley
Shalden
Preston Candover
A339
B3349
ALTON
West Stratton
Chilton Candover
Lower Wield
Anstey
East Stratton
Bentworth
15/10
Brown Candover
Upper Wield
Thedden Grange
Beech
Wivelrod
A31
29
30
Northington
Hattingley
Chawton
Swarraton
Medstead
South Town

HAMPSHIRE

SPECIALIST & GENERAL NURSERIES, GARDEN AND PLANT CENTRES

16/1 THE COACH HOUSE GARDEN CENTRE

16/2 VICARAGE HILL NURSERY

16/3 REDFIELDS GARDEN CENTRE

Ewshot Lane
Church Crookham, Fleet
Hampshire GU13 0UB
01252 624444

Large garden centre and shop. Trees, shrubs, covered plant area. Licensed restaurant. Children's play area. Sheds and conservatories.

Open: All year except Xmas & Boxing Days; 7 days a week; Mon–Sat 9–6 (but Thur 9–8), Sun 11–5.
Wheelchairs: Easy access.
Toilets: Yes.
Dogs: No. **Credit cards:** Yes.

16/4 THE GLEN AND NURSERY

16/5 GARDEN STYLE

16/6 FOREST LODGE GARDEN CENTRE
A very large centre.

16/7 COUNTRY MARKET

16

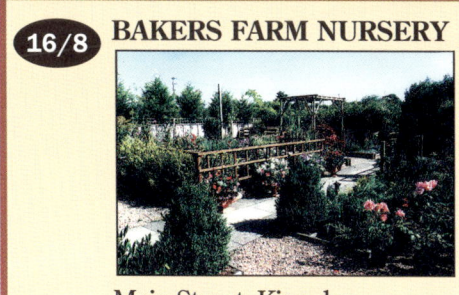

16/8 BAKERS FARM NURSERY

Main Street, Kingsley
Bordon, Hampshire
GU35 9NJ
01420 474718

A small nursery growing summer and winter pot plants, bedding plants, hanging baskets and tubs. Shrubs, herbaceous and house plants.

Open: All year except Xmas–New Year; Mon–Sat 8.30–5, Sun 10–4.
Wheelchairs: Good access.
Toilets: Ask if desperate.
Dogs: No. **Credit cards:** Yes.

WATER GARDEN SPECIALIST

16/9 WYCHWOOD WATERLILY AND CARP FARM

Farnham Road, Odiham
Hook   RG29 1HS
01256 702800
A large range of water plants.

WATER GARDEN

16/10 THE ODIHAM WATERLILY COLLECTION

at Wychwood Carp Farm
Hook, Odiham
The world's largest collection of **hardy nymphaeas.** *Cost: £2.*

GARDEN

16/11 BIRDWORLD

Exotic birds in 25 acres of parkland and gardens.

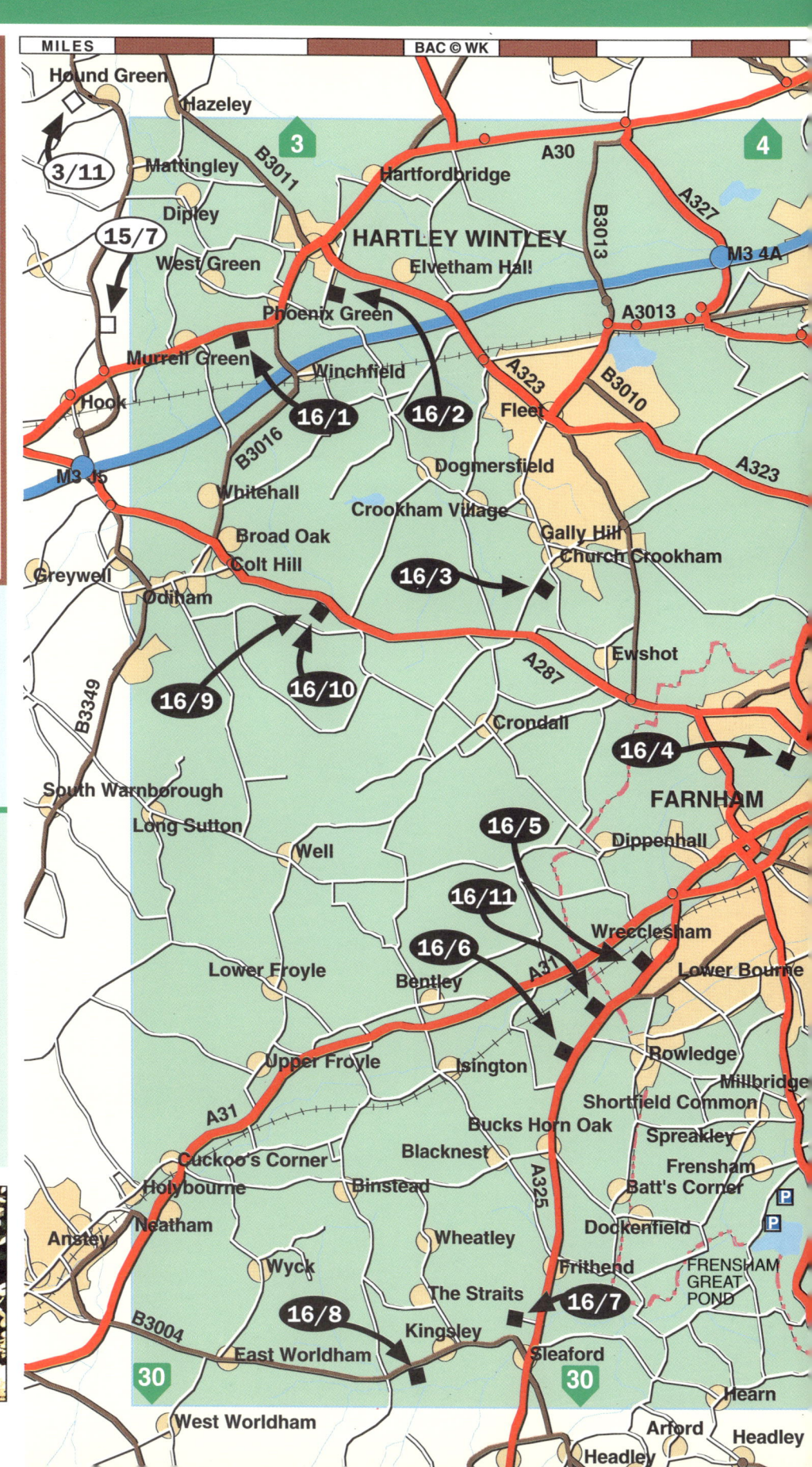

SURREY

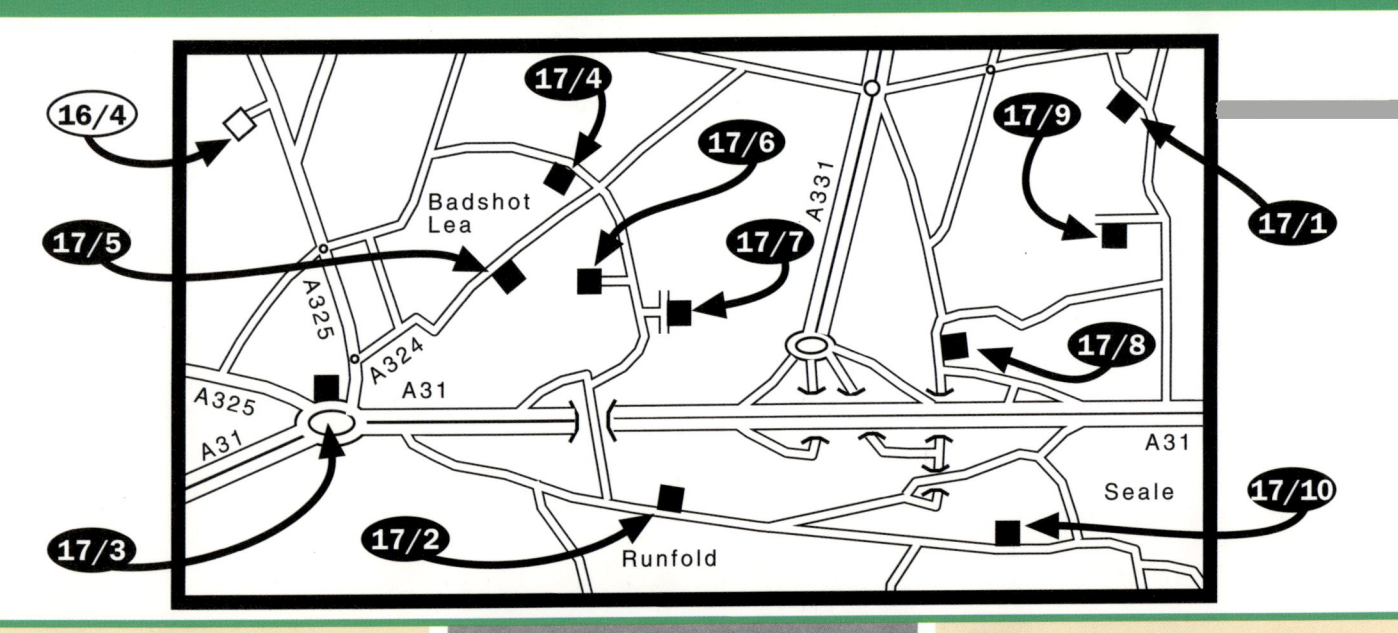

SPECIALIST & GENERAL NURSERIES, GARDEN AND PLANT CENTRES

17/1 OAKS NURSERY
Foreman Road, Ash
Aldershot
Hampshire   GU12 6HD
01252 28590
Trees, shrubs and summer bedding plants. Fresh cut flowers and all floristry work. Personal service and advice if required.
Open: All year except Xmas, Boxing & New Year's Days; 7 days a week, Mon–Sat 9–5.30, Sunday 9–5.
Wheelchairs: Partial access.
Toilets: Ask if desperate.
Dogs: On lead.   **Credit cards:** No.

ARTEFACT SUPPLIERS

17/2 RUNFOLD LANDSCAPES
Stoneyard, Guildford Road
Runfold, Farnham
Surrey   GU10 1PN
01252 782209
Specialists in natural stone for the garden including York flags (old & new), walling, crazy paving, rockery and pond stone.
Open: All year; 6 days a week (CLOSED SUNDAY); Mon–Fri 8–5, Sat (winter) 10–1, (summer) 9–4.
Wheelchairs: Reasonable access.
Toilets: No.
Dogs: On lead.   **Credit cards:** Yes.

17/3 BOURNE BUILDINGS
39–43 Guildford Road
Farnham   GU9 9QB
01252 718481
Garden buildings, stone ornaments.

SPECIALIST & GENERAL NURSERIES, GARDEN AND PLANT CENTRES

17/4 BENNETT'S NURSERY 
2 Church Road
Aldershot
Hampshire
GU11 3PS
01252 310556

Family nursery specialising in over 600 varieties of fuchsias. Shrubs, conifers, all bedding plants, garden ornaments, ponds, fish and accessories.
Open: All year except Xmas Day; 7 days a week, 9–6.
Wheelchairs: Easily accessible.
Toilets: Ask if desperate.
Dogs: On lead.   **Credit cards:** No.

17/5 BADSHOT LEA GARDEN CENTRE
A very large centre.

17/6 LITTLE ACRES NURSERY

17/7 ALDERWOOD NURSERIES 
Runfold St. George
Badshot Lea
Farnham
Surrey   GU10 1PP
01252 782493
Small family nursery specialising in bedding and basket plants. Hanging baskets with refill service. Also woodchip mulch.
Open: March–July; 7 days a week, 10–5.
Wheelchairs: Greenhouses paved.
Toilets: Ask if desperate.
Dogs: On lead.   **Credit cards:** No.

PICK-YOUR-OWN FARM

17/8 MANOR FARM

17

SPECIALIST & GENERAL NURSERIES, GARDEN AND PLANT CENTRES

17/9 LITTLE BROOK FUCHSIAS

Ash Green Lane West
Ash Green
Aldershot
Hampshire
GU12 6HL
01252 29731

Family-run **fuchsia** *nursery, with a wide range of fuchsias, both new & old. Small plants through to standards to baskets.*
Open: 1 Jan–first weekend in July; 5 days a week, Wed–Sun & Bank Holiday Mondays, 9–5.
Wheelchairs: Partial access.
Toilets: Ask if desperate.
Dogs: No.   **Credit cards:** No.

17/10 SEALE NURSERIES (OAK LODGE)

Seale Lane, Seale
Farnham
Surrey GU10 1LD
01252 782410

An old established family nursery with a shrubbery walk. Fuchsias & geraniums. A wide, unusual variety of own-grown plants.
Open: All year except Xmas week; 7 days a week, 9–5.
Wheelchairs: Gravelled car park but easy access elsewhere.
Toilets: Yes.
Dogs: No.   **Credit cards:** Yes.

SPECIALIST & GENERAL NURSERIES, GARDEN AND PLANT CENTRES

17/11 HAZELBANK NURSERY

17/12 FRENSHAM GARDEN CENTRE

The Reeds
Frensham
Surrey GU10 3BP
01252 792545

A country garden centre set in mature woodland with a wide range of trees, shrubs, plants and sundries. Beaton's coffee shop.
Open: All year except Xmas and Boxing Days; 7 days a week, Mon–Sat 9–5.30, Sunday 10.30–4.30.
Wheelchairs: Easy level access.
Toilets: Yes.
Dogs: On lead.   **Credit cards:** Yes.

NURSERY & GARDEN

17/13 MILLAIS NURSERIES
01252 792698
Rhododendron *specialists.*

PICK-YOUR-OWN FARMS

17/14 HYDE ORCHARDS

17/15 AVALON NURSERIES
Tilford Road, Churt, Farnham
GU10 2LL   01428 604842
Garden plant centre & PYO.

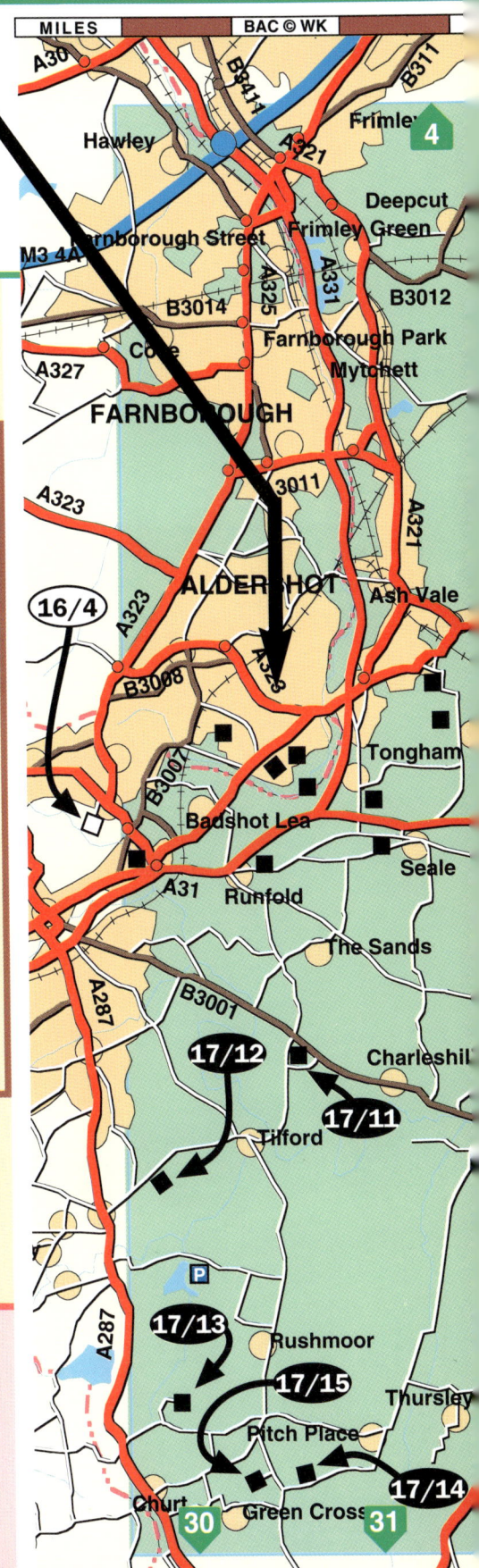

SURREY

SPECIALIST & GENERAL NURSERIES, GARDEN AND PLANT CENTRES

18/1 BARRALETS NURSERY AND GARDEN CENTRE

18/2 TOOBEES EXOTICS
Blackhorse Road, Woking
Surrey GU22 0QT
01483 797534
*Specialists in **succulents**, **cacti** and other exotic plants including **palms & cycads**. Also shrubs & bedding plants.*
Open: 1 Mar–30 Sept; Wed–Sun 10–5 (please phone for times outside these dates).
Wheelchairs: Reasonable access with assistance. **Toilets:** No.
Dogs: On lead. **Credit cards:** No.

18/3 JACKMAN'S GARDEN CENTRE
Egley Road, Woking
Surrey GU22 0NH
01483 714861
Large centre selling plants, shrubs, trees & houseplants. Also tools, stoneware, garden furniture, water garden accessories. Gifts.
Open: All year except Xmas, Boxing & New Year's Days; 7 days a week, Mon–Sat 9–5.30, Sun 10.30–4.30.
Wheelchairs: Are available.
Toilets: Yes.
Dogs: On lead. **Credit cards:** Yes.

18/4 WOKING NURSERY (LOAMPITS) 
99 Westfield Road
Woking
Surrey
GU22 9QR
01483 725646
*Family-run plant centre growing specimen & hard-to-find **trees**, **shrubs**, rhododendrons, azaleas & acers. Topsoil & manure supplies.*
Open: All year except Xmas, Boxing Days & August Sundays; 7 days a week, Mon–Sat 9.15–5.45, Sunday 10–4.
Wheelchairs: Partial access.
Toilets: Ask if desperate.
Dogs: No. **Credit cards:** Yes.

18/5 WOKING NURSERY

18/6 BRIARWOOD NURSERY & GARDEN CENTRE

NURSERY & PICK-YOUR-OWN FARM

18/7 SUTTON GREEN GARDEN NURSERY
Seasonal bedding, shrubs, trees, herbaceous and alpine plants, PYO soft fruit.

SPECIALIST & GENERAL NURSERIES, GARDEN AND PLANT CENTRES

18/8 JUNIPER NURSERIES

18/9 MERRIST WOOD PLANT CENTRE

Merrist Wood College
Holly Lane, Worplesdon
Guildford, Surrey GU3 3PE
01483 235122
A wide range of trees, shrubs, conifers, perennials, climbers, alpines, herbs and bedding, mainly propagated by the students.
Open: All year; Mon–Fri 9–5. Also spring & summer: Sat 10.30–5.30, Sun 10.30–4.30. Other selected weekends – phone for dates.
Wheelchairs: Good access, no steps.
Toilets: Yes.
Dogs: On lead. **Credit cards:** Yes.

18/10 JOHN GUNNER GARDEN CENTRE

18/11 COMPTON NURSERY
Compton, Guildford
Surrey GU3 1DT
01483 811387
*A wide range of **herbaceous perennials**, including some unusual varieties. Bedding plants and hanging baskets.*
Open: All year; 7 days a week, 8.30–5.30, but CLOSED SUNDAY from Xmas to Easter.
Wheelchairs: Paved parking.
Toilets: Yes.
Dogs: On lead. **Credit cards:** No.

18/12 ELM NURSERY
Sutton Green Road
Guildford GU4 7QD
01483 761748
Family-run; own-grown stock.

18/13 TANGLEY GARDENS NURSERY

18/14 ASTOLAT

GARDEN CENTRE & PICK-YOUR-OWN

18/15 SECRETTS GARDEN CENTRE AND PYO

Old Portsmouth Road
Milford, Godalming
Surrey GU8 5HL
Garden centre: 01483 426633
PYO: 01483 426543
A large garden centre with a wide range of house, conservatory & garden plants. New coffee shop. Farm and flower shop. PYO.
Open: 7 days a week:
  Mon–Fri 9–5.30, Sat 9.30–5.30, Sunday 10–4.
Wheelchairs: Accessible.
Toilets: Yes.
Dogs: No. **Credit cards:** Yes.

SPECIALIST & GENERAL NURSERIES, GARDEN AND PLANT CENTRES

18/16 WHEELER STREET NURSERY

18/17 HYDON NURSERIES
Clock Barn Lane
Hydon Heath, Godalming
Surrey GU8 4AZ
01483 860252
***Rhododendron, azalea, camellia and magnolia** specialists. Five Gold Medals at Chelsea Flower Shows.*
Open: All year except Xmas; 6 days a week (CLOSED SUNDAY), 8–12.45 and 2–5.
Wheelchairs: Difficult if unaccompanied. **Toilets:** No.
Dogs: On lead. **Credit cards:** No.

18

ARTEFACT SUPPLIER

18/18 WOODLANDS FARM NURSERY

Woodstreet Village
Guildford
Surrey GU3 3DU
01483 235536

Specialists in antique & reclaimed stone, bricks, flags and garden ornaments. Also mature trees, shrubs & Christmas trees.

Open: All year, except Xmas–New Year; Mon–Sat, by appointment only (please phone first).
Wheelchairs: Flat shingle yard.
Toilets: Yes.
Dogs: Yes. **Credit cards:** No.

GARDENS

18/19 LOSELEY PARK FARMS

Guildford
Surrey
GU3 1HS
01483 304440

Elizabethan family home since 1562. Rose, herb & flower gardens, herbaceous borders & moat walk. Plant sales. Gifts. Restaurant.

Open: 5 May–27 Sept; Wed–Sat & BHs, 11–5. (House: June–Aug only, 2–5.)
Costs: £2, children £1, concessions £1.50.
Wheelchairs: Can tour the gardens.
Dogs: Only in field on lead.
Toilets: Yes. **Credit cards:** No.

18/20 BUSBRIDGE LAKES, WATERFOWL & GARDENS
Phone 01483 421955 for days

18/21 WINKWORTH ARBORETUM (NT)
01483 208477
Hillside woodland, rare trees.

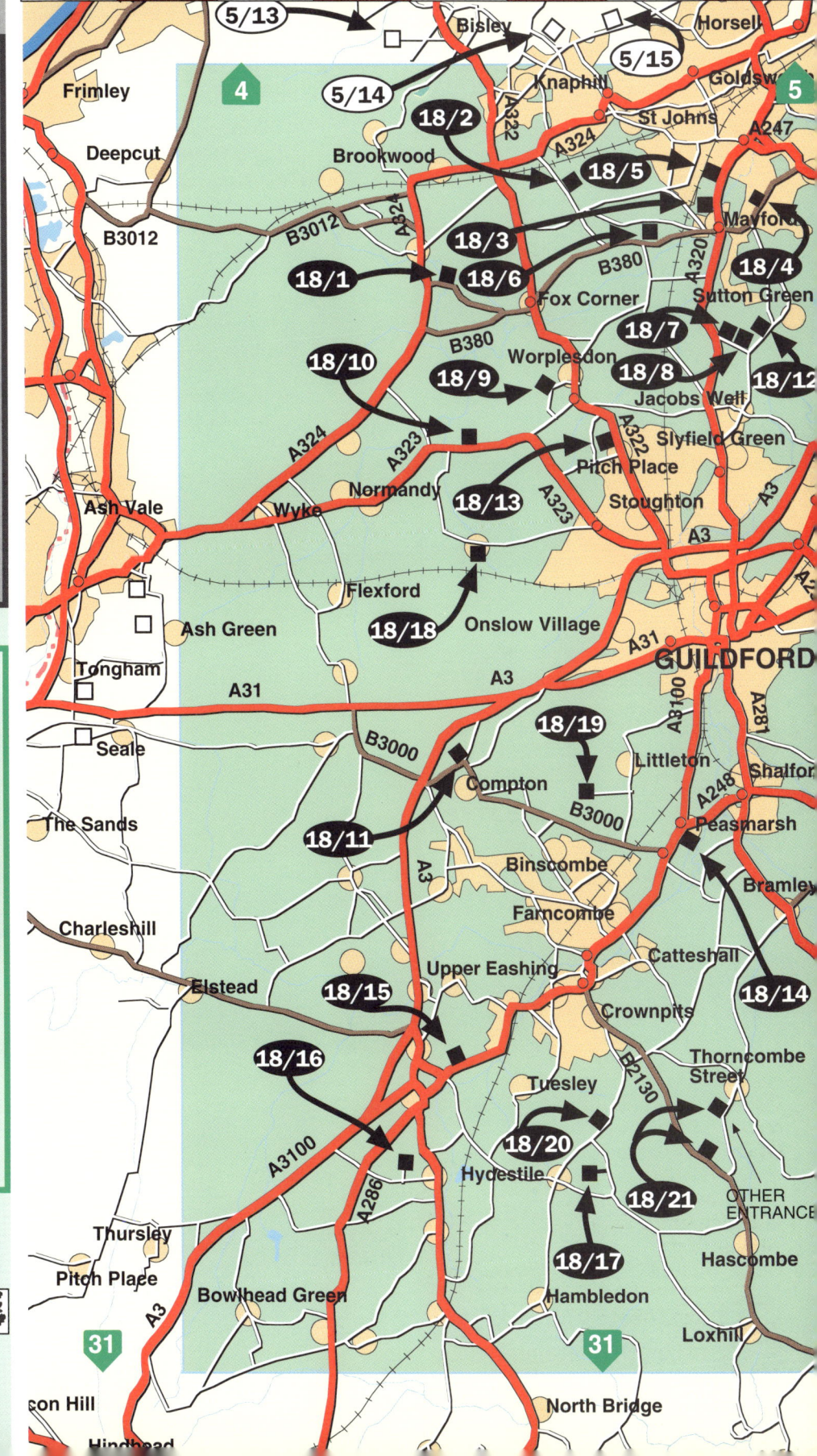

SURREY

SPECIALIST & GENERAL NURSERIES, GARDEN AND PLANT CENTRES

19/1 RIPLEY NURSERIES

19/2 CLANDON PARK GARDEN CENTRE

Clandon Park, West Clandon
Guildford
Surrey   GU4 7RQ
01483 222925

A garden centre specialising in unusual plants, trees and shrubs. An extensive range of roses and herbaceous plants.
Open: All year except Xmas and Boxing Days; 7 days a week, summer 9–6, winter 9–5.
Wheelchairs: Gravelled car park and paths.   **Toilets:** Yes.
Dogs: On lead.   **Credit cards:** Yes.

19/3 SQUIRE'S GARDEN CENTRE

19/4 SEYMOURS GARDEN & LEISURE CENTRE OF STOKE D'ABERNON

(incorporating Peters Plants)
Stoke Road, Stoke D'Abernon
Cobham, Surrey   KT11 3PU
01932 862530

Well known centre moved from Ewell. Plants, aquatics, landscape and leisure centre. Gifts. Large coffee shop.
Open: All year except Xmas & Easter Sunday; Mon–Sat 8.30–5.30, Sunday 10.30–4.30.
Wheelchairs: Paved, ramps and WC.
Toilets: Yes.
Dogs: On lead.   **Credit cards:** Yes.

19/5 DOBBE'S NURSERY

19/6 FOLIAGE & HERB PLANTS

19/7 HEATH NURSERY (Leylandii)

19/8 CEDAR NURSERY
Horsley Road, Cobham
Surrey   KT11 3JX
01932 862473,   fax 01932 867152
E-mail: cedar@netcomuk.co.uk

A country nursery growing a wide range of trees and shrubs. Specialists in garden design and plant sourcing.
Open: All year except Xmas, Boxing and New Year's Days; 7 days a week, Mon–Fri 8–5, Sat 9–5, Sunday 11–4 .
Toilets: Ask if desperate.
Dogs: On lead.   **Credit cards:** No.

19/9 HIGHBANKS NURSERY

19/10 HOMELEIGH NURSERY

19/11 NOTCUTTS GARDEN CENTRE
Guildford Road
Cranleigh GU6 8LT
01483 274222
'For all that's best in gardening.'

19/12 LOWER ROAD PLANT CENTRE

Lower Road, Effingham
Leatherhead
Surrey   KT24 5JP

*A wide range of home grown plants. Specialists in **clematis**, hanging baskets and hardy nursery stock. 'Friendly staff!'*
Open: All year except Xmas & Boxing Days; Mon–Sat 9–5, Sunday 10–4.
Wheelchairs: Good access.
Toilets: Ask if desperate.
Dogs: On lead.   **Credit cards:** Yes.

PICK-YOUR-OWN FARMS

19/13 NUTBERRY FRUIT FARM

19/14 NUTHILL FRUIT FARM

ROYAL HORTICULTURAL SOCIETY GARDEN, WISLEY

GARDENS

19/15 HANNAH PESCHAR SCULPTURE GARDEN
01306 627269 (restricted opening)

19/16 CLANDON PARK (NT)
01483 222482
8 acres; incl. parterre & grotto.

19/17 HATCHLANDS PARK (NT)
01483 222482
18C. garden & pleasure grounds.

19/18 POLESDEN LACEY (NT)
01372 458203
Edwardian style walled gardens.

19/19 ROYAL HORTICULTURAL SOCIETY GARDEN
Wisley, Woking
Surrey GU23 6QB
01483 211113

The Royal Horticultural Society's 240-acre garden. Gardeners' bookshop, plant centre.
Open: All year except Xmas Day, Mon–Sat (MEMBERS ONLY ON SUNDAY); 10–sunset or 7 in summer.
Costs: £5, children £1.75.
Wheelchairs: Standard/electric – phone to book. Good access. **Toilets:** Yes.

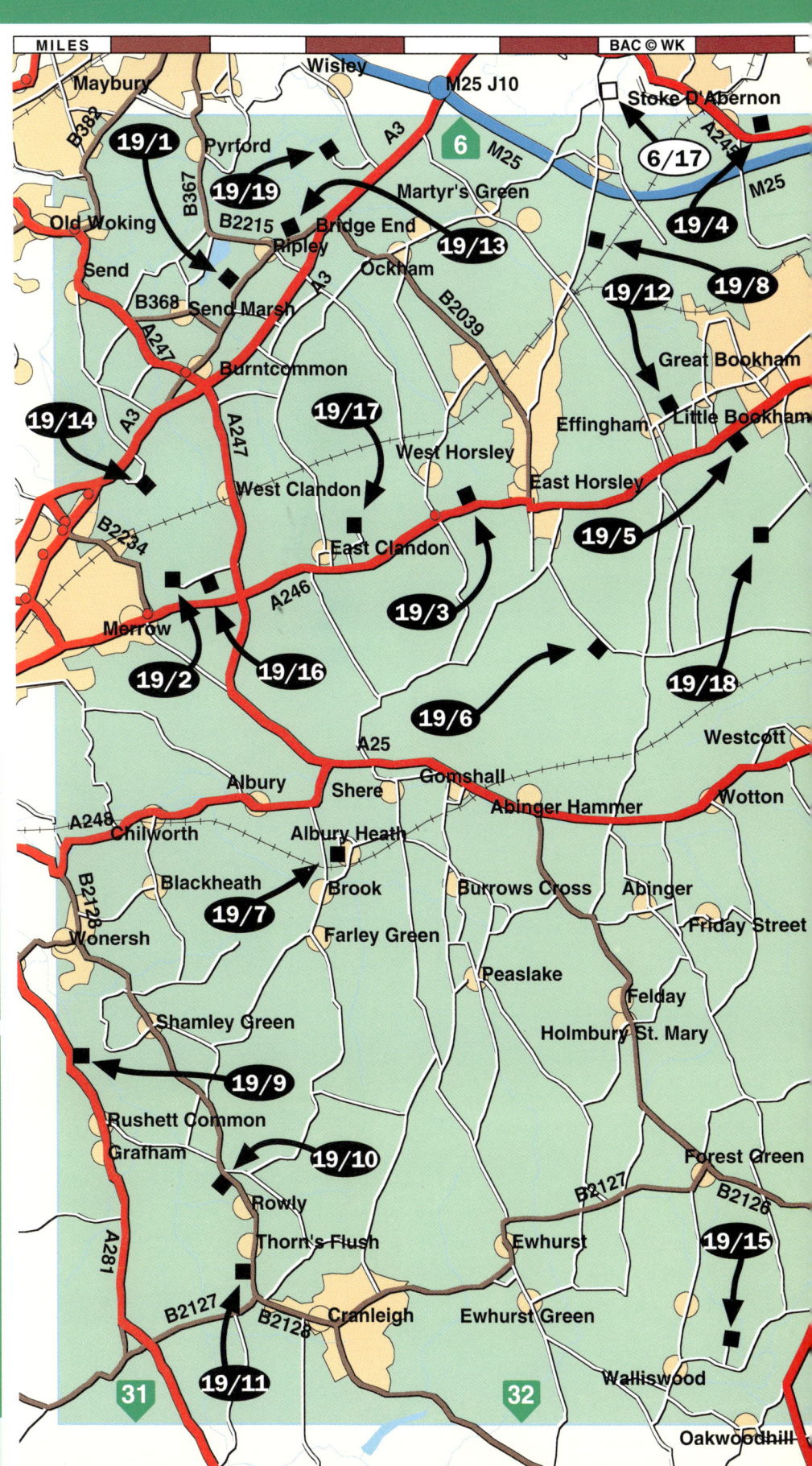

SURREY

SPECIALIST & GENERAL NURSERIES, GARDEN AND PLANT CENTRES

20/1 A. J. DOBBE AND SONS

20/2 FARM LANE NURSERIES
Farm Lane
Ashtead
Surrey KT21 1LY
01372 274400

An enthusiastic family nursery, with an interesting and unusual range of plants and shrubs.

Open: All year except 4 days over Xmas; 6 days a week (CLOSED MONDAY) but open 7 days during summer bedding season, Mon–Sat 8.30–5, Sun 10–5 (or dusk in winter).
Toilets: No.
Dogs: No. **Credit cards:** Yes.

20/3 MARSDEN NURSERY AND GARDEN CENTRE
Pleasure Pit Road
Ashtead
Surrey KT21 1HU
01372 273891

Furniture, sheds, greenhouses, fountains, fencing, silk flowers, barbecues and a full range of trees, shrubs, bedding & sundries.

Open: All year except Xmas, Boxing & New Year's Days; 7 days a week, Mon–Fri 8–5, Sat, Sun and Bank Holidays 9–5.
Wheelchairs: Wide doors, ramps, easy access. **Toilets:** Yes.
Dogs: On lead. **Credit cards:** Yes.

20/4 COUNTRY GARDENS DORKING
Reigate Road, Dorking
Surrey RH4 1WP
01306 884845

Country Gardens

'Good value garden centre with very wide plant selection. Free local delivery. Terracotta pots, compost, seeds, bulbs, furniture.'

Open: All year; Mon–Sat 9–6, Sunday 10.30–4.30. Extended spring hours – phone for information.
Wheelchairs: Easy access.
Toilets: Yes.
Dogs: On lead. **Credit cards:** Yes.

20/5 THE MICHAEL SEYMOUR NURSERY
Station Road,
Betchworth
Surrey RH3 7LX
01737 842099

Hardy nursery stock, shrubs, roses, bedding plants, herbaceous plants, ornamental and fruit trees, conifers, sundries.

Open: All year except Xmas–New Year; Mon–Sat 8–5.30 or dusk if earlier (extended in spring), Sun 10–4.
Wheelchairs: Display areas are paved.
Toilets: Yes.
Dogs: On lead. **Credit cards:** Yes.

20/6 BUCKLAND NURSERIES

20/7 HIGH TREES NURSERIES
Buckland
Reigate RH2 9RE
01737 247217

A long established independent.

20/8 HEATHFIELD NURSERIES

20/9 REIGATE GARDEN CENTRE
143 Sandcross Lane
South Park
Reigate
Surrey
RH2 8HH
01737 248188

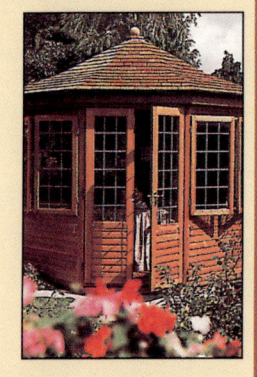

All types of garden furniture, lawnmowers, garden machinery, sheds, garden buildings, landscape materials, ponds, plants & trees.

Open: All year except Xmas & Boxing Days; 7 days a week, Mon–Sat 9–6, Sunday 10.30–4.30.
Wheelchairs: Reasonable access.
Toilets: Yes.
Dogs: Yes. **Credit cards:** Yes.

20/10 CLAY LANE NURSERY THE SURREY FUCHSIA CENTRE
3 Clay Lane, South Nutfield
Redhill, Surrey RH1 4EG
01737 823307

*A specialist **fuchsia** nursery. Rooted cuttings for sale February to mid-April, mature plants May–August.*

Open: Feb–Aug; 6 days a week (CLOSED MONDAY except Bank Hols), 9–5, but phone before travelling in July–Aug.
Toilets: Ask if desperate.
Dogs: No. **Credit cards:** No.

20/11 HILLSIDE SHRUBS & HARDY PLANTS NURSERY
109 Horley Road, Earlswood
Redhill 01737 765645
*Special **roses**, old fashioned plants.*

PICK-YOUR-OWN FARMS

20/12 FANNY'S FARM SHOP

20/13 OCKLEY COURT FARM
Ockley
Dorking
Surrey RH5 5LS
01306 711365

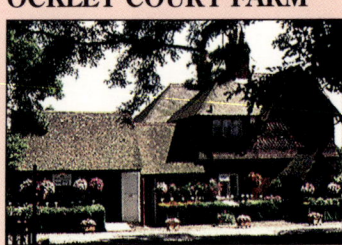

Flower house with hanging baskets, bedding, patio tubs. Farm shop with home grown fruit, salads, vegetables. PYO: soft fruit, vegetables.

Open: Farm shop: all year, 7 days a week, 9–6 (summer), 9–5 (winter). PYO: June–Sept 9–6.
Wheelchairs: Not suitable.
Toilets: Yes. **Dogs:** On lead.
Credit cards: Yes, in shop, not in PYO.

GARDENS

20/14 BOX HILL COUNTRY PARK (NT)
01306 885502
Chalk; views to South Downs.

20

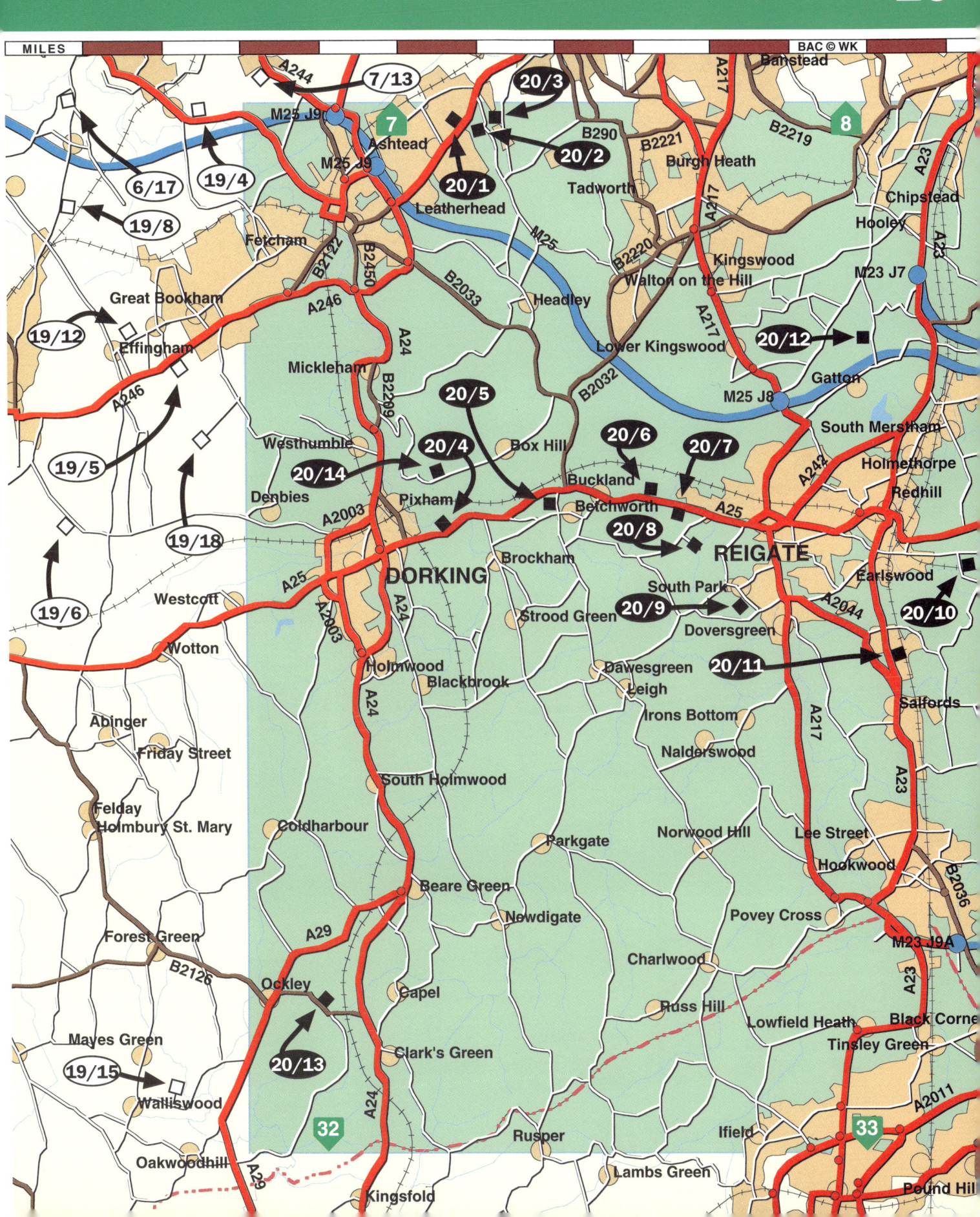

SURREY

SPECIALIST & GENERAL NURSERIES, GARDEN AND PLANT CENTRES

21/1 KNIGHTS GARDEN CENTRE & COFFEE SHOP
Chelsham   CR6 9DZ
01883 622340
'A meeting place for plant lovers.'

21/2 KNIGHTS GARDEN CENTRE & COFFEE SHOP
Woldingham   CR3 7LA
01883 653142
'A meeting place for plant lovers.'

21/3 NUTFIELD NURSERIES

21/4 KNIGHTS GARDEN CENTRE & COFFEE SHOP
Ivy Mill Nursery, Godstone
RH9 8NB   01883 742665
'A meeting place for plant lovers.'

21/5 NETTLETONS NURSERY

21/6 KNIGHTS GARDEN CENTRE
Nag's Hall Nursery, Godstone
RH9 8DB   01883 742275
'A meeting place for plant lovers.'

21/7 WOODHAM NURSERY

21/8 BROOK NURSERY
Eastbourne Road
South Godstone   RH9 8JE
01342 893265
Shrubs, bedding, sheds, trees.

21/9 WALKERS GARDEN LEISURE CENTRE

21/10 OCCASIONALLY YOURS
Centre with farm shop & café.

21/11 WYEVALE GARDEN CENTRE

21/12 DOVES BARN NURSERY

21/13 WILLOW TREE NURSERY
Newchapel Road, Lingfield
Surrey   RH7 6BL
01342 834961
*Award-winning specialist growers of **fuchsias**, hanging baskets and other container plants.*
Open: Feb–Oct (closed Nov–Jan); 6 days a week (CLOSED TUESDAY), Mon–Sat 9.30–5.30, Sunday 9.30–4.30.
Wheelchairs: Good access.
Toilets: Ask if desperate.
Dogs: On lead.   **Credit cards:** No.

21/14 LAURENCE HOBBS ORCHIDS 
Bailiffs Cottage Nursery
Hophurst Lane, Crawley Down
West Sussex   RH10 4LN
01342 715142
Orchids *for growing in the home or heated greenhouse. Send SAE for mail order catalogue. Specialists in orchids for beginners.*
Open: All year except Xmas, Boxing & New Year's Day; 6 days a week (CLOSED FRIDAY) 10–1, 2–5.
Wheelchairs: Yes.
Toilets: Ask if desperate.
Dogs: On lead.   **Credit cards:** Yes.

21/15 HERONS BONSAI NURSERY 
Wiremill Lane, Newchapel
Lingfield
Surrey   RH7 6HJ
01342 832657
*Peter Chan's leading **bonsai** nursery.*
Open: All year except Xmas Day; 7 days a week, Mon–Sat 9.30–dusk (winter), 9.30–5.30 (summer), Sunday 10–4.30.
Wheelchairs: Yes.   **Toilets:** Yes.
Dogs: No.   **Credit cards:** Yes.

21/16 SNOW HILL GARDEN CENTRE
A very large centre.

WATER GARDEN SPECIALISTS

21/17 AQUARIUM & POND CENTRE
At Snow Hill Garden Centre
01342 712545
Ponds, plants, fish & equipment.

21/18 NEWLAKE GARDENS

21/19 WATERSIDE AQUATICS & KOI CENTRE 
Beaver Farm
Eastbourne Road, Newchapel
Lingfield, Surrey   RH7 6HL
01342 835001
Aquatic specialists. Thousands of aquatic plants and fish. Advice on design and construction. Installation service. Café.
Open: All year except Xmas & Boxing Days; 7 days a week, summer 9–6 (Sunday 10–4), winter 10–4.
Wheelchairs: Easy access.
Toilets: Yes.
Dogs: On lead.   **Credit cards:** Yes.

PICK-YOUR-OWN FARMS

21/20 FLOWER FARM
Fruit and vegetables.

PYO FARM & PLANT CENTRE

21/21 PRIORY FARM 
Nutfield, Redhill
Surrey   RH1 4EJ
PYO: 01737 822484
Plant centre: 01737 823500
*Specialist growers of **bedding plants** and hanging baskets, with a good range of potted plants and perennials. Also PYO, farm shop and coffee shop.*
Wheelchairs: Easy access.
Toilets: Yes.   **Dogs:** Only in car parks.
Credit cards: Yes.

SEE PAGE 48 FOR FULL DETAILS OF OPENING DATES AND TIMES

21

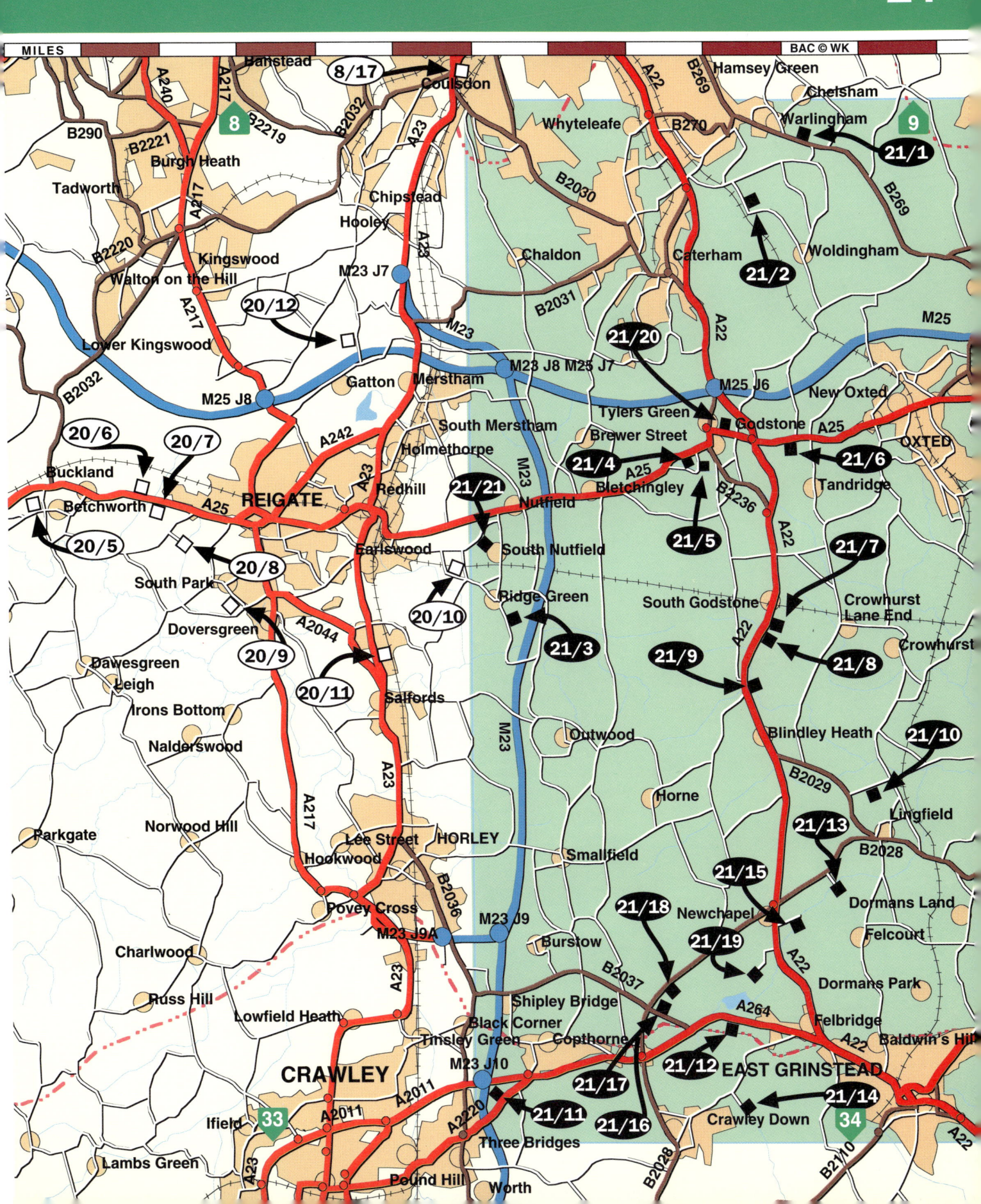

KENT

SPECIALIST & GENERAL NURSERIES, GARDEN AND PLANT CENTRES

22/1 WESTERHAM HEIGHTS NURSERIES

22/2 RING LODGE NURSERY

22/3 FRENCH STREET NURSERIES
Hosey Common Lane
Westerham
Kent   TN16 1PW
01959 563366
Specialist growers of bedding, basket and patio plants, hardy perennials & alpines. Stocks of heathers, conifers, shrubs, sundries.
Open: Jan–Nov (closed Dec); 7 days a week, Mon–Sat 9–1 & 2–5, Sun & Bank Holidays 10–1 & 2–5.
Wheelchairs: Sloping gravel.
Toilets: Yes.
Dogs: On lead.   **Credit cards:** Yes.

22/4 CARE IDE HILL

22/5 NEWLANDS NURSERY
Goathurst Common
Ide Hill, Sevenoaks
Kent   TN14 6DA
01732 750591
Nursery growing shrubs, conifers, summer and winter bedding plants. Specialist **Xmas tree growers.** *HTA gift tokens.*
Open: All year except Xmas–New Year; 7 days a week, Mon–Sat 9–5, Sunday 10–5.
Toilets: Ask if desperate.
Dogs: On lead.   **Credit cards:** Yes.

22/6 SMARTS GARDEN CENTRE

22/7 STARBOROUGH NURSERY
Starborough Road
Marsh Green, Edenbridge
Kent TN8 5RB
01732 865614
Specialist growers of **hardy and unusual shrubs**, *including acers, magnolias and camellias. Some specimen shrubs available.*
Open: All year except Jan & July; 6 days a week (CLOSED SUNDAY), 10–4.
Wheelchairs: All gravel. **Toilets:** Yes.
Dogs: On lead.   **Credit cards:** Yes.

22/8 ROGER PLATTS GARDEN DESIGN & NURSERIES

Photograph by Clive Nichols

Stick Hill, Edenbridge, Kent
TN8 5NH   01732 863318
A traditional nursery with the emphasis on **garden design.** *An interesting range of plants is available, including a wide variety of hardy perennials.*
Open: All year except Xmas & Boxing Days; 7 days a week, 9–5.
Wheelchairs: Flat gravel and paved.
Toilets: No.
Dogs: On lead.   **Credit cards:** Yes.

22/9 ORCHARD NURSERY

22/10 PERRYHILL NURSERIES
Hartfield, East Sussex
TN7 4JP   01892 770377
Nearly 5000 varieties of plants.

PICK-YOUR-OWN FARM

22/11 PERRYHILL ORCHARD

GARDENS

22/12 CHARTWELL (NT)
01732 866368
Sir Winston Churchill's garden.

22/13 SQUERRYES COURT

Westerham, Kent   TN16 1SJ
01959 562345/563118
Lovely gardens surrounding beautiful 17C lived-in manor house (open). Lake, restored formal garden, borders, 18C dovecote.
Open: April–end Sept; Wed, Sat, Sun & Bank Holiday Mondays. Garden 12–5.30. House 1.30–5.30.
Costs: Gardens: adults £2.20, children £1.20, concessions £2.   **Toilets:** Yes.
Wheelchairs: Very limited access.
Dogs: On lead.   **Credit cards:** No.

22/14 EMMETTS GARDEN (NT)
01732 750367
5-acre hillside, shrub garden.

22/15 KNOLE (NT)
01732 450608
Lord Sackville's deer park.

22/16 RIVERHILL HOUSE GARDENS
Riverhill, Sevenoaks
Kent   TN15 0RR
01732 458802/452557
Historic hillside garden. Rhododendrons, azaleas and bluebells in woodland setting.
Open: April–June, Sundays & Bank Holiday weekends, 12–6.
Costs: £2.50, children 50p.
Wheelchairs: not suitable. **Dogs:** No.
Toilets: Yes.   **Credit cards:** No.

22/17 HEVER CASTLE

22/18 CHIDDINGSTONE CASTLE

22/19 PENSHURST PLACE & GARDENS

22/20 HAMMERWOOD PARK

22/21 GROOMBRIDGE PLACE GARDENS

22

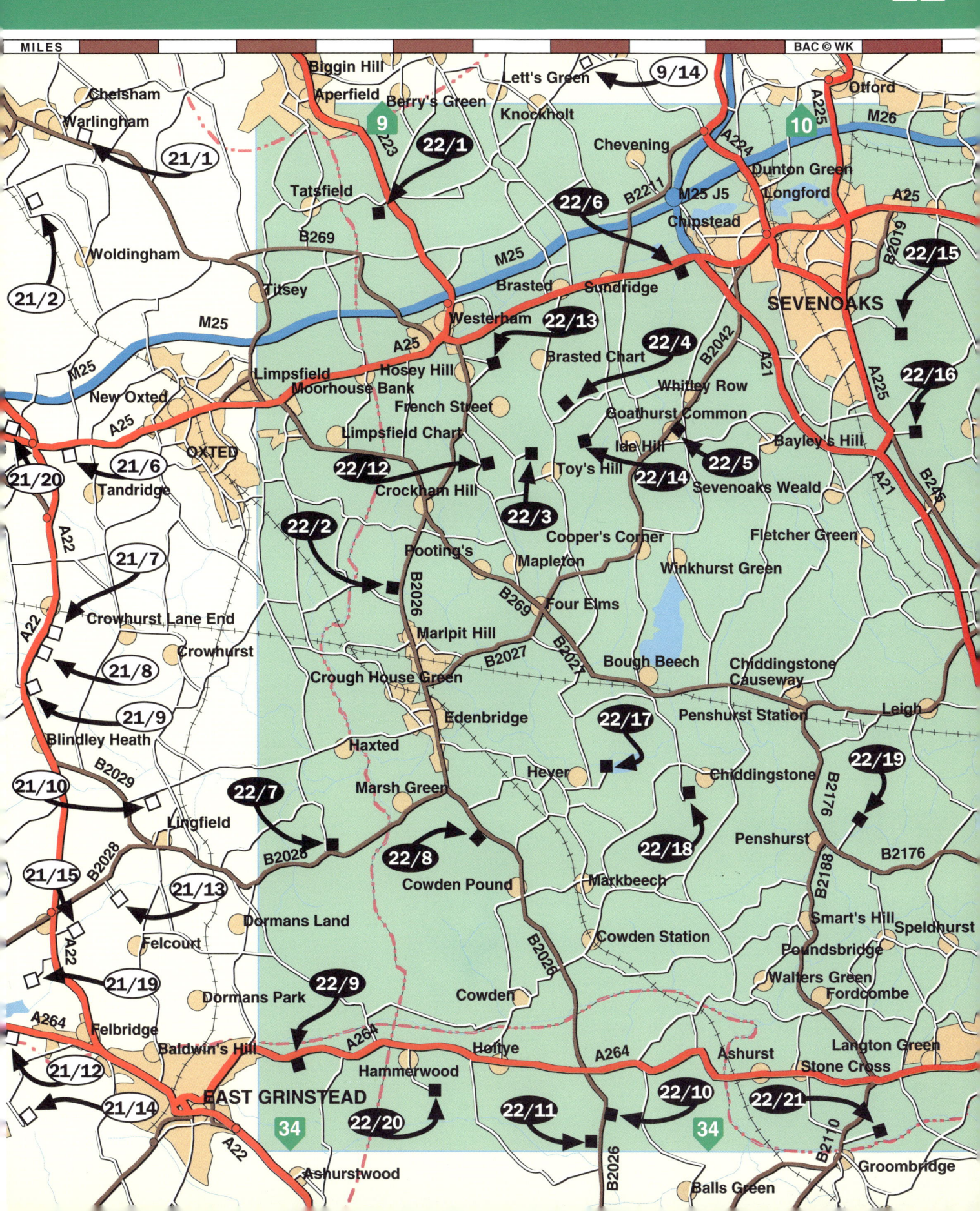

KENT

SPECIALIST & GENERAL NURSERIES, GARDEN AND PLANT CENTRES

23/1 IGHTHAM PLANT CENTRE

23/2 COBLANDS PLANT CENTRE
Sevenoaks Road, Ightham
Sevenoaks
01732 780816
Well stocked plant centre.

23/3 G. REUTHE LTD
Crown Point Nursery
Sevenoaks Road
Ightham, Sevenoaks
Kent   TN15 0HB
01732 810694
Chelsea Gold Medalists. Specialists in **rhododendrons and azaleas**.
A selection of shrubs is also available.
Open: All year; 6 days a week (CLOSED SUNDAY except in April & May), 9.30–4.
Wheelchairs: Difficult.
Toilets: Yes.
Dogs: On lead.   **Credit cards:** Yes.

23/4 PLAXTOL NURSERIES

23/5 HAMPTONS NURSERIES 
Pillar Box Lane
Hadlow, Tonbridge
Kent   TN11 9SW
01732 810633
Set in Victorian walled garden. Unusual herbaceous plants, shrubs, climbers, bedding, fuchsias, geraniums. Basket filling service. Garden advisory visits.
Open: Mar–Oct; 7 days a week, 10–5. Nov–Feb please phone first.
Wheelchairs: Yes.
Toilets: Yes.
Dogs: On lead.   **Credit cards:** Yes.

23/6 HADLOW COLLEGE PLANT CENTRE 
Hadlow College
Hadlow, Tonbridge
Kent   TN11 0AL
01732–851 107
Thousands of plants, many home-grown and guaranteed for one year. Also seeds, bulbs, books, composts, pots and sundries.
Open: All year; 6 days a week (CLOSED SUNDAY), 9–5.
Wheelchairs: Easy access, disabled WC.
Toilets: Yes.
Dogs: No.   **Credit cards:** Yes.

23/7 GATE HOUSE FARM NURSERY

23/8 COBLANDS GARDEN CENTRE 
Eridge Road (A26)
Tunbridge Wells
Kent   TN4 8HP
01892 515234
Extensive well stocked plant area with many specimens. House plants, full range of sundries, terracotta, paving, fencing and sheds.
Open: All year except Xmas, Boxing Days & Easter Sun; 7 days a week, Mon–Sat 8.30–5.30, Sun 10–4.
Wheelchairs: Easy access.
Toilets: Yes.
Dogs: On lead.   **Credit cards:** Yes.
SEE PAGE 49 FOR FULL DETAILS

23/9 NOTCUTTS GARDEN CENTRE
Tonbridge Road, Pembury
TN2 4QN   01892 822636
'For all that's best in gardening.'

23/10 KINGS TOLL NURSERY

PICK-YOUR-OWN FARMS

23/11 SILVERHILL COBNUT PLANTATION
Cobnuts in Sept and Oct.

23/12 BEECHINWOOD FARM 
St. Mary's Platt
Sevenoaks
Kent   TN15 8QN
01732 882037
PYO strawberries, raspberries, gooseberries, other soft fruit and vegetables in season. Farm shop for ready-picked produce etc.
Open: Early June to end September; 7 days a week, 9–6.
Wheelchairs: Reasonable access.
Toilets: Yes.
Dogs: On lead.   **Credit cards:** No.

23/13 DOWNINGBURY PYO FARM

23/14 PIPPINS FRUIT FARM

ARTEFACT SUPPLIER

23/15 PRIMA POTS
Five Oak Green Road
Tonbridge, Kent
01732 367064
Terracotta and glazed pot warehouse.

GARDENS

23/16 IGHTHAM MOTE (NT)
01732 810378
Gardens, lake, woodland.

23

23/17 BROADVIEW GARDENS

At Hadlow College
Hadlow
Tonbridge
Kent
TN11 0AL
01732 850551

"A plantsman's delight" with new design ideas and plant combinations found in a mixture of themed gardens and landscapes.
Open: Mid-March–early November; 5 days a week (CLOSED MON & TUES), 10–5.
Costs: £2, children under 12 free.
Wheelchairs: Difficult access.
Toilets: Yes.
Dogs: No. **Credit cards:** No.

GARDEN AND NURSERY

23/18 GREAT COMP GARDEN & NURSERY

Comp Lane
St. Mary's Platt
Borough Green
Kent   TN15 8QS
01732 882669/886154

Seven-acre 'plantsman's paradise' surrounding 17th century manor. Wide & unusual range of home produced plants.
Open: 1 Apr–31 Oct; daily, 11–6.
Costs: £3, children £1.
Wheelchairs: Good access. Disabled WC.
Toilets: Yes.
Dogs: No. **Credit cards:** No.

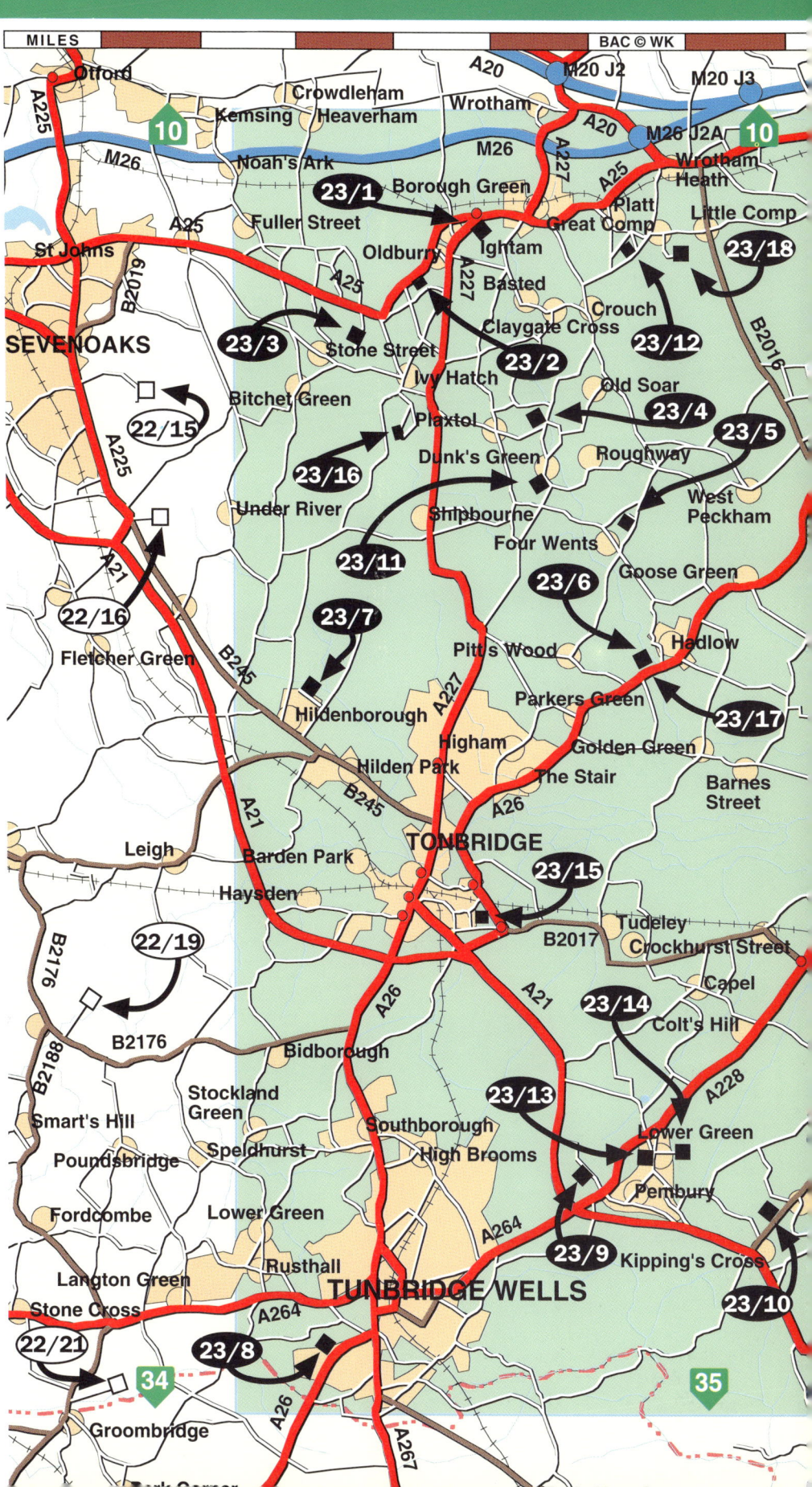

KENT

SPECIALIST & GENERAL NURSERIES, GARDEN AND PLANT CENTRES

24/1 WINDMILL NURSERY
The Street
Mereworth
Maidstone
Kent ME18 5LS

Small nursery with general stock specialising in oriental theme stoneware, steel & wooden bridges & other features.
Open: All year except Xmas–New Year; 6 days a week (CLOSED MON), 10–5. Also CLOSED Tues in Jan/Feb.
Wheelchairs: Reasonable.
Toilets: Ask if desperate.
Dogs: On lead. **Credit cards:** No.

24/2 BIJOU NURSERIES

24/3 CROMAR NURSERY

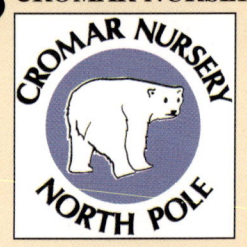

North Pole, Livesey Street
Wateringbury, Maidstone
Kent ME18 5BQ
01622 812380

Shrubs, trees, conifers, extensive range of fruit trees & bushes, perennials, roses, herbs, hanging baskets and patio plants.
Open: All year except Xmas week; 6 days a week (CLOSED WEDNESDAY), 9.30–5.
Wheelchairs: Reasonable access.
Toilets: Ask if desperate.
Dogs: On lead. **Credit cards:** Yes.

24/4 BROOKSIDE GARDEN CENTRE
Seven Mile Lane
East Peckham, Tonbridge
Kent TN12 5JG
01622 871250

Large independent centre est. 1968. A wide range of trees, shrubs, conifers, perennials, alpines, bedding & house plants. Aquatics.
Open: All year except Xmas & Boxing Days; 7 days a week, weekday hours 8.30–5.30.
Wheelchairs: Easy access, ramps and disabled WC. **Toilets:** Yes.
Dogs: No. **Credit cards:** Yes.

24/5 NOTCUTTS GARDEN CENTRE
Bearsted Road, Maidstone
ME14 5LH 01622 739944
'For all that's best in gardening.'

24/6 G & S SMALLHOLDINGS
Wheelers Lane, Linton
ME17 4BN 01622 744273
Hanging baskets, **fuchsias**.

24/7 RALPHS NURSERY & FARM SHOP

Marlpit Farm, Wierton Road
Boughton Monchelsea
Maidstone, Kent ME17 4JW
01622 743851

A family-owned nursery and farmshop specialising in **bedding plants**, *hardy ferns, perennials, shrubs & Xmas trees.*
Open: Mon–Sat 9–5 (closed Mon in Jan & Feb), Sun 9–1 (5pm in May–July). Phone for BH hours.
Wheelchairs: Partial access.
Toilets: Ask if desperate.
Dogs: On lead. **Credit cards:** Yes.

24/8 FOUR SEASONS BONSAI & RHINO ROCK GARDENS

Snoll Hatch
Road
East Peckham
Kent
TN12 5DP
01622 872403

Japanese garden materials, bonsai, rock water features, sculptures, tuition, landscapes – all set in Japanese gardens.
Open: All year except Xmas, Boxing & New Year's Days; 4 days a week, Fri-Mon, 10–5.
Wheelchairs: Accessible.
Toilets: Yes.
Dogs: On lead. **Credit cards:** Yes.

24/9 WYEVALE GARDEN CENTRE

24/10 MARLE PLACE GARDENS

PICK-YOUR-OWN FARMS

24/11 ALDERS FIELD

24/12 TESTON FARM STALL

GARDENS

24/13 BOUGHTON MONCHELSEA PLACE
Elizabethan walled gardens.
Open: Good Friday–mid Oct: Sun & BHs. Also May–Sept, Wed 2–6.
Costs: £3.25, children £1.75, OAPs £2.75.

24/14 YALDING ORGANIC GARDENS
Benover Road
Maidstone
Kent ME18 6EX
01622 814650

A tour through gardening history. 14 individual gardens depict gardening from medieval times to the present day.
Open: May–Sept: BH Mons & Wed–Sun, 10–5 (CLOSED MON, TUES); April & Oct: weekends & BHs, also 10–5. (CLOSED NOV–MARCH.)
Costs: £2.50, children £1.25, concessions £2.
Wheelchairs: Yes. **Toilets:** Yes.
Dogs: No. **Credit cards:** Yes.

Yalding Organic Gardens

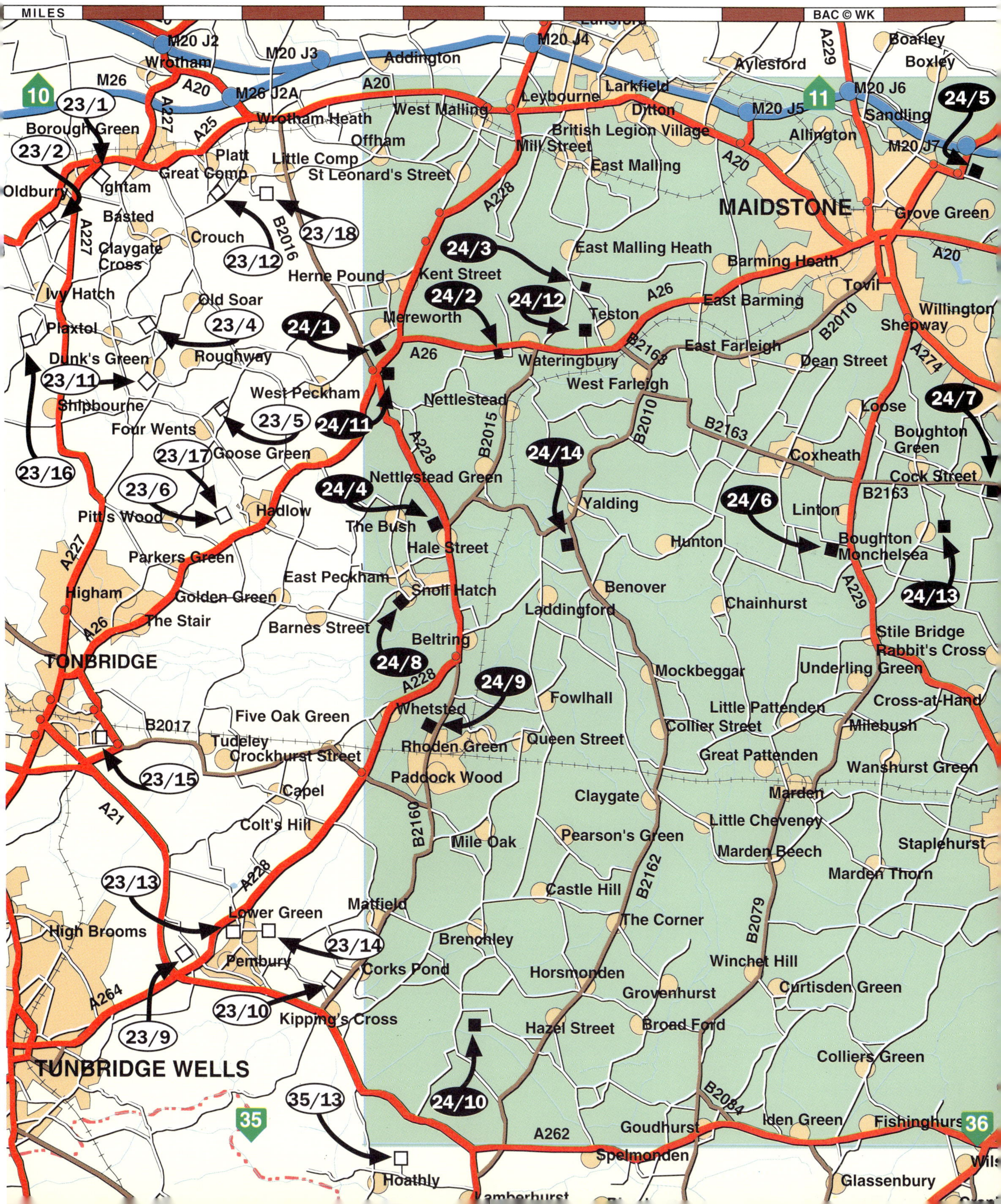
MILES
BAC © WK
M20 J2
Wrotham
M20 J3
Addington
M20 J4
Aylesford
A229
Boarley
Boxley
M26
A20
M26 J2A
A20
Leybourne
Larkfield
M20 J6
Sandling
M20 J5
Ditton
British Legion Village
Allington
M20 J7
Borough Green
A227
A25
Wrotham Heath
West Malling
Offham
Mill Street
East Malling
A20
Oldbury
Platt
Little Comp
Great Comp
St Leonard's Street
Ightham
A228
MAIDSTONE
Grove Green
Basted
A227
B2016
Crouch
Claygate Cross
East Malling Heath
Barming Heath
A20
Kent Street
Herne Pound
Ivy Hatch
Teston
A26
East Barming
Tovil
B2010
Willington
Old Soar
Mereworth
Plaxtol
Shepway
Roughway
B2163
East Farleigh
Dunk's Green
A26
Wateringbury
Dean Street
A274
West Farleigh
Shipbourne
West Peckham
Nettlestead
B2010
Loose
Four Wents
A228
B2015
B2163
Boughton Green
Goose Green
Coxheath
Cock Street
Nettlestead Green
B2163
Hadlow
Yalding
Linton
Pitt's Wood
The Bush
Hunton
Boughton Monchelsea
Hale Street
A227
Parkers Green
East Peckham
Snoll Hatch
Benover
A229
Higham
Golden Green
Laddingford
Chainhurst
The Stair
A26
Barnes Street
Beltring
Stile Bridge
Rabbit's Cross
TONBRIDGE
Mockbeggar
Underling Green
A228
Fowlhall
Little Pattenden
Cross-at-Hand
Whetsted
Collier Street
Milebush
B2017
Five Oak Green
Tudeley
Rhoden Green
Queen Street
Great Pattenden
Wanshurst Green
Crockhurst Street
Paddock Wood
Marden
Capel
Claygate
A21
Little Cheveney
Colt's Hill
B2160
Mile Oak
Pearson's Green
Staplehurst
Marden Beech
Marden Thorn
A228
B2162
Castle Hill
B2079
Lower Green
Matfield
The Corner
High Brooms
Brenchley
Pembury
Winchet Hill
Corks Pond
Horsmonden
Curtisden Green
A264
Grovenhurst
Kipping's Cross
Hazel Street
Broad Ford
TUNBRIDGE WELLS
Colliers Green
B2084
Iden Green
A262
Goudhurst
Fishinghurst
Spelmonden
Hoathly
Glassenbury
10
11
35
36
23/1
23/2
23/4
23/5
23/6
23/9
23/10
23/11
23/12
23/13
23/14
23/15
23/16
23/17
23/18
24/1
24/2
24/3
24/4
24/5
24/6
24/7
24/8
24/9
24/10
24/11
24/12
24/13
24/14
35/13

KENT

SPECIALIST & GENERAL NURSERIES, GARDEN AND PLANT CENTRES

25/1 THE POTTED GARDEN NURSERY
Ashford Road, Bearsted
Maidstone
Kent ME14 4NH
A large family nursery growing shrubs, trees, roses, winter & summer bedding, perennials. Xmas trees. Display gardens.
Open: All year except Xmas–New Year; 7 days a week, summer 9–5.30, winter 9–dusk.
Wheelchairs: Good access.
Toilets: No.
Dogs: On lead.   **Credit cards:** Yes.

25/2 PLEASANT VIEW GARDEN CENTRE

25/3 RUMWOOD NURSERIES & GARDEN CENTRE
Sutton Road, Langley
Maidstone
Kent ME17 3ND
01622 861477
Kent's largest rose growers. Also garden centre with trees, shrubs, special plants, hedging, extensive stoneware etc.
Open: 7 days a week; Mon–Sat 8–5, Sun 10–4. Rose fields open July–Sept, no charge.
Toilets: Yes.
Dogs: On lead.   **Credit cards:** Yes.

25/4 BLOSSOMS NURSERY
Church Hill
Charing Heath
Ashford
Kent TN27 0BU
01233 712886
Offering a wide range of plants – patio, bedding, hanging baskets, perennials, primroses, heathers & many pot plants.
Open: Mid-February–mid-November; 7 days a week, 9–5.
Wheelchairs: Gravel paths.
Toilets: Yes.
Dogs: On lead.   **Credit cards:** Yes.

25/5 WARMLAKE NURSERY & FARM SHOP
North Street
Sutton Valence
Maidstone
Kent
ME17 3LP
01622 844000
Specialist fuchsia growers: up to 1000 varieties as plugs or plants. Also 200 varieties of alpines. Hanging basket plants.
Open: All year except Xmas week; 7 days a week, winter 9–5, summer 8.30–5.30.
Wheelchairs: Reasonable access.
Toilets: Ask if desperate.
Dogs: On lead.   **Credit cards:** Yes.

25/6 CHURCH HILL COTTAGE GARDENS & NURSERY

25/7 CROFTERS NURSERY
Church Hill, Charing Heath
TN27 0BU   01233 712798
Fruit and ornamental trees.

25/8 GRAFTY GARDEN CENTRE

25/9 HEADCORN FLOWER CENTRE

25/10 IDEN CROFT HERBS

25/11 BUMBLE'S NURSERY
Tolehurst Farm, Frittenden
Cranbrook
Kent TN17 2BN
01580 715319
Specialist growers of bedding and perennial plants. 150 varieties of roses, large range of conifers, trees and shrubs.
Open: All year except Xmas & Boxing Days; 7 days a week, 8.30–5.
Wheelchairs: Partial access.
Toilets: No.
Dogs: No.   **Credit cards:** Yes.

25/12 THE COTTAGE GARDEN
Cranbrook Road, Staplehurst,
TN12 0EU   01580 891312
Perennials, bedding & baskets.

25/13 BIDDENDEN NURSERIES

25/14 MADRONA NURSERY
Pluckley Road
Bethersden
Kent
TN26 3DD
01223 820100

Unusual, rare and new plant varieties displayed on a spectacular and unique nursery site. Catalogue available.
Open: Mid-March–end October; Sat, Sun, Mon & Tues only, 10–5. (CLOSED WED–FRI).
Wheelchairs: Gravel paths.
Toilets: Yes.
Dogs: On lead.   **Credit cards:** No.

25/15 TORRENS GARDEN CENTRE

ARTEFACT SUPPLIER

25/16 GARDEN CRAFTS
Biddenden   01580 292070
Specialists in garden ornaments and furniture.

GARDENS

25/17 STONEACRE (NT)
01622 862871
Herb and cottage style garden.

25/18 LEEDS CASTLE

25/19 SISSINGHURST CASTLE GARDEN (NT)
01580 715330
Vita Sackville-West's garden.

25

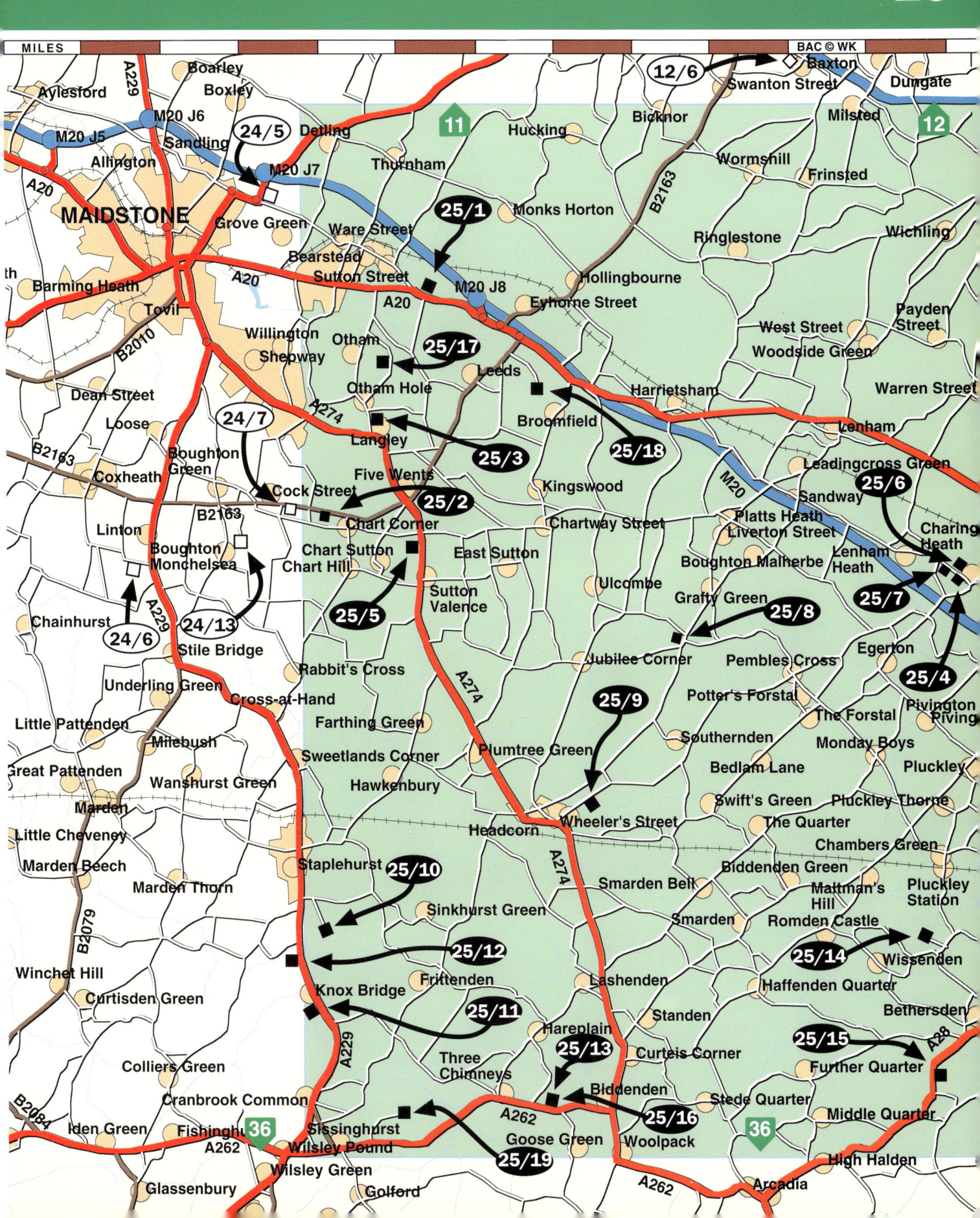

KENT

SPECIALIST & GENERAL NURSERIES, GARDEN AND PLANT CENTRES

26/1 LONGACRE NURSERY
Perrywood, Selling
Faversham ME13 9SE
01227 752254
Hardy perennials & *shrubs.*

26/2 WYEVALE GARDEN CENTRE

26/3 PICKARD'S MAGNOLIA GARDENS

26/4 MERRYFIELD NURSERIES

26/5 VICTORIANA NURSERY GARDENS

Challock, Ashford
Kent TN25 4DG
01233 740480
Family nursery under construction growing **fuchsias** *(350 varieties), citrus, bonsai, aquatics, unusuals, trees, shrubs and plants.*
Open: All year except Xmas & Boxing Days; Mon–Fri, 9–5 (phone for weekends and Bank Holidays).
Wheelchairs: Phone for information.
Toilets: Ask if desperate.
Dogs: No.   **Credit cards:** Yes.
SEE PAGE 48 FOR FULL DETAILS

26/6 OLANTIGH GARDEN NURSERIES
Little Olantigh Road, Wye
Own-grown **bedding plants***, cut flowers & fresh vegetables.*

26/7 THOMPSONS PLANT & GARDEN CENTRE

26/8 ORCHARD NURSERIES
Stone Street, Petham
CT4 5PR   01227 700375
Conifer *specialists, shrubs.*

26/9 RICHARD G. BAKER
Mill House, Stelling Minnis
CT4 6BD   01227 709398
Named *begonias & delphiniums.*

26/10 COUNTRY GARDENS ASHFORD
Hythe Road
Willesborough, Ashford
Kent TN24 0NE
01233 502136
'Good value garden centre with very wide plant selection. Free local delivery. Buildings, paving and walling.'
Open: All year; Mon–Sat 9–6. Sunday 10.30–4.30. Extended spring hours – phone for information.
Wheelchairs: Easy access.
Toilets: Yes.
Dogs: On lead.   **Credit cards:** Yes.

26/11 FARTHING COMMON PLANT CENTRE

26/12 OLDBURY NURSERIES
Brissenden Green
Bethersden, Ashford
Kent TN26 3BJ
01233 820416
Specialist nursery growing **fuchsias & pelargoniums** *– over 400 varieties. Winners of five Chelsea Gold Medals.*
Open: Feb–late June (CLOSED LATE JUNE–JAN); 7 days a week, 9.30–5.
Toilets: No.
Dogs: No.   **Credit cards:** Yes.

GARDEN AND NURSERY

26/13 BEECH COURT GARDENS
Challock   01233 740735
Woodland gardens.
Open: March–Oct; Mon–Fri 10–5.30, Sat & Sun 12–6.

GARDENS

26/14 DODDINGTON PLACE GARDEN

26/15 BELMONT

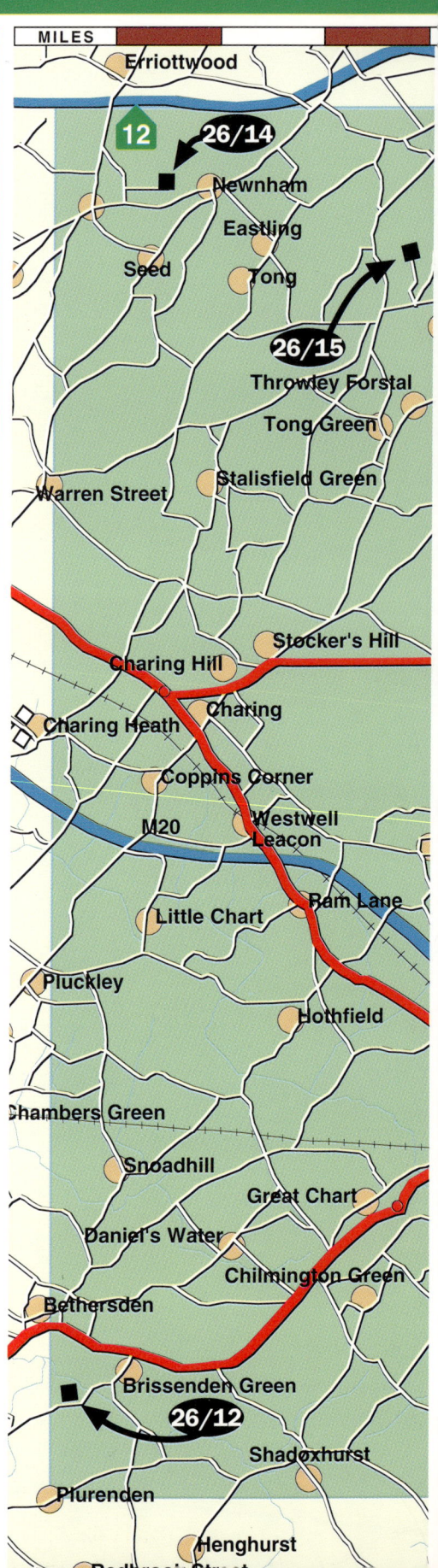

26

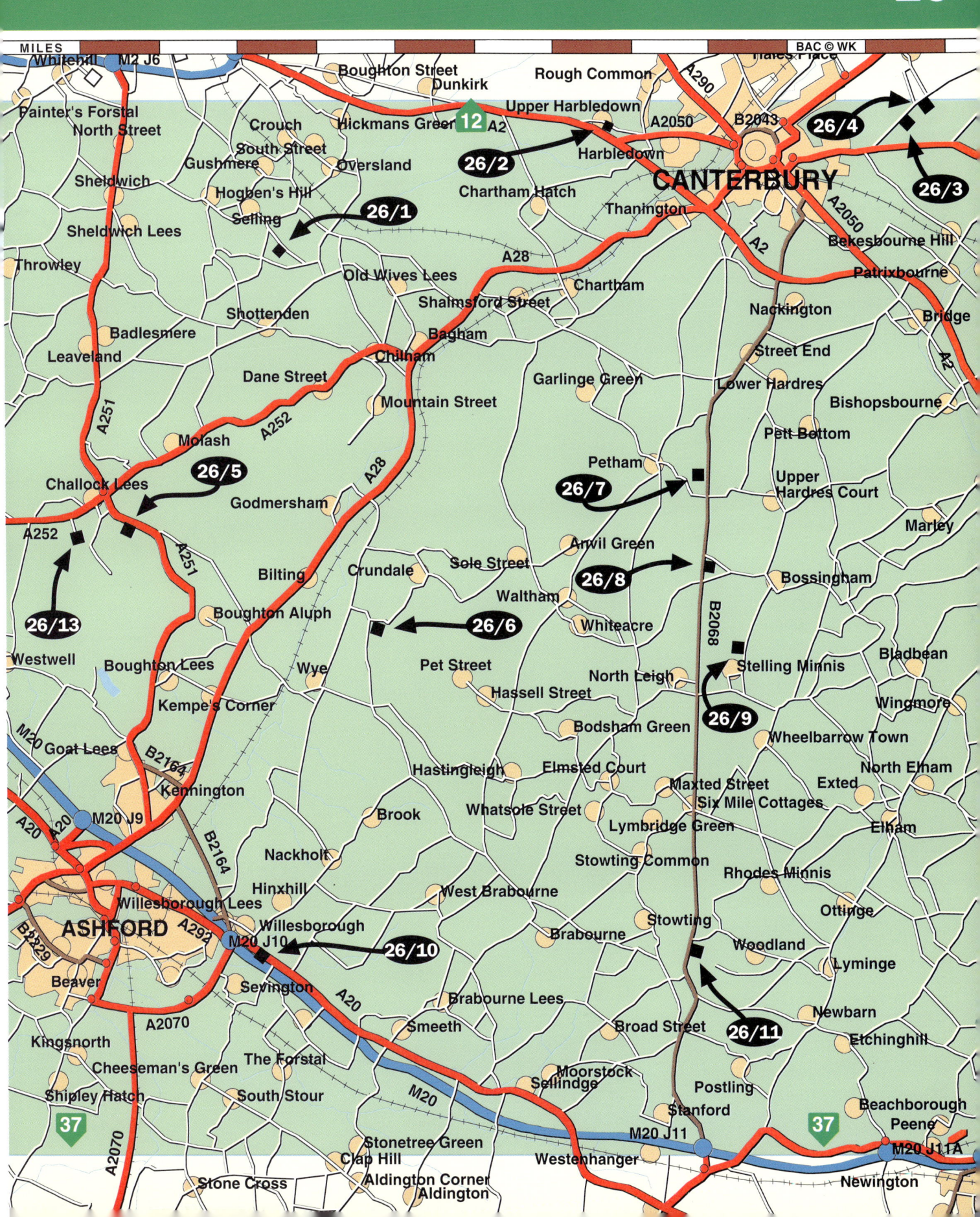

KENT

SPECIALIST & GENERAL NURSERIES, GARDEN AND PLANT CENTRES

27/1 SUMMERFIELD NURSERIES
Barnsole Road, Staple
CT3 1LD   01304 812549
A plant-orientated centre.

27/2 LAYHAM GARDEN CENTRE
Lower Road, Staple
Canterbury
Kent   CT3 1LH
01304 813267
*Specialist **rose** growers and a wide selection of herbaceous plants, conifers, flowering trees and shrubs.*
Open: All year except Xmas, Boxing & New Year's Days; 7 days a week, 9–5.
Wheelchairs: Easy access.
Toilets: Yes.
Dogs: On lead.   **Credit cards:** Yes.

27/3 SAUNDERS HOUSE NURSERY

27/4 ARCHERS LOW NURSERY
Ash Road, Sandwich
Kent   CT13 9JB
01304 613150
*Old-established nursery growing shrubs, trees and **border perennials**. Full nursery stock.*
Open: All year except Xmas & Boxing days, 6 days a week (CLOSED TUESDAY), 9–5.30.
Wheelchairs: Good access.
Toilets: No.
Dogs: On lead.   **Credit cards:** Yes.

27/5 TREVORS NURSERY
Dover Road, Sandwich
Kent   CT13 0DG
01304 614377
Perennials, shrubs, ferns, climbers, grasses, alpines, bedding, silver and grey foliage, Mediterranean plants, ornaments. Tea garden.
Open: All year except Xmas–New Year; March–Oct: 7 days a week, 10–5. Nov–Feb: Mon–Fri only, 10–2.
Wheelchairs: Gravel, but no steps.
Toilets: Ask if desperate.
Dogs: On lead.   **Credit cards:** No.

WATER GARDEN SPECIALIST

27/6 SOUTH EAST WATER GARDENS
Dover Road, Sandwich
Kent   CT13 0DG
01304 614963
Display ponds and pond fish. Everything for the pond keeper. Also a large selection of tropical fish.
Open: All year except Xmas week; 6 days a week (CLOSED MONDAY), winter 10–5, summer 10–5.30.
Wheelchairs: Good access.
Toilets: Ask if desperate.
Dogs: On lead.   **Credit cards:** Yes.

SPECIALIST & GENERAL NURSERIES, GARDEN AND PLANT CENTRES

27/7 MARTINS NURSERY
Poison Cross Nursery, Eastry
Sandwich   01304 611262
Plant centre and farm shop.

27/8 RINGWOULD ALPINES

27/9 ALKHAM VALLEY GARDEN CENTRE
Alkham Valley Road
South Alkham   01303 893351
Garden centre, PYO & farm shop.

27/10 MACFARLANES NURSERY & GARDEN CENTRE
Swingfield, Folkestone
CT15 7HX   01303 844244
A wide range of garden stock.

PICK-YOUR-OWN FARM

27/11 LITTLE CROCKSHARD PYO & FARM SHOP

GARDENS

27/12 GOODNESTONE PARK

12/13 NORTHBOURNE COURT GARDEN

27/14 WALMER CASTLE & GARDENS
A Penelope Hobhouse garden.

27/15 THE PINES GARDEN

27/16 RUSSELL GARDENS

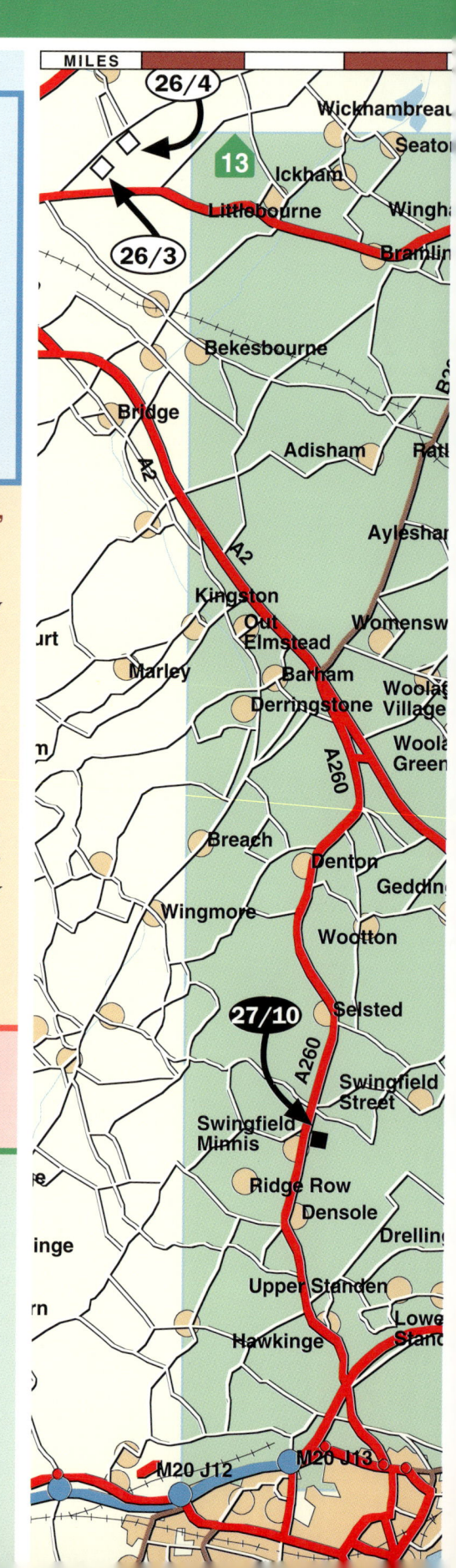

27

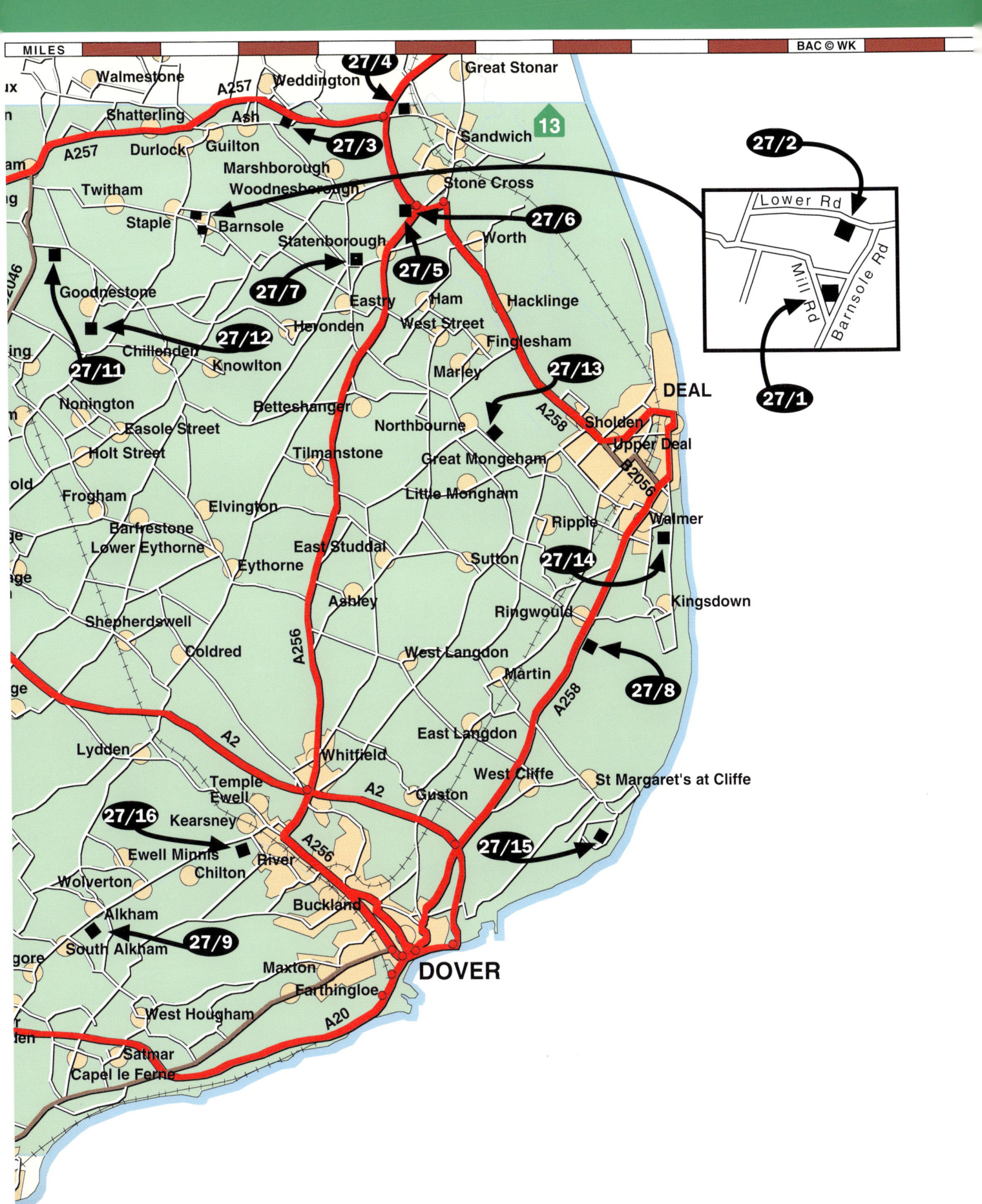

HAMPSHIRE

SPECIALIST & GENERAL NURSERIES, GARDEN AND PLANT CENTRES

28/1 B & W NURSERIES

28/2 POCOCK'S NURSERY AND ROSE CENTRE
Sherfield English, Romsey
SO51 6DT   01794 323514
Roses a speciality.

28/3 MacGREGORS PLANTS
Carters Clay Road, Lockerly
Romsey
Hampshire   SO51 0GL
01794 340256
Specialist nursery growing **Phygelius (National Collection)** & less common shrubs & perennials, particularly for shade.
Open: March–Oct: Fri, Sat & Sun (& Bank Holidays) only, 10–4. Other times by appointment.
Wheelchairs: Nursery paths narrow.
Toilets: Ask if desperate.
Dogs: No.   Credit cards: No.

GARDENS

28/4 MOTTISFONT ABBEY GARDEN (NT)
01794 340757
National Collection of old roses.

NURSERIES AND CENTRES

28/5 RIVERSIDE NURSERY & PLANT CENTRE

28/6 CHOICE PLANTS 
Stockbridge Road, Tilnsbury
Romsey
Hampshire   SO51 0NB
01794 368895
Nursery specialising in **hanging baskets**, planted containers. Refill service: spring, summer & autumn. Good range of plants.
Open: March–July & Sept–Oct;
7 days a week, Mon–Sat 9–5,
Sun 10.30–4.30.
Wheelchairs: Good access.
Toilets: Ask if desperate.
Dogs: On lead.   Credit cards: Yes.

28/7 HILLIER GARDEN CENTRE
Botley Road, Romsey
SO51 8AG   01794 513459
'The heart of good gardening.'

28/8 CEDAR NURSERIES

28/9 HILLIER GARDEN CENTRE
Jermyns Lane, Ampfield,
Romsey   SO51 0QA
01794 68407
'The heart of good gardening.'

WATER GARDEN SPECIALISTS

28/10 WORLD OF WATER

28/11 MILL WATER GARDENS

PICK-YOUR-OWN FARM

28/12 GANGER FARM PYO
Jermyns Lane, Romsey
Hampshire   SO51 0QA
01794 513345 (answerphone)
Family-run PYO for strawberries, raspberries, currants, gooseberries and a wide selection of fresh vegetables.
Open: June–Sept; 7 days a week, 10–6, but closed on Mondays after strawberry season has finished.
Wheelchairs: Limited access.
Toilets: Ask if desperate.
Dogs: On lead.   Credit cards: No.

GARDENS

28/13 THE SIR HAROLD HILLIER GARDENS & ARBORETUM
01794 368787
One of the finest collections of hardy trees & shrubs in Britain.

28/14 HOUGHTON LODGE GARDEN & HYDROPONICUM

28

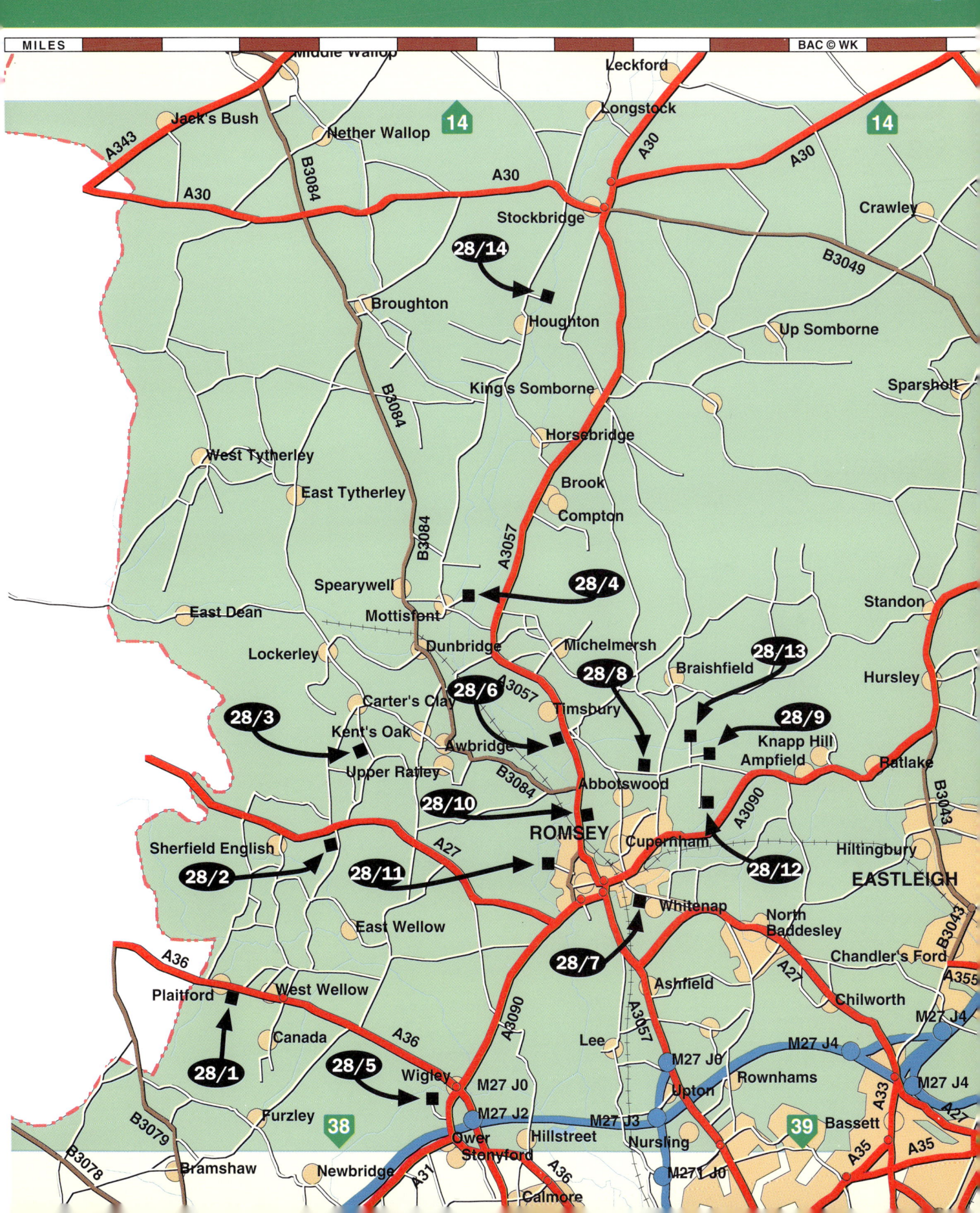

HAMPSHIRE

SPECIALIST & GENERAL NURSERIES, GARDEN AND PLANT CENTRES

29/1 HOOKER'S GARDEN CENTRE

29/2 HILLIER GARDEN CENTRE
Romsey Road, Winchester
SO22 5DN   01962 842288
'The heart of good gardening.'

WATER GARDEN SPECIALIST

29/3 WINCHESTER PET & AQUATIC CENTRE
At Hillier Garden Centre
Winchester   01962 856753
Fish, plants, pumps and ponds.

SPECIALIST & GENERAL NURSERIES, GARDEN AND PLANT CENTRES

29/4 GEORGE BECKETT NURSERIES

29/5 BRAMBRIDGE PARK GARDEN CENTRE

29/6 SANDYFIELDS NURSERIES
Main Road, Colden Common
SO21 1TB   01962 712218
Wide range of garden plants.

29/7 COUNTRY GARDENS FAIR OAK
Winchester Road
Fair Oak, Eastleigh
Hampshire   SO50 7HD
01703 600392

Country Gardens

'Good value garden centre with very wide plant selection. Free local delivery. Aquatics centre, paving. Coffee shop.'
Open: All year; Mon–Sat 9–6. Sunday 10.30–4.30. Extended spring hours – phone for information.
Wheelchairs: Easy access.
Toilets: Yes.
Dogs: On lead.   **Credit cards:** Yes.

29/8 FIELDFARE OF FAIR OAK

29/9 ORCHARDLEIGH NURSERIES

29/10 CONIGER NURSERIES

29/11 ARTURI'S GARDEN CENTRE

29/12 ALLINGTON NURSERY

29/13 WATER MEADOW NURSERY & HERB FARM

Water Meadows
Cheriton, Alresford
Hampshire   SO24 0QB
01962 771895
Award-winning nursery. **Water-related plant specialists**. *Unusual hardy perennials, fragrant climbers.* **Herbs.** *Teas when fine.*
Open: March–Oct; 3 days a week: Fri, Sat (& Bank Holidays) 9–5, Sun 2–5. (CLOSED NOV–FEB.)
Wheelchairs: Access to part of garden, terrace and sales area.
Toilets: Ask if desperate.
Dogs: No.   **Credit cards:** No.

29/14 EASTFIELD PLANT CENTRE

Paice Lane
Medstead, Alton
Hampshire   GU34 5PR
01420 563640
Attractive nursery with wide selection of mostly home-grown shrubs, herbaceous plants, trees, roses and conifers. Bedding.
Open: All year; 7 days a week, 9–5, but phone to check Nov–Feb.
Wheelchairs: Gravelled car park.
Toilets: No.
Dogs: No.   **Credit cards:** No.

PICK-YOUR-OWN FARM

29/15 PARK HOUSE PYO

GARDEN

29/16 HINTON AMPNER (NT)
01962 771305
'Formal design, informal planting.'

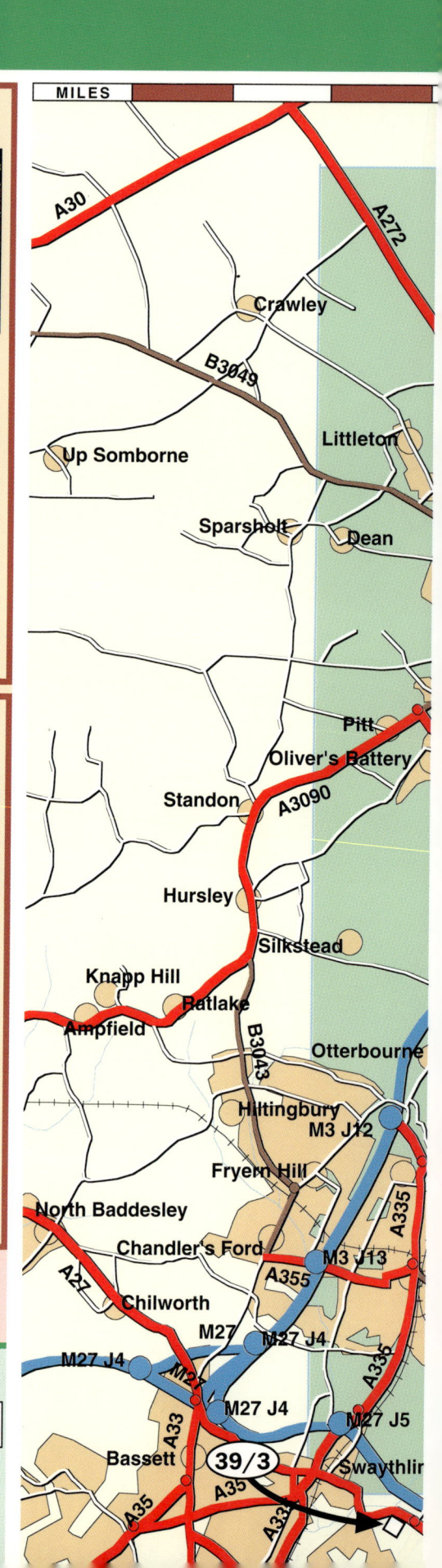

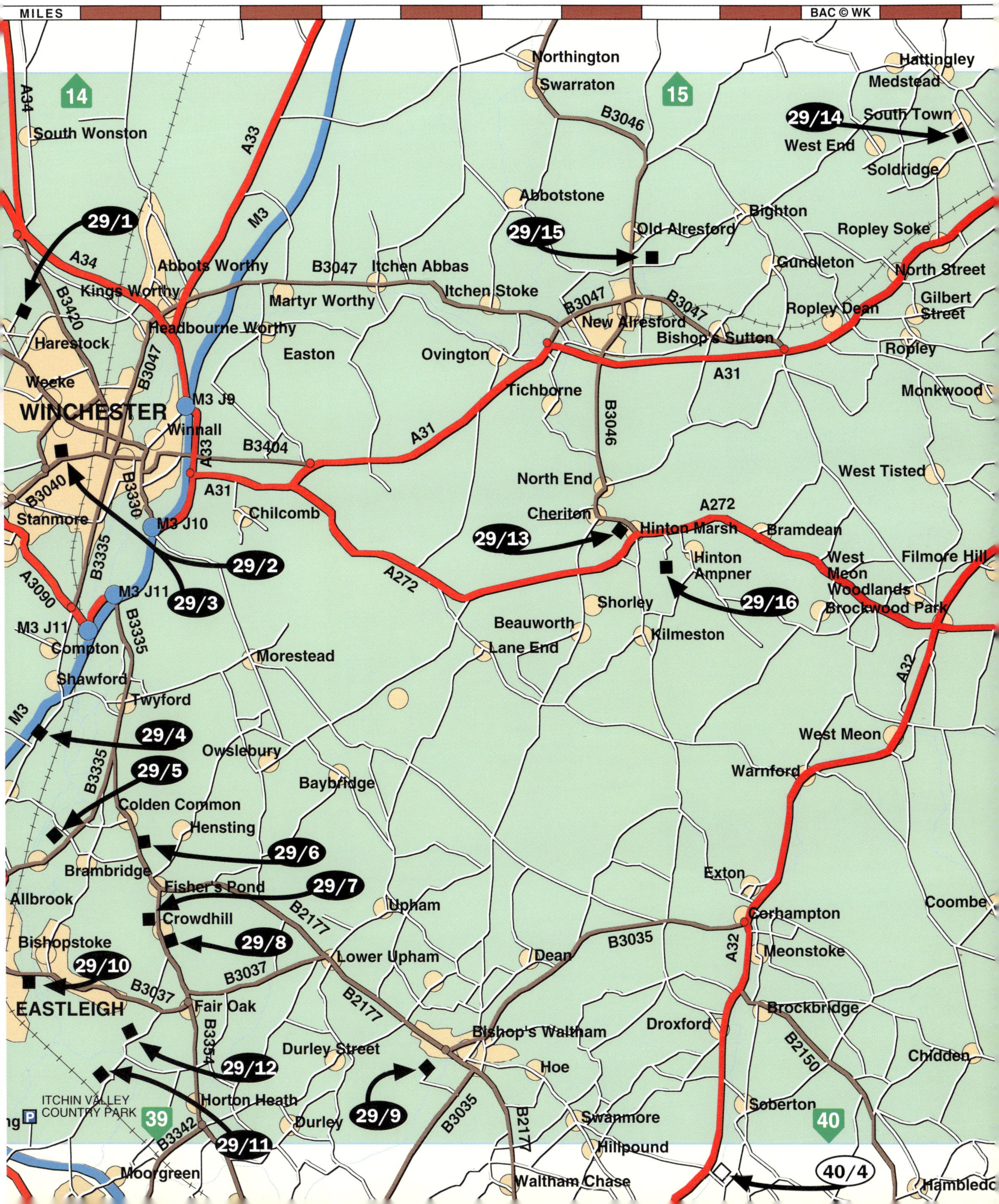
MILES
BAC © WK
14
15
39
40
A34
South Wonston
A33
M3
Northington
Swarraton
B3046
Hattingley
Medstead
South Town
West End
Soldridge
29/14
Abbotstone
Bighton
Old Alresford
Ropley Soke
29/15
29/1
A34
Abbots Worthy
B3047
Itchen Abbas
Gundleton
North Street
Kings Worthy
Itchen Stoke
Martyr Worthy
B3047
B3047
Ropley Dean
Gilbert Street
B3420
Headbourne Worthy
New Alresford
Bishop's Sutton
Harestock
Easton
Ovington
Ropley
Weeke
B3047
A31
Tichborne
Monkwood
WINCHESTER
M3 J9
Winnall
B3046
A33
B3404
A31
North End
West Tisted
B3040
B3330
A31
Chilcomb
A272
Cheriton
Hinton Marsh
Bramdean
Stanmore
M3 J10
29/13
29/2
Hinton Ampner
West Meon Woodlands
Filmore Hill
B3335
A272
A3090
M3 J11
29/3
Shorley
29/16
Brockwood Park
M3 J11
B3335
Beauworth
Compton
Lane End
Kilmeston
Morestead
A32
Shawford
Twyford
M3
29/4
West Meon
Owslebury
B3335
29/5
Warnford
Baybridge
Colden Common
Hensting
29/6
Brambridge
Exton
Fisher's Pond
29/7
Allbrook
Upham
Coombe
Crowdhill
B2177
Corhampton
Bishopstoke
29/8
B3035
Meonstoke
A32
Lower Upham
29/10
Dean
B3037
B3037
EASTLEIGH
Fair Oak
B2177
Brockbridge
Droxford
B3354
Bishop's Waltham
B2150
Durley Street
Hoe
Chidden
29/12
29/9
ITCHIN VALLEY COUNTRY PARK
Horton Heath
B3035
B2177
Soberton
B3342
Durley
Swanmore
29/11
Hillpound
Moorgreen
40/4
Waltham Chase
Hambledon

HAMPSHIRE

SPECIALIST & GENERAL NURSERIES, GARDEN AND PLANT CENTRES

30/1 GARTHOWEN GARDEN CENTRE & NURSERIES
Alton Lane
Four Marks, Alton
Hampshire GU34 5AJ
01962 773225
Shrubs, ornamental trees, fruit trees, conifers, alpines, perennials, roses, heathers, bedding plants, tubs and pots. Sundries.
Open: All year except Xmas & Boxing Days; 7 days a week, 9–5.
Wheelchairs: Easy access.
Toilets: Ask if desperate.
Dogs: No.   **Credit cards:** Yes.

30/2 GALES NURSERY

30/3 OAKLEIGH NURSERIES
Petersfield Road
Monkwood, Alresford
Hampshire SO24 0HB
01962 773344
Fuchsia & pelargonium specialists. The nurseries have been awarded 14 Gold Medals at Chelsea Flower Shows.
Open: March–June: 7 days a week, 10–4. July: Mon–Fri only, 10–4.
Wheelchairs: Yes.
Toilets: Ask if desperate.
Dogs: On lead.   **Credit cards:** Yes.

30/4 RUMSEY GARDENS
117 Drift Road
Clanfield, Waterlooville
Hampshire PO8 0PD
01705 593367
Traditional nursery & plant centre. Five acres of plants on display including international collection of cotoneasters.
Open: All year except 25 Dec–2 Jan; 7 days a week, 9–5.
Wheelchairs: Gravel paths (well rolled).
Toilets: Ask if desperate.
Dogs: No.   **Credit cards:** No.

30/5 SHRUBLANDS
St. Patrick's Lane
Rake, Liss
Hampshire GU33 7HQ
01730 892094
Offering screening alternatives & a wide range of ornamental coloured conifers, fresh from the ground or in pots.
Open: All year except Xmas & Boxing Days; 7 days a week, 9–5.30 or dusk if earlier.
Wheelchairs: Difficult.
Toilets: No.
Dogs: On lead.   **Credit cards:** No.

30/6 LANGLEY BOXWOOD NURSERY

30/7 PRINCES GARDEN CENTRE

30/8 HILLIER GARDEN CENTRE
Farnham Road, Liss
GU33 6LJ   01730 892196
'The heart of good gardening.'

WATER GARDEN SPECIALIST

30/9 LISS PET & AQUATIC CENTRE
at Hillier Garden Centre
Farnham Road, Liss GU33 6LJ
01730 894135
Fish, plants, pumps & liners.

SPECIALIST & GENERAL NURSERIES, GARDEN AND PLANT CENTRES

30/10 AYLINGS OF TROTTON
Trotton
Rogate, Petersfield
Hampshire GU31 5ES
01730 813621
Very large range of shrubs and herbaceous plants, terracotta, ceramics and pot plants. Coffee shop.
Open: All year except Xmas & Boxing Days (open other Bank Holidays): Mon–Sat 8–5, Sun 10.30–4.30.
Wheelchairs: Access.
Toilets: Yes.
Dogs: On lead.   **Credit cards:** Yes.

30/11 ROTHERHILL NURSERIES & GARDEN CENTRE

30/12 JARDINIQUE

PICK-YOUR-OWN FARM

30/13 DURLEIGHMARSH PYO & FARM SHOP
Rogate Road, Petersfield
Hampshire GU31 5AX
01730 821626
PYO: soft fruit, vegetables, herbs, flowers. Farm shop: fresh fruit, veg (incl. asparagus) and local home made produce (cheeses etc).
Open: PYO: June–Oct.
Shop: all year, 7 days a week;
June–Aug 9–7, Sept–May
9–5.30 (but winter Sundays 9–1).
Wheelchairs: Some areas accessible.
Toilets: Yes.
Dogs: No.   **Credit cards:** No.

GARDENS

30/14 GILBERT WHITE'S HOUSE & GARDEN

30/15 GREATHAM MILL

Greatham
Hampshire GU33 6HH
01420 538245
Riverside garden and mill. Rare plants in five acres. Extensive season from narcissi to winter flowering clematis. Tearooms and nursery garden.
Open: 1 Feb–30 Sept; 7 days a week, 10–6 (tea room: weekends & Bank Hols from Easter, 2–6).
Costs: £2.   **Wheelchairs:** Limited.
Toilets: Yes.
Dogs: No.   **Credit cards:** No.

30/16 UPPARK (NT)
01730 825317
Downland garden with views.

30/17 FITZHALL
9-acre manor house garden. Teas.
Open: All year;
7 days a week, 10–6.
Costs: £2, children £1.

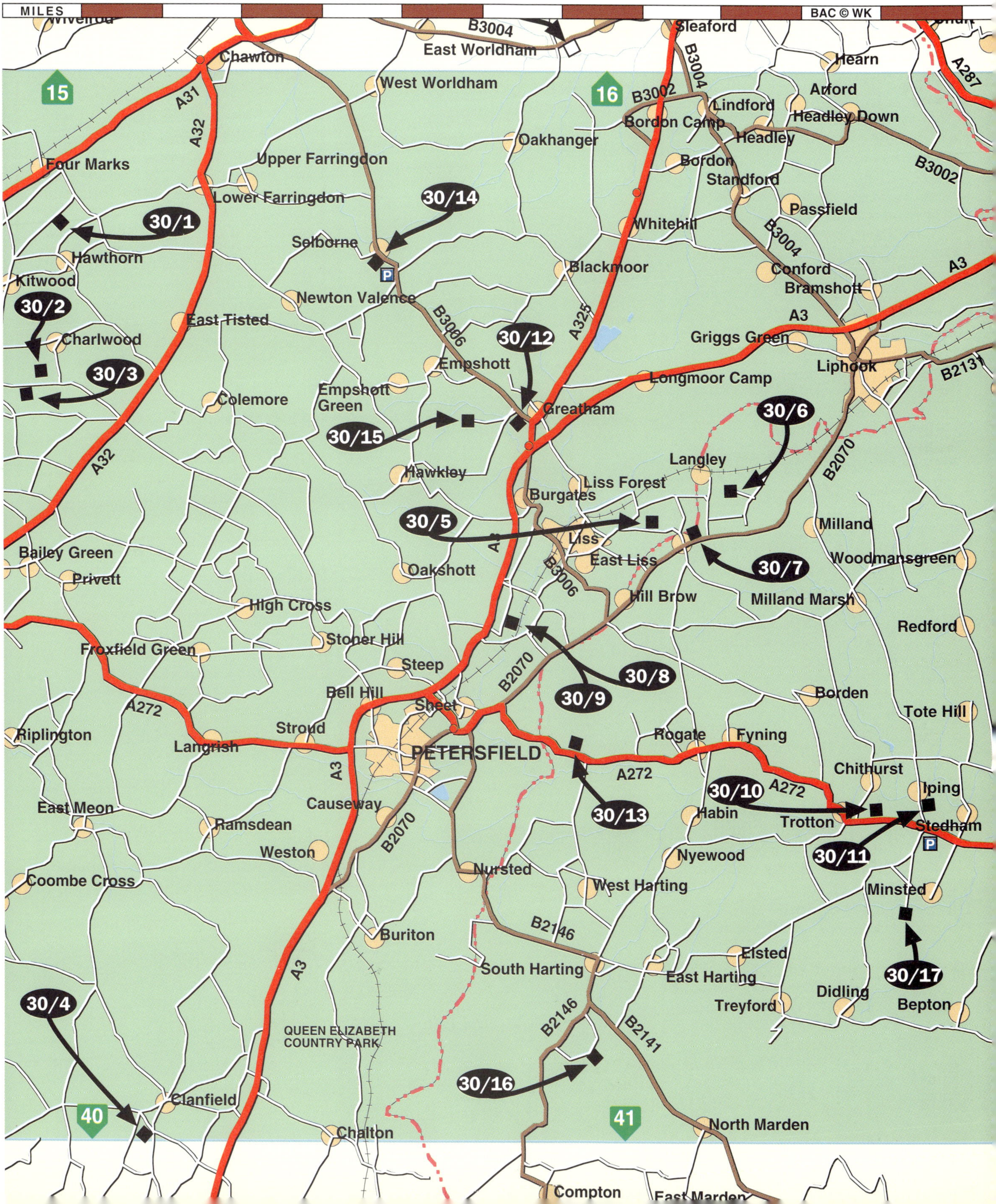
MILES
BAC © WK
B3004
East Worldham
Sleaford
B3004
Chawton
Hearn
A31
A32
West Worldham
16
B3002
Lindford
Arford
Bordon Camp
Headley Down
Headley
A287
15
Oakhanger
Four Marks
Upper Farringdon
Bordon
Standford
B3002
Lower Farringdon
30/14
Whitehill
Passfield
30/1
Selborne
B3004
Hawthorn
Blackmoor
Conford
Kitwood
Bramshott
A3
30/2
Newton Valence
East Tisted
B3006
A325
A3
Charlwood
30/12
Griggs Green
Liphook
Empshott
B2131
30/3
Longmoor Camp
Colemore
Empshott Green
Greatham
30/6
30/15
A32
Langley
Hawkley
Liss Forest
B2070
Burgates
30/5
Milland
Liss
A3
East Liss
Woodmansgreen
Bailey Green
30/7
Privett
Oakshott
B3006
Hill Brow
Milland Marsh
High Cross
Redford
Stoner Hill
Froxfield Green
Steep
30/8
Bell Hill
B2070
30/9
Borden
A272
Sheet
Tote Hill
Ripplington
Stroud
Rogate
Fyning
Langrish
PETERSFIELD
A3
A272
Chithurst
30/10
A272
Iping
Causeway
Habin
Trotton
Stedham
East Meon
30/13
Ramsdean
B2070
30/11
Weston
Nyewood
Minsted
Coombe Cross
Nursted
West Harting
B2146
Buriton
Elsted
A3
South Harting
East Harting
30/17
Didling
Treyford
Bepton
30/4
B2146
B2141
QUEEN ELIZABETH COUNTRY PARK
30/16
Clanfield
40
41
Chalton
North Marden
Compton
East Marden

SURREY & WEST SUSSEX

SPECIALIST & GENERAL NURSERIES, GARDEN AND PLANT CENTRES

31/1 COUNTRY GARDENS ALFOLD
Horsham Road, Alfold
Cranleigh
Surrey   GU6 8JE
01403 752359
'Good value garden centre with very wide plant selection. Free local delivery. Terracotta pots, compost, seeds, buildings.'
Open: All year; Mon–Sat 9–6. Sunday 10.30–4.30. Extended spring hours – phone for information.
Wheelchairs: Easy access.
Toilets: Yes.
Dogs: On lead.   **Credit cards:** Yes.

31/2 LOXWOOD NURSERIES
31/3 TANGLEWOOD
31/4 GREENWAYS NURSERY
31/5 WALLABIES NURSERY

Kirdford Road
Wisborough Green
Billingshurst
West Sussex   RH14 0DD
01403 700147
Specialities: **wild flower plants**, *hanging baskets, summer & winter bedding. Picked strawberries, raspberries and ogen melons.*
Open: All year except Xmas and Boxing Days; 6 days a week (CLOSED THURSDAY), 9–5.
Wheelchairs: Paved access.
Toilets: Ask if desperate.
Dogs: On lead.   **Credit cards:** No.

31/6 COUNTRY GARDENS PULBOROUGH
Stopham Road
Pulborough
West Sussex   RH20 1DS
01798 872981
'Good value garden centre with very wide plant selection. Free local delivery. Garden buildings. Coffee shop.'
Open: All year; Mon–Sat 9–6, Sunday 10.30–4.30. Extended spring hours – phone for information.
Wheelchairs: Easy access.
Toilets: Yes.
Dogs: On lead.   **Credit cards:** Yes.

31/7 BLACKGATE LANE NURSERY

31/8 THE CITRUS CENTRE
Marehill Nursery
West Mare Lane
Pulborough
West Sussex   RH20 2EA
01798 872786
Specialist **citrus** *growers. Many varieties including rare and unusual ones. Citrus feed. Mail order welcome. Featured on "Gardeners' World".*
Open: All year except Xmas Day–New Year's Eve; Wed–Sun, 9.30–5.30.
Wheelchairs: Easy access.
Toilets: No.
Dogs: On lead.   **Credit cards:** Yes.

31/9 MURRELLS NURSERY
Broomers Hill Lane
Pulborough
West Sussex   RH20 2DU
01798 875508
Extensive range (incl. some unusual varieties) of shrubs, herbaceous, bedding plants, trees and fruit trees. **Bonsai.**
Open: All year, except Xmas, Boxing, New Year's Days & Easter Sun; 7 days a week, Mon–Sat, winter 9–5, summer 9–5.30. Sun 10–4.
Wheelchairs: Good access.
Toilets: No.
Dogs: On lead.   **Credit cards:** Yes.

PICK-YOUR-OWN FARM

31/10 BROOKFIELD FARM
River
Petworth
West Sussex
01798 861235
Over 20 fruit and vegetable crops in an attractive rural location.
'The more you pick, the lower the price'.
Open: June–September; 7 days a week, 10–5.
Wheelchairs: Not accessible.
Toilets: No.
Dogs: No.   **Credit cards:** No.

31/11 TULLENS FRUIT FARM

GARDENS

31/12 RAMSTER
01428 644422

31/13 PETWORTH PARK (NT)
01798 343929
650-acre deer park, pleasure grounds.

31

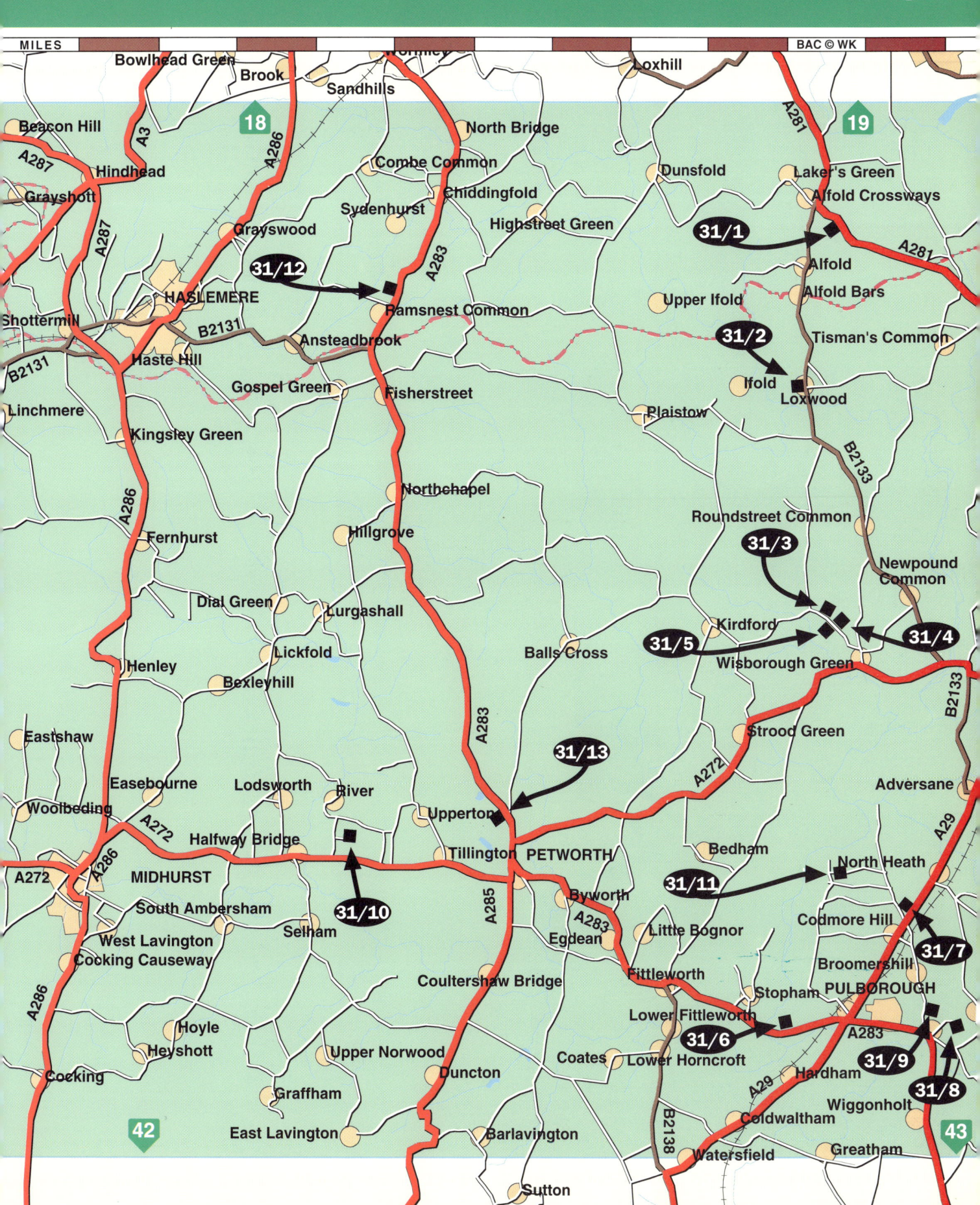

WEST SUSSEX

SPECIALIST & GENERAL NURSERIES, GARDEN AND PLANT CENTRES

32/1 THE VILLAGE NURSERIES
Sinnocks
West Chiltington
Pulborough
West Sussex
RH20 2JX
01798 813040

Nursery-grown shrubs, bedding plants, basket and patio plants, perennials, climbers, conifers and roses in a beautiful country setting.
Open: All year; 7 days a week, 9–6 (close at dusk in winter).
Wheelchairs: No steps; paved and gravel.   **Toilets:** No.
Dogs: Yes.   **Credit cards:** Yes.

32/2 MAYFIELD NURSERY
West Chiltington Lane
Broadford Bridge
Billingshurst, West Sussex
RH14 9EA   01403 741224

Bedding plants, hanging baskets: April–Aug. Freshly picked strawberries: May–July. Freshly picked raspberries: June–Aug.
Open: Beginning of April–mid August; 7 days a week, 8–6.
Wheelchairs: Grass walkway.
Toilets: Ask if desperate.
Dogs: No.   **Credit cards:** No.

32/3 CAMELIA BOTNAR GARDEN & CRAFT CENTRE
Littleworth Lane
West Grinstead, Horsham
West Sussex   RH13 8NA
01403 864773

Garden centre and nursery. Ornamental garden ironwork and pine furniture from own workshops.
Open: All year except Xmas, Boxing & New Year's Days; 7 days a week, Mon–Fri 9–5, Sat 10–5, Sun 10.30–4.30.
Wheelchairs: Easy access and WC.
Toilets: Yes.
Dogs: On lead.   **Credit cards:** Yes.

32/4 HOLLY GATE CACTUS NURSERY AND GARDEN

32/5 OLD BARN NURSERIES
Modern garden centre.

32/6 BROOKSIDE CACTUS NURSERY

32/7 KINGSFOLD NURSERY PLANT CENTRE
Dorking Road
Kingsfold, Horsham
West Sussex   RH12 3SD
01306 627614

A very large selection of plants, the majority produced on site. Knowledgeable staff available for expert advice.
Open: All year except Xmas–2 Jan; 7 days a week (including Bank Holidays), 9.30–5.30.
Wheelchairs: Good access.
Toilets: No.   **Credit cards:** Yes.
Dogs: Guide dogs only.

32/8 NEWBRIDGE NURSERIES
Billingshurst Road
Broadbridge Heath, Horsham
01403 272686
'The garden centre that grows.'

32/9 BOURNE HILL NURSERY

32/10 OAKDEAN NURSERY
Sedgwick Lane,
Horsham
West Sussex   RH13 6QE
01403 252897

Fuchsia *specialists (350 varieties). Baskets, bedding plants, shrubs, climbers, dwarf conifers, perennials and alpines.*
Open: Mar–23 Dec; 6 days a week (CLOSED MONDAY), Tues–Sat 9–5, Sunday 10–4.
Wheelchairs: Partial access.
Toilets: No.
Dogs: On lead.   **Credit cards:** No.

32/11 ARCHITECTURAL PLANTS
Cooks Farm, Horsham
RH13 6LH   01403 891772
Please phone for catalogue.

32/12 HOWARDS NURSERY

32/13 HILLIER GARDEN CENTRE
Brighton Road, Horsham
RH13 6QA   01403 210113
'The heart of good gardening.'

WATER GARDEN SPECIALISTS

32/14 HORSHAM WATER GARDENS
at Hillier Garden Centre,
Horsham   01403 268152
Fish, filtration and fountains.

32/15 ARCHER-WILLS

PICK-YOUR-OWN FARM

32/16 CHURCHFIELD FARM
West Chiltington
Pulborough
West Sussex   RH20 2JS
01798 812353

A peaceful, attractive location with 30 quality fruit and vegetable crops to pick from the field. 'The more you pick, the lower the price.'
Open: 7 days a week; May 11–5, June to mid-Aug, 10–6, mid-Aug to Sept, 11–5.
Wheelchairs: Not accessible.
Toilets: Yes.
Dogs: On lead.   **Credit cards:** No.

GARDEN & NURSERY

32/17 COOMBLAND GARDENS
Coneyhurst, Billingshurst
West Sussex
RH14 9DY   01403 741727

Interesting five-acre garden. Roses & choice herbaceous plants. **National Collection of hardy geraniums**. *Seed list available.*
Open: Garden: first 4 Sats in June (groups can book in spring). Nursery: March–end October, Mon–Fri 2–4 (CLOSED SAT, SUN & BHs). Other times phone.
Costs: Garden £2, nursery free.
Wheelchairs: Limited access.
Toilets: Ask if desperate.
Dogs: No.   **Credit cards:** No.

GARDEN

32/18 LEONARDSLEE GARDENS
01403 891212
World-famous rhododendron and azalea gardens.

NURSERY

32/19 LEONARDSLEE PLANTS

32

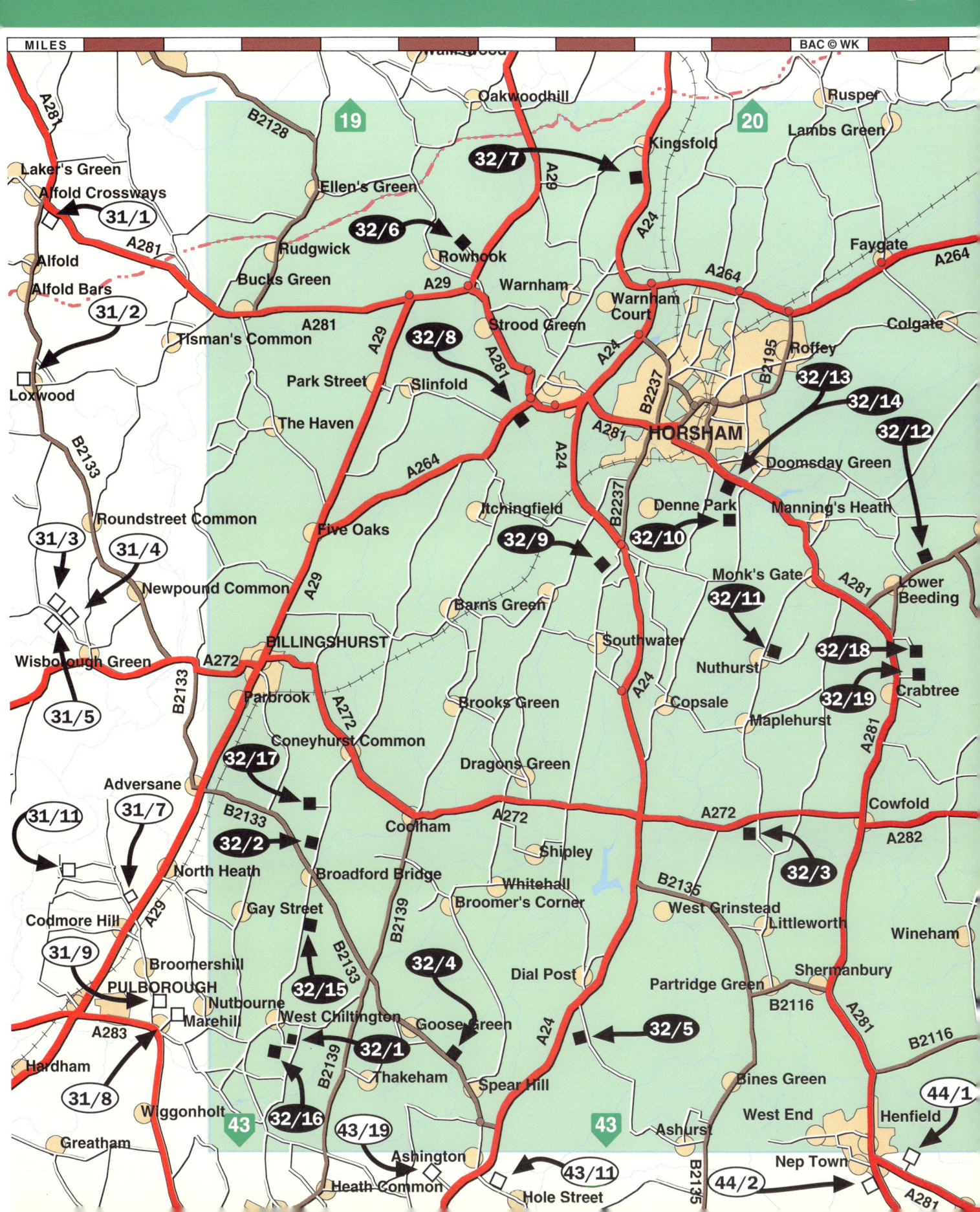

WEST SUSSEX

SPECIALIST & GENERAL NURSERIES, GARDEN AND PLANT CENTRES

33/1 CHEALS GARDEN CENTRE

33/2 COUNTRY GARDENS HANDCROSS
London Road, Handcross
West Sussex
RH17 6BA
01444 400725
Country Gardens
'Good value garden centre with very wide plant selection. Free local delivery. Garden buildings, aquatic centre.'
Open: All year; Mon–Sat 9–6. Sunday 10.30–4.30. Extended spring hours – phone for information.
Wheelchairs: Easy access.
Toilets: Yes.
Dogs: On lead. **Credit cards:** Yes.

33/3 STANBRIDGE VIEW NURSERY

33/4 BOLNEY NURSERY
Cowfold Road, Bolney
RH17 5QR 01444 881784
Trees, nursery stock, sheds & pots.

33/5 MARYLANDS NURSERY

33/6 HIGH BEECHES NURSERY

33/7 PLANTS 'N' GARDENS 
at World of Water
Turners Hill Road, Worth
Crawley, W Sussex RH10 4PE
01293 882992
Recently opened garden centre offering friendly, expert advice. Specialists in herbaceous plants, ornamental grasses.
Open: All year except Xmas, Boxing and New Year's Days; 7 days a week, Mon–Sat, 9–5 (winter), 9–6 (summer). Sun 10.30–4.30.
Wheelchairs: Easy paved access with ramps. **Toilets:** Yes.
Dogs: On lead. **Credit cards:** Yes.

33/8 STONEHURST ORCHID & CAMELLIA NURSERY

33/9 SCAYNES HILL NURSERY

33/10 W. E. Th. INGWERSEN
Birch Farm Hardy Plant Nursery
Gravetye Estate
East Grinstead
West Sussex RH19 4LE
01342 810236
Award winning hardy plant nursery: alpines, rock plants, dwarf shrubs and conifers.
Open: March–Sept: 7 days a week, Mon–Fri 9–1 & 1.30–4; Sat, Sun & BHs 10–1 & 1.30–4. Winter: Mon–Fri only.
Wheelchairs: Possible, but on hill.
Toilets: Yes.
Dogs: On lead. **Credit cards:** No.

33/11 GARDEN PRIDE GARDEN CENTRE

WATER GARDEN SPECIALIST

33/12 WORLD OF WATER

ARTEFACT SUPPLIER

33/13 POTS AND PITHOI 
The Barns
East Street
Turners Hill
West Sussex RH10 4QQ
01342 714793
Hand-made terracotta pots from Crete for the garden, patio and conservatory. Up to 5ft high. Huge choice.
Open: All year except Xmas–New Year; 7 days a week, 10–5.
Wheelchairs: Yes.
Toilets: Yes.
Dogs: No. **Credit cards:** Yes.

PICK-YOUR-OWN FARMS

33/14 PATERNOSTERS FRUIT FARM
Sloughgreen Lane, Warninglid
Haywards Heath 01444 461474
Extensive range of soft fruit.

33/15 TULLEYS FARM 
Turners Hill Road
Turners Hill
Crawley
West Sussex
RH10 4PD

PYO:
01342 715365
Shop:
01342 718472

A wide range of fruit & vegetables to pick from April–Oct. Scenic views. Farm shop and country food in Farmhouse Kitchen.
Wheelchairs: Yes.
Toilets: Yes. **Credit cards:** Yes.
Dogs: In car park, not in PYO.
SEE PAGE 48 FOR FULL DETAILS

GARDENS

33/16 HIGH BEECHES GARDENS
20 acres of woodland gardens.
Open: Spring & autumn: phone 01444 400589 for dates.
Costs: £3, children free.

33/17 BORDE HILL GARDEN
Family day out. 01444 450326.
Open: All year; daily, 10–6.
Costs: £2.50, children £1.

33/18 NYMANS GARDEN (NT)
01444 400321
A great garden of S.E. England.

33/19 WAKEHURST PLACE

Ardingly
Haywards Heath
West Sussex
RH17 6TN
01444 892701
(24-hour
enquiry line
0181 332 5066)

National Botanic Garden *noted for one of the finest collections of rare trees and flowering shrubs. Restaurant.*
Open: All year except Xmas & New Year's Days; Nov–Jan 10–4, Feb 10–5, March & Oct 10–6, April–Sept 10–7.
Costs: £4, children £1.50, concessions £2.
Wheelchairs: Good access. Wheelchairs are available on free loan.
Toilets: Yes.
Dogs: No.   **Credit cards:** No.

Wakehurst Place

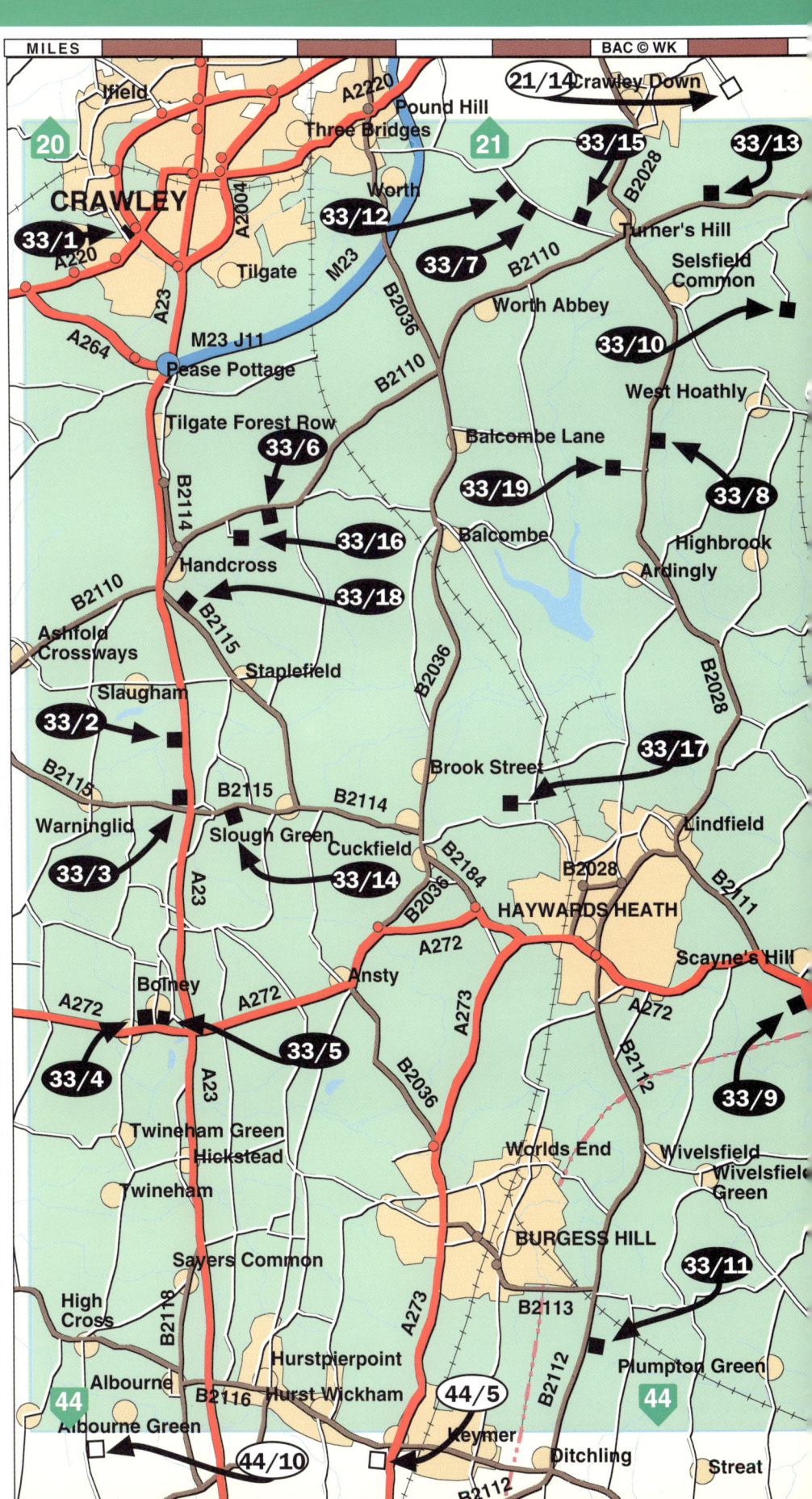

EAST SUSSEX

SPECIALIST & GENERAL NURSERIES, GARDEN AND PLANT CENTRES

34/1 GEMA NURSERY

34/2 ROYAL MIRES NURSERY
London Road
Lye Green, Crowborough
East Sussex   TN6 1UU
01892 668850
Specialists in summer and winter **hanging baskets**, *bedding plants, large shrub area, terracotta pots & stoneware.*
Open: All year except Xmas & Boxing Days; 7 days a week, March–Nov 9–5.30, winter 9–5.
Wheelchairs: Yes.
Toilets: Ask if desperate.
Dogs: On lead.   **Credit cards:** Yes.

34/3 ASHDOWN FOREST GARDEN CENTRE & NURSERY

34/4 REGGIES PLANTS

34/5 ROCKINGTON NURSERY

34/6 MILLBROOK GARDEN CENTRE
Rotherfield Road
Jarvis Brook, Crowborough
East Sussex   TN6 3RJ
01892 663822
Modern centre within the high weald. Full range of plants, garden sundries and gifts. Award-winning landscapers. Restaurant.
Open: All year except Xmas, Boxing, New Year's Days; 7 days a week, Mon–Sat: 9–5.30 (summer), 9–5 (winter). Sunday 10.30–4.30.
Wheelchairs: Sloping with ramps.
Toilets: Yes.
Dogs: On lead.   **Credit cards:** Yes.

34/7 BLACKBOYS NURSERY
Lankhurst Oak
Blackboys, Uckfield
East Sussex   TN22 5LS
01825 890858
Nursery growing perennials, herbs, alpines, geraniums, patio plants, fuchsias, bedding and vegetable plants. **Hanging baskets.**
Open: March–Nov; 7 days a week (but CLOSED MONDAY in July & August), 9–5.30.
Wheelchairs: Good access.
Toilets: No.
Dogs: On lead.   **Credit cards:** No.

34/8 STAVERTON NURSERY
Eastbourne Road, Halland,
BN8 6PU   01825 840249
Home-grown **bedding** *& shrubs.*

34/9 MATHEWS NURSERY

34/10 CHUBBS NURSERY
Littleworth
Cooksbridge
Lewes
East Sussex   BN8 4TD
01273 400218
Long established nursery. Shrubs, roses, herbaceous plants, trees, fruit trees and bushes. Alpines and garden sundries.
Open: All year except Xmas & Boxing days; 7 days a week, 8.30–5.
Wheelchairs: Easy access.
Toilets: Yes.
Dogs: On lead.   **Credit cards:** Yes.

34/11 NUTLIN NURSERY
Hydrangea *specialists.*
Open: By appointment, phone 01825 712670 evenings.

34/12 IMBERHORNE LANE NURSERY
Imberhorne Lane
East Grinstead
01342 321175
Bedding, herbaceous, sundries.

34/13 WARRENORTH NURSERY
East Grinstead Road
North Chailey   BN8 4JD
01825 723266
Fuchsia & pelargonium *specialists.*

34/14 SHEFFIELD PARK NURSERY

ARTEFACT SUPPLIER

34/15 DOMA FARM NURSERY
Statuary.

PICK-YOUR-OWN FARMS

34/16 CHERRY GARDENS FARM
01892 864348
Wide range of soft fruit & vegetables.
Open: April–October.

34/17 OAST FARM
Buxted, Uckfield
01825 733446
PYO fruit. Farm shop & café.

GARDENS

34/18 STANDEN (NT)
01342 323029
Hillside garden and walks.

34/19 MOORLANDS
3-acre water garden in a valley.
Open: April–Oct; Wed 11–5.
Also some Suns (01892 652474).

GARDEN & GARDEN ARTEFACTS

34/20 WILDERNESS WOOD

Hadlow Down
Uckfield
East Sussex   TN22 4HJ
01825 830509
Wood furniture and products from the grower/maker: seats, trellis, hurdles, poles, etc. Lovely walks, playground, shop, teas, picnics.
Open: All year; daily, 10–dusk.
Costs: £1.90, children 80p, OAPs £1.50.
Wheelchairs: Partial access.
Toilets: Yes.
Dogs: On lead.   **Credit cards:** No.

GARDENS

34/21 BENTLEY WILDFOWL & MOTOR MUSEUM
Halland, Lewes, East Sussex
BN8 5AF   01825 840573
Formal gardens (designed as a series of rooms), park & woodlands. Waterfowl collection in 23 acres. Tearoom etc.
Open: Mid-March–end Oct: 7 days a week, 10.30–4.30 (July/August 10.30–5). Winter: weekends only, 10.30–4 (BUT CLOSED JAN).
Costs: £4.10, children £2.50, concessions £3.10, families £12.
Wheelchairs: Pre-bookable: special facilities.   **Toilets:** Yes.
Dogs: No.   **Credit cards:** Yes.

34/22 SHEFFIELD PARK GARDEN (NT)
01825 790231
100 acres of rare trees & shrubs.

34

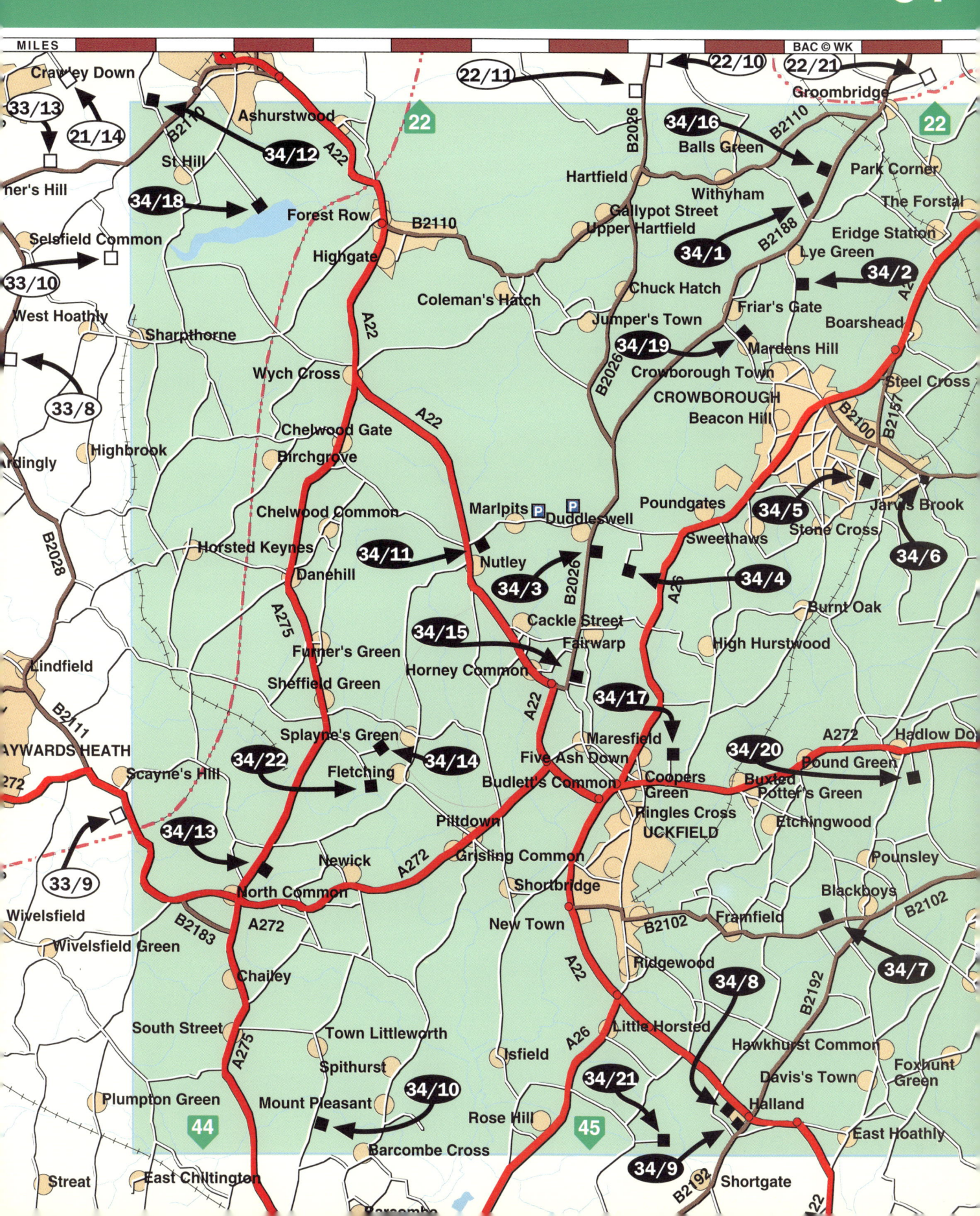

EAST SUSSEX

SPECIALIST & GENERAL NURSERIES, GARDEN AND PLANT CENTRES

35/1 FLOWER POWER

35/2 SUSSEX COUNTRY GARDENS
Eastbourne Road
Mark Cross, Crowborough
East Sussex TN6 3PJ
01892 852828
Extensive ranges of plants, terracotta, stoneware & sundries. Hardwood furniture. Expert and friendly advice and service.
Open: All year except Xmas & Boxing Days; 7 days a week, Mon–Sat 9–5.30, Sun 10–5.
Wheelchairs: Easy access.
Toilets: Yes.
Dogs: Yes. **Credit cards:** Yes.

35/3 MOYSES NURSERIES

35/4 THORPE GARDEN CENTRE
Little London Road
Horam, Heathfield
01435 812455
Nursery-based garden centre.

35/5 BROAD OAK GARDEN CENTRE

35/6 BARTRAM'S GARDEN CENTRE & NURSERY

35/7 K. R. SHANKS 
Old Orchard Nursery
Heathfield Road
Burwash Common
East Sussex TN19 7NE
01435 882060
*Specialists in select **shrubs, trees, hardy plants and climbers**. Bedding and indoor plants also on sale.*
Open: All year except Xmas; 6 days a week (CLOSED MONDAY), Tues–Sat 9–5, Sunday 10–4.
Wheelchairs: Paved but sloping.
Toilets: Ask if desperate.
Dogs: No. **Credit cards:** Yes.

35/8 SUNNY RISE NURSERIES
North Trade Road, Battle
TN33 0HW 01424 772685
Nursery stock & house plants.

35/9 KNOWLE GRANGE NURSERIES

35/10 A P NURSERY
Nettlesworth Lane
Vines Cross, Heathfield
East Sussex TN21 9EN
01435 812965
*Specialists in **standard plants incl. geraniums and fuchsias**. Wide range of bedding plants and perennials. Hanging baskets made up to order.*
Open: April–July: 7 days a week, 9–5; Aug–March: 5 days a week, Mon–Fri, 10–4.
Toilets: Ask if desperate.
Dogs: On lead. **Credit cards:** Yes.

GARDEN & GARDEN CENTRE

35/11 MERRIMENTS GARDENS & NURSERY 
Hurst Green
East Sussex TN19 7RA
01580 860666
'Four-acre show garden – one of the finest in the country'. Nursery selling many rare plants. Café for lunches and teas.
Open: Garden: Easter–Oct; 7 days a week, 10–5. Nursery: all year except Xmas day–10 Jan approx; 7 days a week, 9–5.30.
Costs: Gardens £1.50.
Wheelchairs: When dry.
Toilets: Yes.
Dogs: On lead. **Credit cards:** Yes.

GARDENS

35/12 BATEMANS (NT)
01435 882302
Rudyard Kipling's garden.

35/13 OWL HOUSE GARDENS
16 acres of beautiful, informal gardens planned by the Marchioness of Dufferin.

35/14 SCOTNEY CASTLE GARDEN (NT)
01892 891081
Romantic landscape garden.

35/15 FINCHCOCKS MUSICAL MUSEUM & GARDEN
Beautiful garden, 18C manor.
Open: April–Oct: phone 01580 211702.

35/16 BEDGEBURY NATIONAL PINETUM & FOREST
Open: Daily. 01580 211044.

35/17 PASHLEY MANOR GARDENS 
Pashley Manor
Ticehurst
East Sussex TN5 7HE
01580 200692
'A garden of great age, steeped in romance, where all you hear is the sound of splashing water and birdsong.'
Open: Mid-April–end Sept; Tues, Wed, Thur, Sat & BH Mons, 11–5.
Costs: £3.50, concessions £3.
Wheelchairs: With difficulty.
Toilets: Yes.
Dogs: No. **Credit cards:** No.

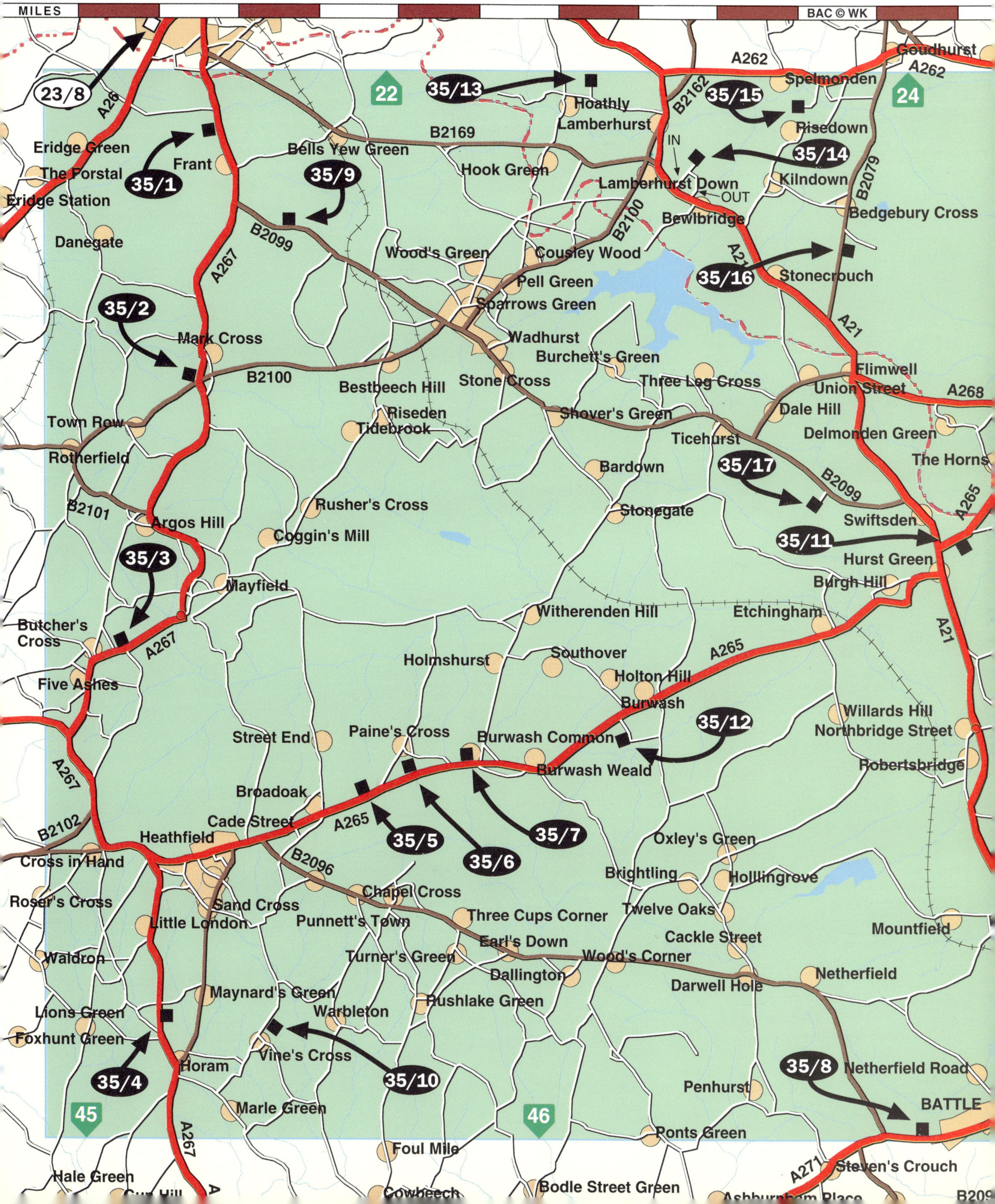
MILES
BAC © WK
23/8
A26
Eridge Green
The Forstal
Eridge Station
Frant
35/1
Danegate
Bells Yew Green
35/9
B2099
A267
B2169
Hook Green
22
35/13
Hoathly
Lamberhurst
A262
Goudhurst
A262
Spelmonden
24
B2162
35/15
Risedown
IN
35/14
Kilndown
B2079
Lamberhurst Down
OUT
Bewlbridge
B2100
Bedgebury Cross
Wood's Green
Cousley Wood
Pell Green
Sparrows Green
35/16
Stonecrouch
A21
Wadhurst
Burchett's Green
35/2
Mark Cross
B2100
Bestbeech Hill
Stone Cross
Three Leg Cross
Flimwell
Union Street
A268
Dale Hill
Delmonden Green
The Horns
Town Row
Riseden
Tidebrook
Shover's Green
Ticehurst
Rotherfield
Bardown
35/17
B2099
B2101
Rusher's Cross
Argos Hill
Stonegate
Swiftsden
A265
Coggin's Mill
35/3
35/11
Hurst Green
Burgh Hill
Mayfield
Butcher's Cross
Witherenden Hill
Etchingham
A267
A21
Five Ashes
Holmshurst
Southover
A265
Holton Hill
Burwash
Willards Hill
Northbridge Street
35/12
Street End
Paine's Cross
Burwash Common
Robertsbridge
Burwash Weald
A267
Broadoak
B2102
Cade Street
A265
35/5
35/6
35/7
Heathfield
Oxley's Green
Cross in Hand
B2096
Brightling
Hollingrove
Roser's Cross
Sand Cross
Chapel Cross
Little London
Punnett's Town
Three Cups Corner
Twelve Oaks
Cackle Street
Mountfield
Waldron
Turner's Green
Earl's Down
Wood's Corner
Netherfield
Dallington
Darwell Hole
Maynard's Green
Rushlake Green
Lions Green
Warbleton
Foxhunt Green
Vine's Cross
35/10
35/8
Netherfield Road
Horam
35/4
Penhurst
45
Marle Green
46
BATTLE
A267
Ponts Green
Foul Mile
A271
Steven's Crouch
Hale Green
Cowbeech
Bodle Street Green

EAST SUSSEX & KENT

SPECIALIST & GENERAL NURSERIES, GARDEN AND PLANT CENTRES

36/1 UCKHAM LANE NURSERY

36/2 WASHFIELD NURSERY

36/3 BODIAM NURSERY
Bodiam, Robertsbridge
TN32 5RA 01580 830811
Over 2000 plant varieties.

36/4 BODIAM BONSAI
Ewhurst Green, Robertsbridge
TN32 5RJ 01580 830644
Bonsai nursery.

36/5 PHOENIX NURSERY
Sunflower Gardens
Staplecross
East Sussex TN32 5QA
01580 830701
*Recently established nursery specialising in **hardy perennials**, many unusual or new. Also climbers, shrubs, roses, bedding plants.*
Open: March–Xmas only; 6 days a week (CLOSED MONDAY), Tues–Fri 10–3, Sat & Sun 9–5.
Wheelchairs: Gravel surfaces.
Toilets: No.
Dogs: Yes. **Credit cards:** No.

36/6 STAPLECROSS SHRUB CENTRE
Brambles Cripps Corner
Robertsbridge 01580 830678
Family nursery – all garden plants.

36/7 BLACKBROOKS GARDEN CENTRE
Main A21
Sedlescombe, Hastings
East Sussex TN33 0RJ
01424 870710/870673
Large range of indoor & outdoor plants, shrubs and trees (incl. 30ft. specimens). Fish, ponds, fountains & ornaments. Café.
Open: All year except 25 Dec–1 Jan; 7 days a week, Mon–Fri 8–5.30, Sat 8–5, Sun 10.30–4.30.
Wheelchairs: Chair available.
Toilets: Yes.
Dogs: No. **Credit cards:** Yes.

36/8 BEXHILL FARM NURSERY

36/9 TILE BARN NURSERY
Standen Street, Benenden
TN17 4LB 01580 240221
Hardy cyclamen species (National Collection).

36/10 LAURELS NURSERY
Dingleden, Benenden
01580 240463
Trees, wisteria, shrubs. Designs.
Open: Mon–Fri & Sat am.

36/11 JUST ROSES
Beales Lane, Northiam
01797 252355
*Specialist in all types of **roses**.*

36/12 HARBOROUGH NURSERIES
The Thorne (Rye Road)
Guestling, Hastings
East Sussex TN35 4LU
01424 814220
*Long established family-run nursery. An exceptionally wide range of **hardy plants**, fruit, trees, shrubs and much more.*
Open: All year except 2 weeks at Xmas; 7 days a week, Feb–Oct 10–5, Nov–Jan 10–4.
Wheelchairs: Gravel.
Toilets: Ask if desperate.
Dogs: No. **Credit cards:** Yes.

NURSERY & GARDEN

36/13 AXLETREE NURSERY
Starvecrow Lane
Peasmarsh, Rye
East Sussex TN31 6XL
01797 230470
*A wide variety of unusual herbaceous perennials especially **hardy geraniums**. One-acre plantsman's garden.*
Open: Mid-March to end Sept; Wed–Sat 10–5.
Costs: Garden free.
Toilets: Yes.
Dogs: On lead. **Credit cards:** No.

GARDEN

36/14 GREAT DIXTER GARDENS & NURSERY
01797 252878
Christopher Lloyd's garden.

WATER GARDEN SPECIALISTS

36/15 WORLD OF WATER

Hastings Road (A28)
Rolvenden
Kent TN17 4PL
01580 241771
One of the largest in the S.E. Everything for the pond and tropical fish enthusiast. Showgardens. Expert advice. Café.
Open: All year except Xmas & Boxing Days; 7 days a week, Mon–Sat 9–5.30, Sunday 10.30–4.30.
Wheelchairs: Easy paved access.
Toilets: Yes.
Dogs: On lead. **Credit cards:** Yes.

36/16 THE NISHIKIGOI CENTRE

Hawkhurst Fish Farm
Hastings Road, Hawkhurst
Kent TN18 4RT
01580 754030
Koi and filtration specialists, extensive coldwater fish, Japanese style, and water plants, set in 42 acres. Tea rooms.
Open: All year; 6 days a week (CLOSED MONDAY except Bank Holidays), 9–5.30 (summer), 10–4.30 (winter).
Wheelchairs: Partial access.
Toilets: Yes.
Dogs: No. **Credit cards:** Yes.

GARDEN

36/17 BRICKWALL HOUSE AND GARDENS
Open: Restricted opening.

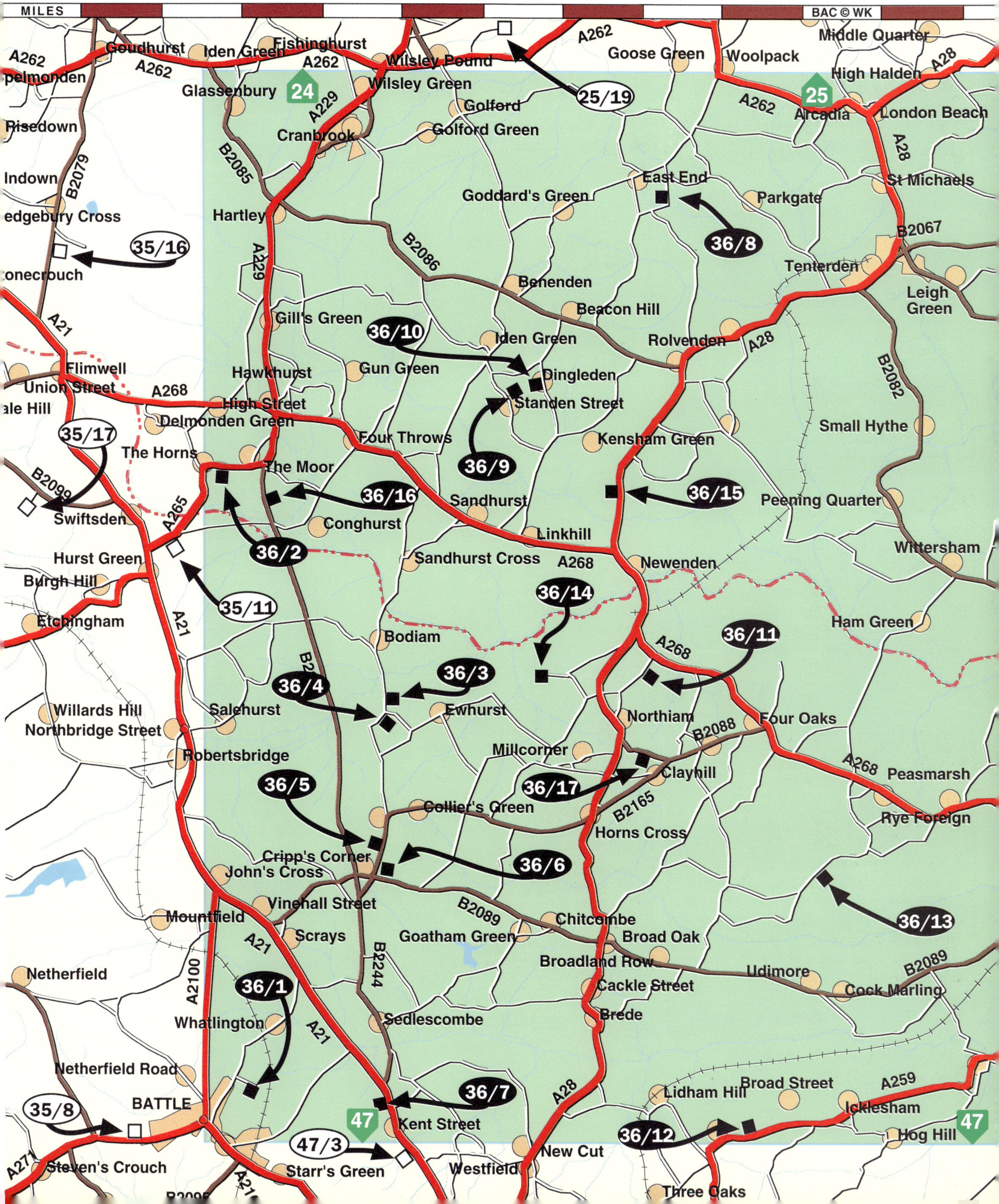
MILES
BAC © WK
A262
Goudhurst
Iden Green
Fishinghurst
A262
Wilsley Pound
Wilsley Green
Glassenbury
24
A229
Cranbrook
Golford
Golford Green
B2085
Hartley
Goddard's Green
B2086
B2079
Risedown
Lamberhurst Down
Bedgebury Cross
35/16
Stonecrouch
A229
Gill's Green
36/10
Iden Green
Dingleden
Hawkhurst
Gun Green
A21
Flimwell
Union Street
A268
High Street
Delmonden Green
Standen Street
Four Throws
36/9
35/17
The Horns
The Moor
B2099
36/16
Sandhurst
Swiftsden
Conghurst
A265
Linkhill
36/2
Hurst Green
Burgh Hill
35/11
Sandhurst Cross
A268
36/14
Etchingham
A21
Bodiam
36/4
36/3
Salehurst
Ewhurst
Willards Hill
Northbridge Street
Robertsbridge
Millcorner
36/5
36/17
Collier's Green
Cripp's Corner
John's Cross
36/6
Vinehall Street
Mountfield
A21
Scrays
B2089
Goatham Green
B2244
Netherfield
A2100
36/1
Whatlington
A21
Sedlescombe
Netherfield Road
BATTLE
35/8
36/7
47
Kent Street
47/3
A271
Steven's Crouch
Starr's Green
Westfield
A21
B2095
A262
Goose Green
Woolpack
Middle Quarter
25/19
High Halden
A28
A262
25
Arcadia
London Beach
A28
East End
St Michaels
Parkgate
36/8
B2067
Tenterden
Benenden
Leigh Green
Beacon Hill
Rolvenden
A28
B2082
Small Hythe
Kensham Green
36/15
Peening Quarter
Wittersham
Newenden
36/11
Ham Green
A268
Northiam
Four Oaks
B2088
Clayhill
A268
Peasmarsh
B2165
Rye Foreign
Horns Cross
36/13
Chitcombe
Broad Oak
Broadland Row
Udimore
B2089
Cackle Street
Cock Marling
Brede
A28
Lidham Hill
Broad Street
A259
Icklesham
36/12
47
Hog Hill
New Cut
Three Oaks

KENT

SPECIALIST & GENERAL NURSERIES, GARDEN AND PLANT CENTRES

37/1 PINECOVE NURSERIES

37/2 TENTERDEN GARDEN CENTRE
Reading Street
Tenterden
Kent TN30 7HT
01233 758510

Plant centre specialising in a wide range of **unusual shrubs & herbaceous plants**. Garden sundries, fencing and furniture.
Open: All year except Xmas week; 7 days a week, summer Mon–Fri 9.30–6 (Sat 6.30), winter 9.30–5 (Sat 5.30). All year, Sun 10.30–4.30.
Wheelchairs: Easy access.
Toilets: Yes.
Dogs: On lead. **Credit cards:** Yes.

37/3 ROMNEY MARSH GARDEN CENTRE

37/4 NEWINGREEN NURSERIES

N.N.

Cydonia, Ashford Road
Newingreen
Hythe
Kent CT21 4JD
01303 260863

A family-run nursery growing a large range of **hardy nursery stock**: trees, shrubs, herbaceous perennials, conifers, herbs and seasonal bedding plants.
Open: All year except Xmas Day; 7 days a week, 9–6.
Wheelchairs: Difficult access.
Toilets: No.
Dogs: No. **Credit cards:** No.

37/5 LONGACRE NURSERIES
St. Mary's Road
West Hythe
Kent CT21 4NU
01303 265132

A wholesale and retail nursery for **geraniums, bedding plants, fuchsias** etc. Hanging baskets, cyclamen, poinsettias and pot chrysanthemums.
Open: All year except Xmas & Boxing Days; 7 days a week, 10–5.
Wheelchairs: Good access.
Toilets: Ask if desperate.
Dogs: On lead. **Credit cards:** Yes.

37/6 PETER J. GODDARD LANDSCAPES
New Romney Landscape Centre
Cockreed Lane
01797 363908
Display gardens & retail sales.

37/7 KENNEDYS GARDEN CENTRE
Ingles Meadow
Jointon Road, Folkestone
Kent CT20 2RS
01303 258100

Garden centre catering for all garden needs. Giftware, pet shop, aquatics. Café and scenic gardens.
Open: All year except Xmas & Boxing Days; 7 days a week, Mon–Sat 9–5.30 (winter), 9–6.30 (summer), Sun 10.30–4.30.
Wheelchairs: Easy access.
Toilets: Yes. **Credit cards:** Yes.
Dogs: Guide dogs only.

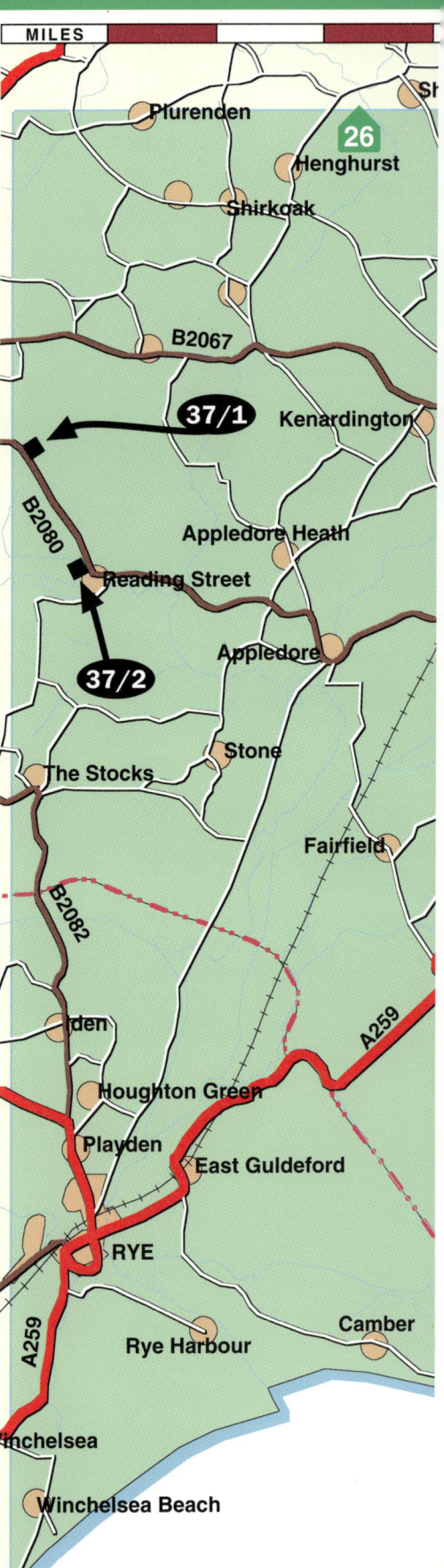

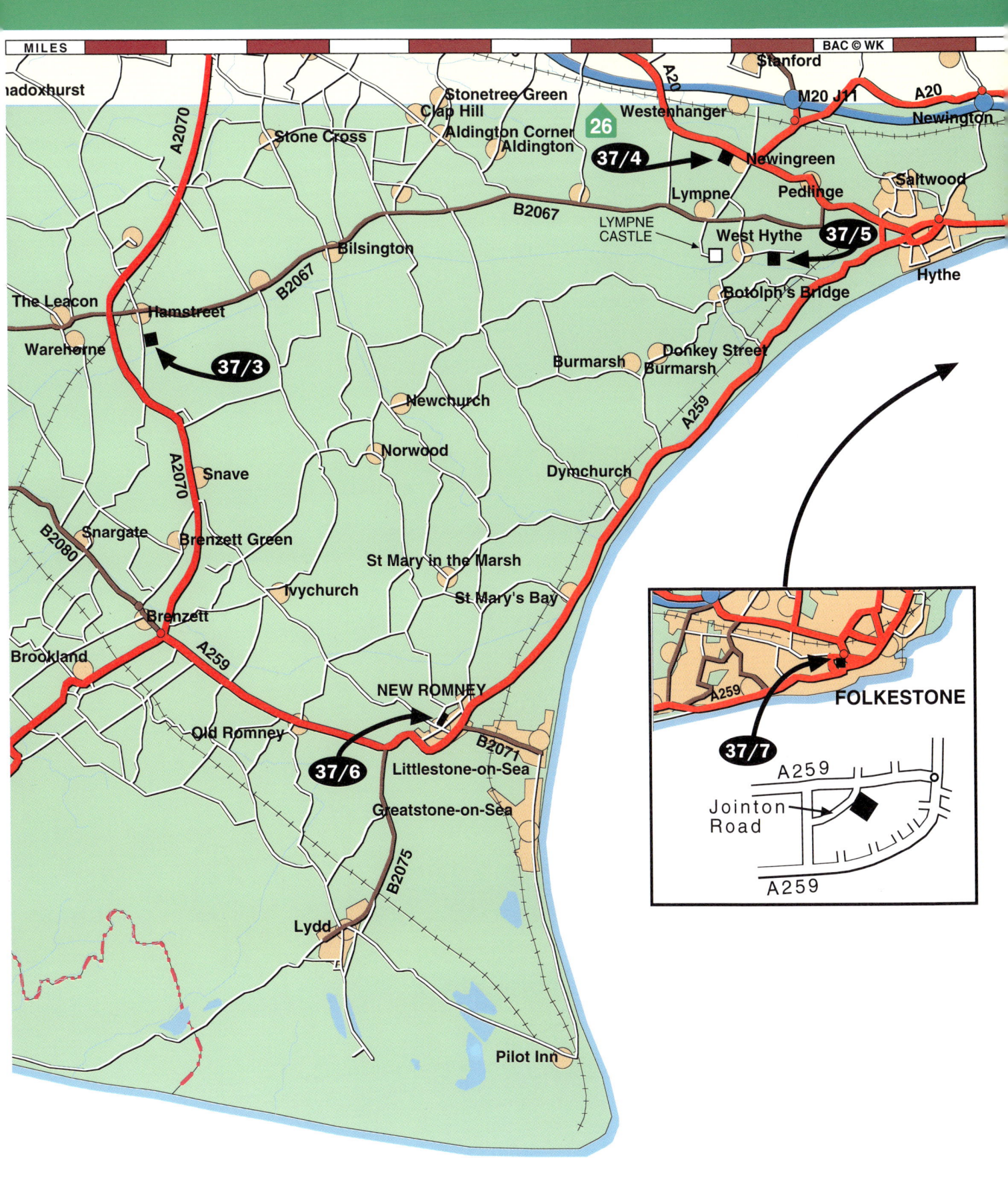

37

HAMPSHIRE

SPECIALIST & GENERAL NURSERIES, GARDEN AND PLANT CENTRES

38/1 DRYSDALE NURSERY
01425 653010
Bamboos.

38/2 BARNHAWK NURSERY

38/3 MACPENNYS NURSERY

38/4 GARDEN COTTAGE NURSERY
New Lane, Bashley
New Milton BH25 5TE
01425 613029
Summer and winter bedding.

38/5 REDCLIFFE GARDEN CENTRE

38/6 AGAR'S NURSERY

NURSERY & GARDEN

38/7 APPLE COURT NURSERY

Hordle Lane
Hordle, Lymington
Hampshire SO41 0HU
01590 642130
Walled garden with **famous hosta walk***. Attractive plantings of day lilies, ferns and grasses. Theatrical white garden. Well stocked specialist nursery.*
Open: Feb–June & Sept–Oct, Thur–Mon; July–Aug, all week. 9.30–1 & 2–5.
Costs: Garden £1.50, children 50p.
Wheelchairs: In garden yes, but not in nursery.   **Credit cards:** No.
Toilets: Ask if desperate. **Dogs:** No.

SPECIALIST & GENERAL NURSERIES, GARDEN AND PLANT CENTRES

38/8 ABBEY GARDEN CENTRE

38/9 STEVEN BAILEY LTD
Silver Street, Sway
Lymington, Hampshire
01590 682227
Alstroemeria, carnations, pinks.

38/10 HOLLINS NURSERY

38/11 LYMINGTON PLANT CENTRE
Pitmore Lane, Pennington
Lymington   01590 682611
Family nursery: bedding etc.

38/12 HOLLY BUSH GARDEN CENTRE

38/13 NEW FOREST WINE
Hollybush Vineyard
Brockenhurst SO42 7UF
01590 622246
Vines for sale. Wine tasting.

38/14 NORTHFIELD NURSERY

38/15 FAIRWEATHER GARDEN CENTRE

PICK-YOUR-OWN FARM

38/16 HAZELCOPSE FARM

GARDEN & NURSERY

38/17 SPINNERS GARDEN
School Lane
Boldre, Lymington
Hampshire SO41 5QE
01590 673347
Well known woodland garden and nursery. An exceptional selection of **rare and unusual hardy plants***, shrubs and trees for sale.*
Open: All year; Tues–Sat, 10–5.
Costs: Garden £1.50, nursery free.
Wheelchairs: Not suitable.
Toilets: Yes.
Dogs: No.   **Credit cards:** No.

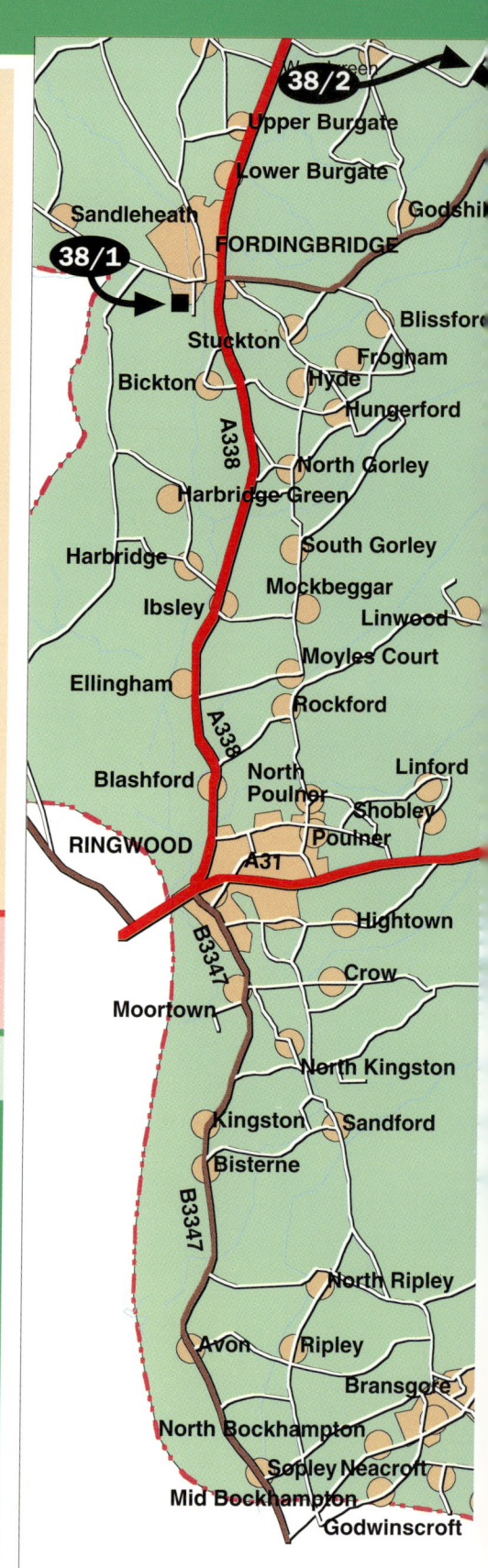

38

HAMPSHIRE

GARDEN & PLANT CENTRE

39/1 EXBURY GARDENS
Exbury
Southampton
Hampshire SO45 1AZ
01703 891203
200 acres of woodland garden providing a dazzling display of colour. Well stocked plant centre, gift shop and tea rooms.
Open: March–early Nov; 7 days a week, 10–5.30 or dusk if earlier.
Costs: £2.20–£4.80.
Wheelchairs: Some available.
Toilets: Yes.
Dogs: On lead.   **Credit cards:** Yes.

SPECIALIST & GENERAL NURSERIES, GARDEN AND PLANT CENTRES

39/2 HASKINS GARDEN CENTRE
A very large centre.

39/3 HILLIER GARDEN CENTRE
Woodhouse Lane, Botley
Southampton   01489 782306
'The heart of good gardening.'

39/4 KEILEEN NURSERIES
Brook Avenue, Warsash
01489 573660
Bedding & *pot plant growers.*
Open: April–May & Oct only.

39/5 MEDINA NURSERIES
Warsash, Southampton
SEE PAGE 50 FOR FULL DETAILS

39/6 BRIDGE ROAD NURSERIES

39/7 ST. MARGARET'S FUCHSIA NURSERIY
St. Margaret's Lane
Titchfield, Fareham
Hampshire   PO14 4BG
01329 846006
Over 600 varieties of **fuchsia** *grown: rooted cuttings to standards. Display garden. Hanging baskets, patio and bedding plants.*
Open: Feb–Nov; 7 days a week, 9–5 (dusk in winter). Dec–Jan, 5 days a week (CLOSED MON & TUES).
Wheelchairs: Access to most areas.
Toilets: Yes.
Dogs: On lead.   **Credit cards:** Yes.

39/8 HAMBROOKS GARDEN CENTRE
135 Southampton Road
Titchfield, Fareham
Hampshire   PO14 4PR
01489 572285
A wide range of plants including many unusual varieties. Show gardens, working water features, paving, fencing, greenhouses, sheds, stoneware, sundries.
Open: All year; 7 days a week, summer 9–6, winter 9–5, Sun 10.30–4.30.
Wheelchairs: Easy access.
Toilets: Yes.
Dogs: On lead.   **Credit cards:** Yes.

39/9 ABBEY GARDEN CENTRE

39/10 TITCHFIELD MILLS

39/11 LEYDENE GARDENS NURSERY
Polyanthus and primroses. Summer & autumn **bedding**.
Open: 7 days a week; 9–12.30, 2–5.

39/12 FONTLEY NURSERIES & GARDEN CENTRE

39/13 PARK PLACE FARM NURSERY
Titchfield Lane
Wickham
Hampshire   PO17 5HB
01329 834991
Commercial nursery open to the public, specialising in **basket & patio plants**. *Hundreds of varieties to choose from.*
Open: All year; 7 days a week, 9–5.
Wheelchairs: All concreted.
Toilets: Ask if desperate.
Dogs: On lead.   **Credit cards:** No.

39/14 ABBEY CROFT NURSERIES

39/15 HOLLAM NURSERIES

39/16 SOLENT NURSERIES
Fontley Road, Titchfield
Fareham   01329 843036
A wide range of nursery stock.

39/17 SILVER SPRING NURSERIES

39/18 CHERYLDENE NURSERY

39/19 LYMORE VALLEY HERB GARDEN

39/20 EVERTON NURSERIES

WATER GARDEN SPECIALIST

39/21 EVERTON WATER GARDEN CENTRE
Newlands Manor
Everton, Lymington
Hampshire   SO41 0JH
01590 644405
Water garden centre in the grounds of Newlands Manor with fine display gardens and ponds. Design & building service available. Ancilliary sales.
Open: Feb–Nov; 7 days a week, 9.30–5.30.
Wheelchairs: Good access.
Toilets: Yes.
Dogs: No.   **Credit cards:** Yes.

39

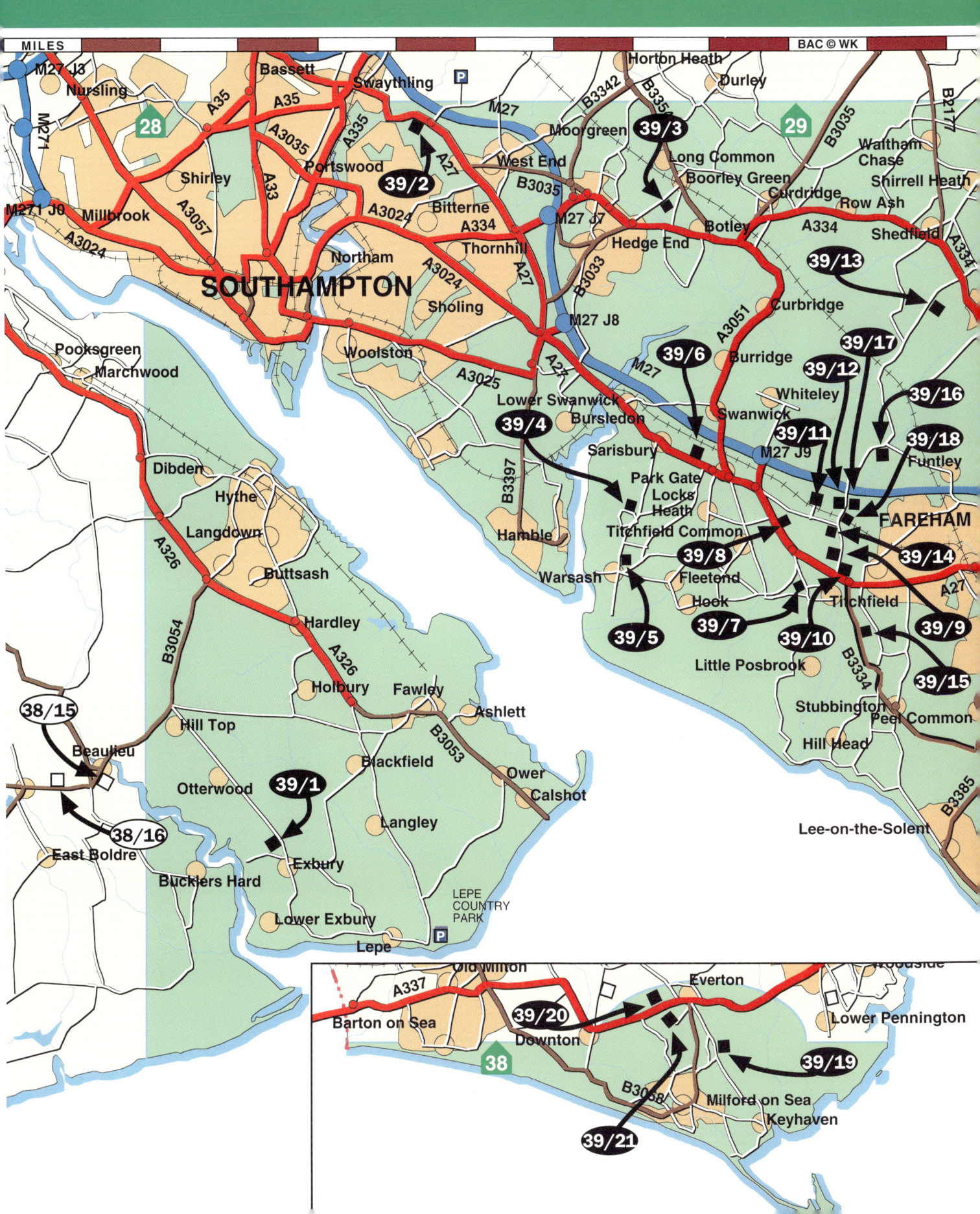

HAMPSHIRE

SPECIALIST & GENERAL NURSERIES, GARDEN AND PLANT CENTRES

40/1 MUD ISLAND NURSERIES

Southwick Road
Wickham, Fareham
Hampshire   PO17 6JF
01329 834407

A family-owned garden nursery, in delightful surroundings, producing a wide variety of quality plants. Extensive alpine section. Coffee shop.
Open: All year except Xmas week; 7 days a week 9–5, spring 9–6.
Wheelchairs: Easy access.
Toilets: Yes.
Dogs: No.   **Credit cards:** Yes.

40/2 MOUNT FOLLY NURSERIES

Southwick Road, Wickham
01329 832294
Fuchsia, patio plant *specialists.*

40/3 LODGE HILL NURSERY

Lodge Hill
Newtown, Wickham
Hampshire   PO17 6LG
01329 834753
Herb & hardy perennial *specialists. Also bedding, patio and basket plants. Herbaceous borders and herb garden.*
Open: Mid-March–June, 7 days a week; July–mid-Nov, 5 days a week, (CLOSED TUES & WED), 10–5.
Wheelchairs: Flat gravel.
Toilets: No.
Dogs: On lead.   **Credit cards:** No.

40/4 KINGFISHER PLANTS

Selworth Lane, Soberton
01489 877100
Shrubs, trees, general stock.

40/5 MEON VALLEY NURSERIES

Soberton Heath
Southampton
SEE PAGE 49 FOR FULL DETAILS

40/6 DENMEAD GERANIUM NURSERIES

Hambledon Road, Waterlooville
01705 240081
Pelargonium *specialist.*
Open: Mon–Fri, 9–1 & 2–5.

40/7 HAYWARDS CARNATIONS

40/8 RUSTLINGS NURSERY & PLANT CENTRE

104 Catherington Lane,
Horndean   01705 594832
Bedding, *pot plants, shrubs, roses.*

GARDEN

40/9 SIR GEORGE STAUNTON COUNTRY PARK

01705 453405
Landscaped parkland. Tropical plants under glass. Restored walled garden.

SPECIALIST & GENERAL NURSERIES, GARDEN AND PLANT CENTRES

40/10 KEYDELL NURSERIES

Havant Road, B2149
Horndean, Waterlooville
Hampshire   PO8 0UU
01705 593839
Well established garden centre with a wide range of stock. Bedding plants. Trees. Wooden garden furniture.
Open: All year except Xmas & Boxing Days; 7 days a week, 9–5. Late nights in summer.
Wheelchairs: Easy access.
Toilets: Yes.
Dogs: On lead.   **Credit cards:** Yes.

40/11 MEADOW FARM NURSERY

Woodgason Lane
Hayling Island
Hampshire   PO11 0RL
01705 461570
Family-run nursery in an attractive rural setting offering a comprehensive range of quality plants. Friendly advice given.
Open: All year except Xmas Day–New Year; 7 days a week, 9–6 (summer), 9–5 (winter).
Wheelchairs: Good access.
Toilets: Ask if desperate.
Dogs: On lead.   **Credit cards:** Yes.

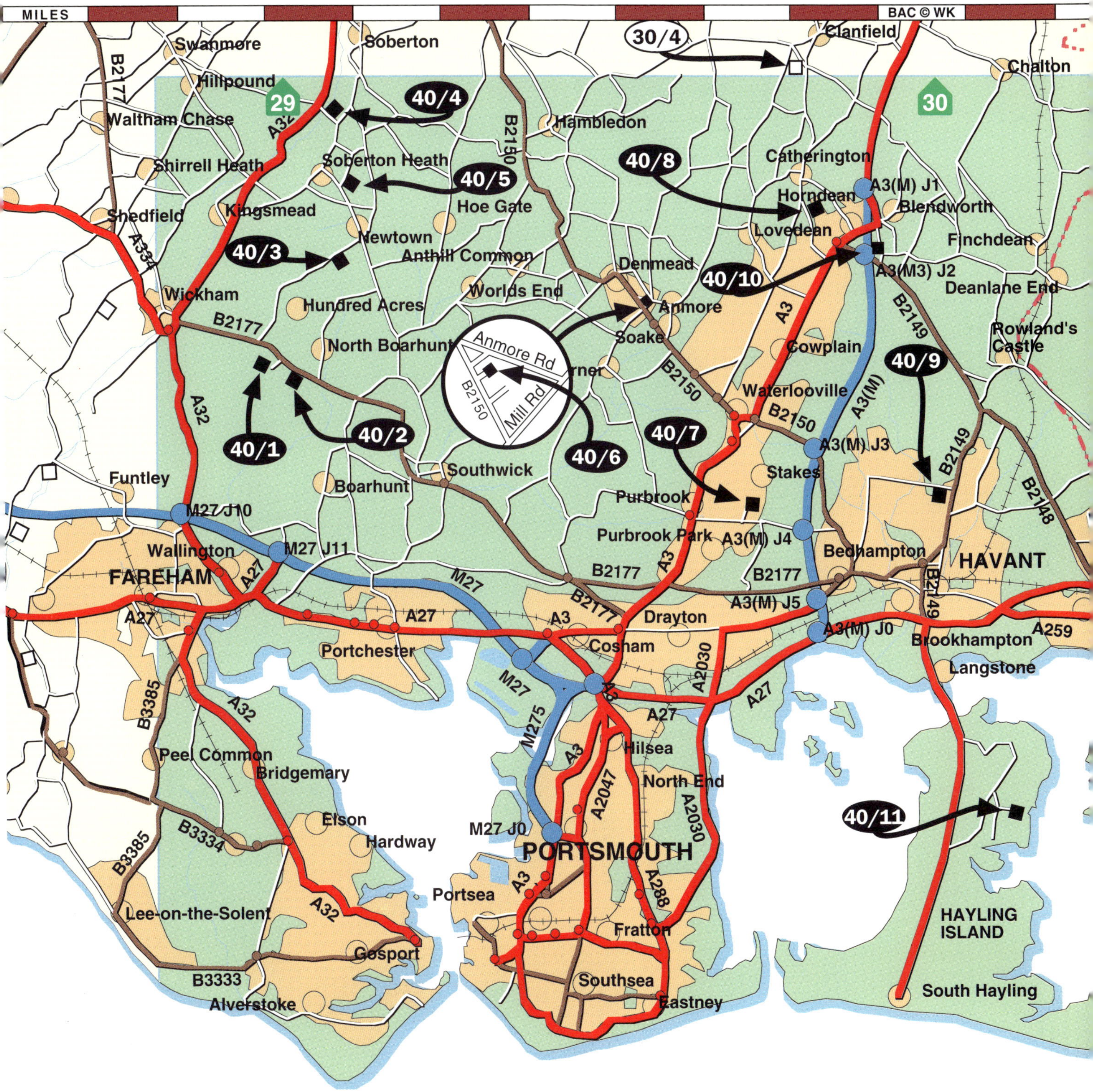
MILES
BAC © WK
Swanmore
Soberton
30/4
Clanfield
Chalton
Hillpound
29
40/4
30
Waltham Chase
Hambledon
B2150
Shirrell Heath
Soberton Heath
40/8
Catherington
40/5
A3(M) J1
Horndean
Blendworth
Hoe Gate
Shedfield
Kingsmead
Lovedean
Newtown
Finchdean
40/3
Anthill Common
A3(M3) J2
Denmead
40/10
Deanlane End
Wickham
Worlds End
Anmore
Hundred Acres
B2177
Rowland's Castle
Soake
North Boarhunt
Anmore Rd
Mill Rd
Cowplain
40/9
Waterlooville
B2150
40/1
40/2
40/6
40/7
A3(M) J3
Southwick
Stakes
B2149
Funtley
Boarhunt
Purbrook
M27 J10
Purbrook Park
A3(M) J4
B2148
Wallington
M27 J11
Bedhampton
HAVANT
FAREHAM
M27
B2177
A27
A3
B2177
A3(M) J5
Drayton
A3(M) J0
A259
Portchester
Cosham
Brookhampton
Langstone
A2030
M27
A3
A27
A32
B3385
M275
A27
Hilsea
Peel Common
Bridgemary
North End
A2047
A2030
Elson
40/11
Hardway
M27 J0
B3334
PORTSMOUTH
B3385
A288
Portsea
A3
HAYLING ISLAND
Lee-on-the-Solent
A32
Fratton
Gosport
Southsea
South Hayling
B3333
Eastney
Alverstoke
A32
A334
A3

HAMPSHIRE & WEST SUSSEX

ARTEFACT SUPPLIER

41/1 NEW DAWN FURNITURE

Rose Cottage
Commonside
Westbourne
Emsworth
Hampshire
PO10 8TD
01243 375535

Teak garden furniture, hand-crafted in the joinery workshop and on view in the showroom.
Open: All year except Xmas & Boxing Days; 7 days a week, 10–5.30.
Wheelchairs: Reasonable access.
Toilets: Yes.
Dogs: Yes. **Credit cards:** Yes.

PICK-YOUR-OWN FARM

41/2 WESTON APPLE FARM

SPECIALIST & GENERAL NURSERIES, GARDEN AND PLANT CENTRES

41/3 BARRY'S BLOOMING BASKETS

112 Main Road, Emsworth
01243 379929
Hanging baskets, *bedding, shrubs.*

41/4 GREENACRE NURSERY

A259, Main Road
Chidham, Chichester
West Sussex   PO18 8TP
01243 572441

A nursery growing **bedding**, *fuchsias, geraniums, pansies, polys and hanging baskets, shrubs, conifers and roses.*
Open: All year except Xmas and Boxing Days; 7 days a week, 9.30–5.30.
Wheelchairs: The whole area, including car park, is concreted.
Toilets: Ask if desperate.
Dogs: No. **Credit cards:** Yes.

41/5 BRINKMANS GARDEN CENTRE

41/6 BEACHLANDS NURSERY

Newells Lane
West Ashling
West Sussex   PO18 8DD
01243 573117

Recently established nursery growing plants, including vegetable plants, and shrubs. Hanging baskets.
Open: All year except Xmas & Boxing Days; 6 days a week (CLOSED TUESDAY), 9–5.
Wheelchairs: Good access.
Toilets: Ask if desperate.
Dogs: No. **Credit cards:** No.

41/7 BELLFIELD NURSERY

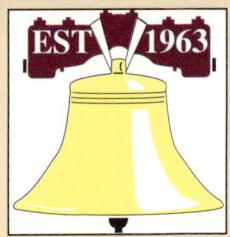

EST 1963

Bell Lane
Birdham, Chichester
West Sussex   PO20 7HY
01243 512333

A family nursery growing geraniums, bedding plants, perennials, fuchsias and hanging basket plants.
Open: All year except Xmas & Boxing Days; 6 days a week (CLOSED TUES): 8–5.30 (winter), 8–6.30 (summer).
Wheelchairs: Outside areas only.
Toilets: No.
Dogs: No. **Credit cards:** No.

41/8 BRAMBER NURSERY
2000 varieties of **trees & shrubs**.

41/9 KELLY'S NURSERY

41/10 RUSSELL'S GARDEN CENTRE

41/11 EAST ASHLING NURSERIES

Lye Lane, East Ashling
Chichester
West Sussex   PO18 9DD
01243 575523

A family nursery growing a wide variety of **perennials**. *Summer and winter bedding plants, hanging baskets, shrubs, clematis.*
Open: March–June, 7 days a week; July–Feb, 6 days a week (CLOSED SUNDAY), 8–5.
Wheelchairs: Concrete. **Toilets:** No.
Dogs: On lead. **Credit cards:** No.

41/12 TAWNY NURSERIES
Bell Lane, Birdham
Chichester   01243 512168
Bedding *plant specialists.*

41/13 THE CUCKOO'S NEST NURSERY

125 Third Avenue
Almodington
Chichester
West Sussex
PO20 7LB
01243 512541

Well established nursery specialising in **patio container plants**. *Also shrubs, alpines etc. in attractive courtyard garden.*
Open: March–June, 7 days a week, 9–5. Sept–mid-Nov, 7 days a week, 10–4.
Wheelchairs: Gravel parking.
Toilets: Ask if desperate.
Dogs: On lead. **Credit cards:** No.

41/14 RICHARDSON'S NURSERY

41/15 APULDRAM ROSES
Apuldram Lane, Dell Quay
Chichester   01243 785769
Rose *nursery & display garden.*

41/16 FUCHSIA WORLD

Cedar Nursery
Birdham Road
Chichester, West Sussex
PO20 7EQ
01243 776822

A plant centre specialising in producing **fuchsias** *– 30000 in 125 varieties – geraniums and patio plants.*
Open: Mid-March–November; 7 days a week, 10–5.
Wheelchairs: Level concrete paths – easy access. **Toilets:** Yes.
Dogs: On lead. **Credit cards:** Yes.

41/17 THE APULDRAM CENTRE

WATER GARDEN SPECIALIST

41/18 LOCKSACRE AQUATIC NURSERY
Wophams Lane, Birdham,
Chichester   01243 512472
Fish, plants and pools.

GARDENS

41/19 GARDEN IN MIND
Ivan Hick's BBC2 garden in the grounds of Stanstead Park.
Open: June–Sept; Sunday pm.

41/20 FISHBOURNE ROMAN PALACE
01243 785859
Restored Roman garden.
Open: Mid-Feb–mid-Dec, daily 10–5.

41/21 WEST DEAN GARDENS
West Dean
Chichester   PO18 0QZ
01243–818 210/811 301
Kitchen garden and arboretum.

West Dean Gardens

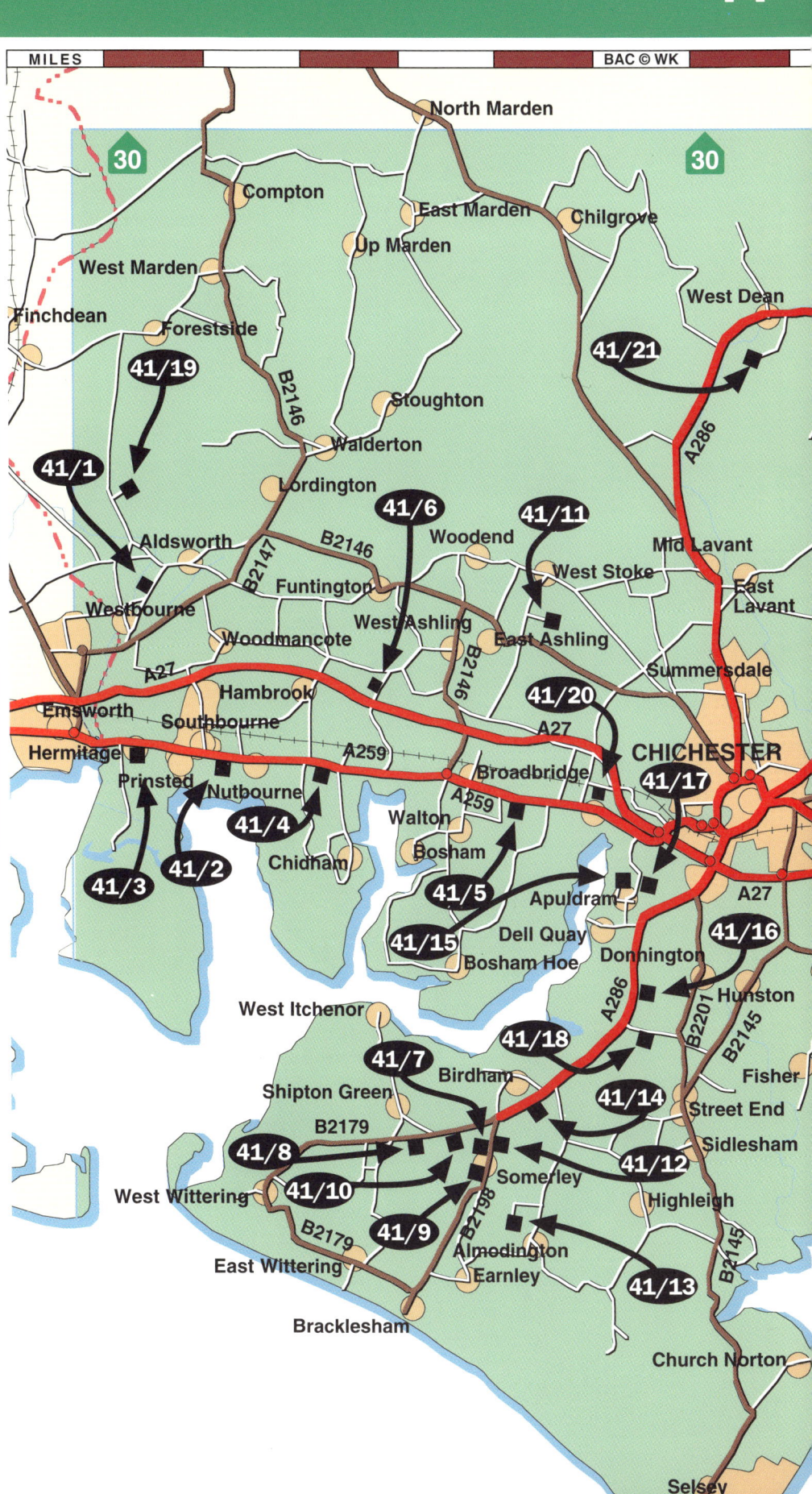

WEST SUSSEX

SPECIALIST & GENERAL NURSERIES, GARDEN AND PLANT CENTRES

42/1 MAUDLIN NURSERY

42/2 BRICK KILN NURSERY

42/3 MANOR NURSERY

42/4 SHOPWHYKE NURSERIES & SUPPLIES
Shopwhyke Road, Chichester
01243 783123
Trees, shrubs, bedding plants.

42/5 COUNTRY GARDENS CHICHESTER
Bognor Road
Merston, Chichester
West Sussex PO20 6EG
01243–789 276
'Good value garden centre with very wide plant selection. Free local delivery. Garden buildings. Coffee shop.'
Open: All year; Mon–Sat 9–6. Sunday 10.30–4.30. Extended spring hours – phone for information.
Wheelchairs: Easy access.
Toilets: Yes.
Dogs: On lead. **Credit cards:** Yes.

42/6 ALDINGBOURNE COUNTRY CENTRE

42/7 THE LILLIES NURSERY

42/8 PUMPKIN COTTAGE

42/9 CROFTWAY NURSERY
Hardy geraniums and irises.

42/10 MANOR NURSERY, BARNHAM (MAPLETREES)

25 Yapton Road
Bognor Regis
West Sussex PO22 0BQ
01243 552028
Large, old established family nursery with all stock grown on the premises. Specialists in **hanging baskets**.
Open: All year except Xmas, Boxing & New Year's Days; 7 days a week, Mon–Sat 8–5, Sun 9–5.
Wheelchairs: Paved access.
Toilets: Yes.
Dogs: Yes. **Credit cards:** Yes.

42/11 CINDERS LANE NURSERY

42/12 HILLSIDE NURSERIES

42/13 ARUNDEL ARBORETUM

42/14 FAIRHAVEN NURSERY
Toddington Lane, Littlehampton
BN17 1LY   01903 725642
Seasonal **bedding**, *hanging baskets.*

42/15 CHALCROFT NURSERIES AND GARDEN CENTRE
Chalcraft Lane
Bognor Regis
West Sussex PO21 5TS
01243 863346
Home-grown shrubs, conifers, herbaceous and bedding plants, ornamental and fruit trees. Garden supplies. Free advice.
Open: All year except Xmas, Boxing and New Year's Days; 7 days a week. Summer: Mon–Sat 9–5.30, Sun 9–5. Winter: Mon–Sat 9–5, Sun 9–4.
Wheelchairs: Flat paved and gravel areas. **Toilets:** Ask if desperate.
Dogs: No. **Credit cards:** Yes.

WATER GARDEN SPECIALIST

42/16 TROPIKOI – AQUATIC CENTRE

Chalcroft Nurseries
Chalcroft Lane
North Bersted, Bognor Regis
West Sussex P021 5UA
01243 842660
Everything for the water garden and aquarium, including koi, marines and fresh water tropicals.
Open: All year except Xmas & Boxing Days; 6 days a week (CLOSED MON except BHs). Summer: Tues–Sat 9–5.30, Sun 9–5. Winter: Tues–Sat 9–5, Sun 9–4.
Toilets: Ask if desperate.
Dogs: No. **Credit cards:** Yes.

PICK-YOUR-OWN FARM

42/17 RUNCTON FARM PYO

GARDEN

42/18 DENMANS GARDEN
Costs: £2.50, children £1.50, concessions £2.25.

42

WEST SUSSEX

SPECIALIST & GENERAL NURSERIES, GARDEN AND PLANT CENTRES

43/1 MANOR NURSERY
High Street, Angmering
BN16 4AU   01903 786977
Garden centre, plant specialists.

43/2 ROUNDSTONE GARDEN CENTRE
Roundstone By-pass, Angmering
BN16 4RD   01903 776481/2/3
A very large centre. 'The centre with a difference.'

43/3 THREE ACRES GARDEN CENTRE

WATER GARDEN SPECIALIST

43/4 WORLD OF WATER

SPECIALIST & GENERAL NURSERIES, GARDEN AND PLANT CENTRES

43/5 ST. DENYS NURSERY
Dappers Lane, Angmering
BN16 4EN   01903 773240
Bedding *plants and compost.*

43/6 LOWERTREES NURSERY
Roundstone By-pass, Angmering
BN16 4BD   01903 770457
Seasonal **bedding**, *baskets.*

43/7 COUNTRY FAYRE

43/8 COUNTRY GARDENS WORTHING
Littlehampton Road
Ferring, Worthing
West Sussex BN12 6PG
01903 242003
'Good value garden centre with very wide plant selection. Free local delivery. Garden buildings. Coffee shop.'
Open: All year; Mon–Sat 9–6. Sunday 10.30–4.30. Extended spring hours – phone for information.
Wheelchairs: Easy access.
Toilets: Yes.
Dogs: On lead.   **Credit cards:** Yes.

43/9 GREENGOLD TREE FARM

43/10 WYEVALE GARDEN CENTRE

43/11 HOLE STREET NURSERIES

43/12 CASTLE NURSERY

43/13 FERRING NURSERY
A259, Littlehampton Road
Ferring, Worthing
West Sussex   BN12 6PN
01903 241122
Family nursery specialising in summer and autumn **bedding** *plants including perennials, patio plants, fuchsias and shrubs. Large car park.*
Open: Spring & autumn; 7 days a week, 9–5.
Wheelchairs: Very flat ground.
Toilets: No.   **Credit cards:** No.

43/14 WASHINGTON GARDEN CENTRE (ENGLISH WATER GARDENS) 
London Road
Washington, West Sussex
RH20 3BL
01903 892006
A large garden centre specialising in trees, shrubs and water gardens. Stoneware. Pets. Coffee shop.
Open: All year except Xmas Day; 7 days a week, Mon–Sat 9–5.30, Sun 10.30–4.30.
Wheelchairs: Easy paved access, wheelchair available.   **Toilets:** Yes.
Dogs: On lead.   **Credit cards:** Yes.

GARDENS

43/15 HIGHDOWN GARDENS
Unique chalk garden, free entry.

43/16 PARHAM ELIZABETHAN HOUSE AND GARDENS

Gold border at Parham

NURSERY

43/17 SPITHANDLE NURSERY 
Spithandle Lane
Ashurst, Steyning
West Sussex   BN44 3DY
01903 816299
A working nursery hidden in the bluebell woods. Wide variety of herbs, bedding, basket plants and geraniums, some new and unusual.
Open: 7 days a week; March–end June & Sept–end Oct, 9–5 (or later). Closed July, Aug & Nov–Feb.
Wheelchairs: Flat but gravel.
Toilets: Ask if desperate.
Dogs: No.   **Credit cards:** No.

PICK-YOUR-OWN FARMS

43/18 ROUNDSTONE PYO & FARM SHOP 
Roundstone Farm
Littlehampton Road, Ferring
West Sussex   BN12 6PW
PYO: 01903 770670/501663
Shop: 01903 783817
Over 30 PYO fruit & vegetable crops. Plenty of free car parking. Tractor rides to each PYO crop. Large picnic area, drinks & ice creams.
Open: PYO: June–Oct, 7 days a week, 9–5. Shop: All year; 7 days a week, Mon–Sat 9–5, Sun 10–4.
Toilets: Yes.
Dogs: No.   **Credit cards:** No.

43/19 SPRING GARDENS PYO

43/20 ROCK FARM
The Hollow, Washington
RH20 3DA   01903 892412
Soft fruit and vegetables.

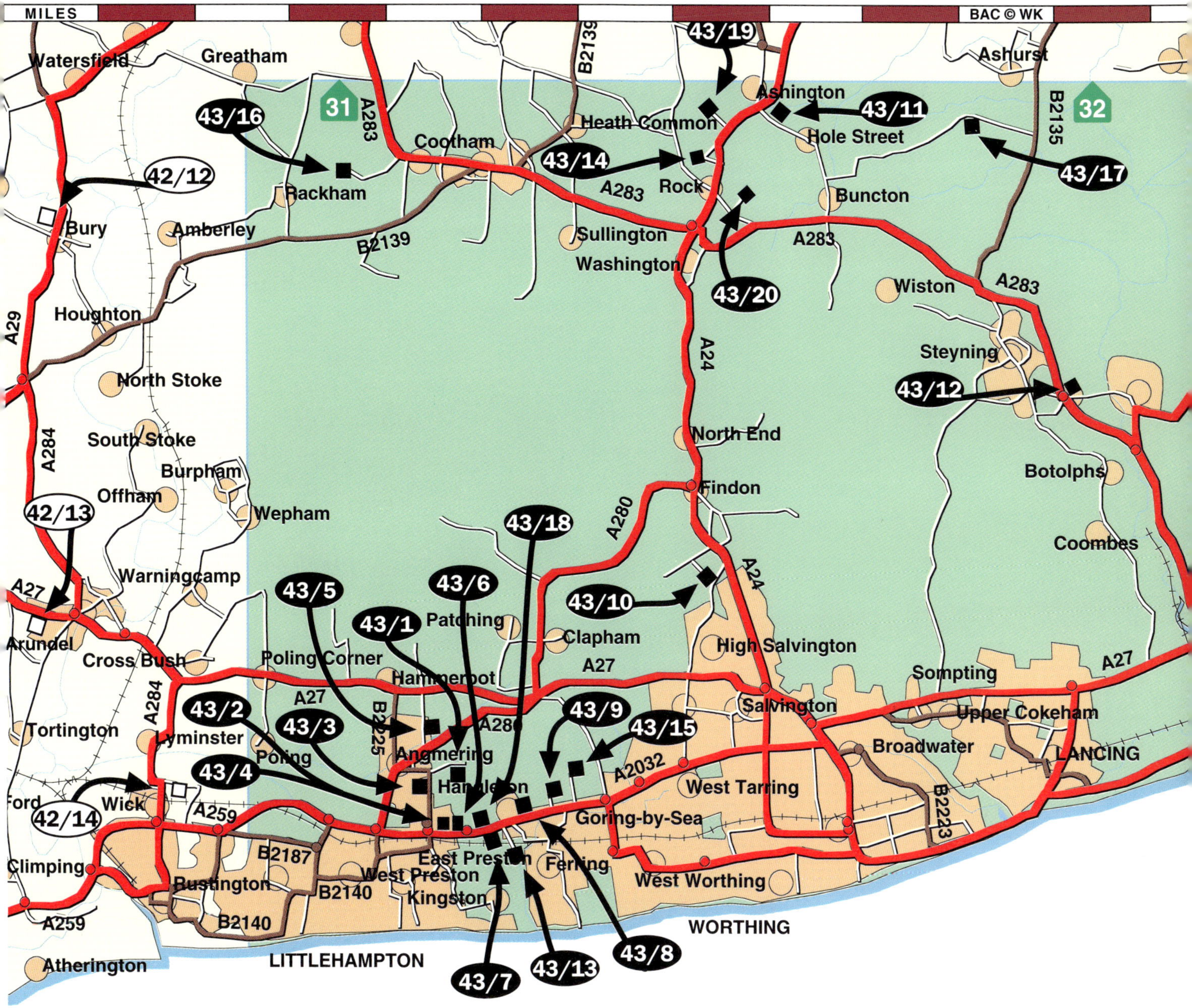
MILES
BAC © WK
Watersfield
Greatham
Ashurst
43/19
B2139
31
32
A283
Ashington
43/11
B2135
43/16
Heath Common
Hole Street
Cootham
43/14
43/17
42/12
Rackham
A283
Rock
Buncton
Bury
Amberley
B2139
Sullington
A283
Washington
Wiston
A283
43/20
A29
Houghton
A24
Steyning
North Stoke
43/12
A284
South Stoke
North End
Burpham
Botolphs
Offham
Findon
42/13
Wepham
A280
43/18
Coombes
Warningcamp
A24
A27
43/5
43/6
43/10
43/1
Patching
Clapham
Arundel
High Salvington
Cross Bush
Poling Corner
A27
Hammerpot
A27
Sompting
A27
43/2
A27
B2225
A280
43/9
Salvington
43/15
Upper Cokeham
A284
43/3
Tortington
Lyminster
Broadwater
Angmering
A2032
LANCING
Poling
43/4
Hangleton
West Tarring
Ford
Wick
A259
B2223
42/14
Goring-by-Sea
B2187
East Preston
Climping
Ferring
West Preston
Rustington
West Worthing
B2140
Kingston
A259
B2140
WORTHING
43/8
43/13
Atherington
LITTLEHAMPTON
43/7

WEST & EAST SUSSEX

SPECIALIST & GENERAL NURSERIES, GARDEN AND PLANT CENTRES

44/1 SWAINS FARM

44/2 BARROW HILL NURSERY

Shoreham Road
Henfield
West Sussex   BN5 9DN
01273 492733

Attractive nursery in farmyard setting. Extensive choice of plants, many home produced. Stoneware, terracotta etc.
Open: All year except Xmas–New Year; 7 days a week, 9–5.30.
Wheelchairs: Accessible.
Toilets: No.
Dogs: On lead.   **Credit cards:** Yes.

44/3 HILL BROOK NURSERY

44/4 RUSHFIELDS PLANT CENTRE

Henfield Road
Poynings
Brighton
West Sussex
BN45 7AY
01273 857445

A wide range of mostly own-grown plants throughout the year. Light snacks and lunches in the Greenhouse Café.
Open: All year except Xmas–New Year, 7 days a week. Summer 9–5.30; winter 10–4.30.
Wheelchairs: Easy paved access.
Toilets: Yes.
Dogs: On lead.   **Credit cards:** Yes.

44/5 W. RUSSELL & SON

44/6 KINGS GARDEN CENTRE

44/7 McBEAN'S ORCHIDS

44/8 WYEVALE GARDEN CENTRE

44/9 COUNTRY GARDENS BRIGHTON

Warren Road
Brighton
East Sussex BN2 2XX
01273 607888

'Good value garden centre with very wide plant selection. Free local delivery. Garden buildings. Coffee shop.'
Open: All year; Mon–Sat 9–6. Sunday 10.30–4.30. Extended spring hours – phone for information.
Wheelchairs: Easy access.
Toilets: Yes.
Dogs: On lead.   **Credit cards:** Yes.

PICK-YOUR-OWN FARM

44/10 ALBOURNE FARM PYO
01273 833683
Strawberries, raspberries, red & black currants, gooseberries.

ARTEFACT SUPPLIER

44/11 STUDIO FORGE

Offham
Lewes
East Sussex
BN7 3QD
01273 474173

Old established forge making wrought iron garden furniture, arches, obelisks, benches, gazebos, tunnels, plant stands. Various urns.
Open: All year except Xmas Day; 6 days a week (CLOSED SUN except by appointment), 9–4.
Wheelchairs: Rear access.
Toilets: Ask if desperate.
Dogs: On lead.   **Credit cards:** No.

44

EAST SUSSEX

SPECIALIST & GENERAL NURSERIES, GARDEN AND PLANT CENTRES

45/1 GOLDCLIFF NURSERIES

45/2 CLAYHILL NURSERIES
Uckfield Road, Ringmer, Lewes
BN8 5RU   01273 812409
Hardy plants & *landscaping.*

GARDEN CENTRE & GARDEN

45/3 PARADISE FAMILY LEISURE PARK

Avis Road, Newhaven
East Sussex   BN9 0DH
01273 512123
24-hr info 01273 616006
One of the largest garden centres in the south, alongside the Newhaven Botanic Garden and two acres of leisure grounds.
Open: All year except Xmas & Boxing Days; 7 days a week.
Costs: Garden centre free; gardens £2.75, children £1.99, OAPs £2.50.
Wheelchairs: Flat & level. **Dogs:** No.
Toilets: Yes.   **Credit cards:** Yes.

NURSERIES & CENTRES

45/4 A P NURSERY (LAUGHTON)
Lewes Road, Laughton
01435 812965
Bedding plants and perennials.

45/5 LITLINGTON NURSERY
Alfriston   BN26 5RB
01323 871211
'Unusual plants..and staff!'

45/6 ROBINS NURSERY

45/7 KENNEDYS GARDEN CENTRE
A22, Lower Dicker, Hailsham
East Sussex   BN27 4BJ
01323 844834
Garden centre with wide range of plants and garden products. Giftware, pet shop, aquatics and conservatories. Café.
Open: All year but Xmas/Boxing Days; 7 days a week, Mon–Sat 9–5.30 (winter), 9–6.30 (summer), Sun 10.30–4.30.
Wheelchairs: Easy access.
Toilets: Yes. **Dogs:** Guide dogs only.
Credit cards: Yes.

45/8 ROSSLOW ROSES

North Street Farm
North Street, Hellingly
East Sussex   BN27 4DZ
01323 440888
Small rose nursery growing 130 varieties, including the new English roses of Austins.
Open: WEEKENDS ONLY, all year & Bank Holiday Mondays, 9–5.
Wheelchairs: Accessible.
Toilets: Ask if desperate.
Dogs: Yes.   **Credit cards:** Yes.

45/9 COLDHARBOUR NURSERY
Coldharbour Rd, Lower Dicker
Hailsham   01323 846753
Patio & basket, bedding, vegetables.

45/10 HEMPSTEAD NURSERIES
01323 843183
Small nursery: lots of plants.
Open: Weekends: March–Nov.

45/11 WILLINGDON GARDEN CENTRE
197 Willingdon Road,
Eastbourne   01323 503455
Eastbourne's oldest garden centre.

WATER GARDEN SPECIALIST

45/12 WORLD OF WATER

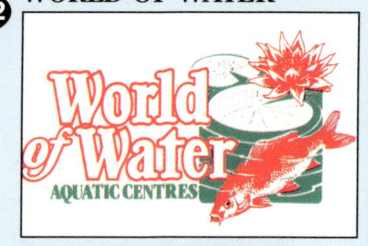

Ersham Road, Hailsham
East Sussex   BN27 2RH
01323 442400
Specialists in everything for the garden pond. Large tropical fish department. Expert advice.
Open: All year except Xmas & Boxing Days; 7 days a week, Mon–Sat 9–5.30, Sun 10.30–4.30.
Wheelchairs: Easy paved access.
Toilets: Yes.
Dogs: On lead.   **Credit cards:** Yes.

PICK-YOUR-OWN FARMS

45/13 ROOKERY WOOD FRUIT FARM

45/14 TUTTI FRUTTI PYO

45/15 MEADOW FARM PYO
Coldharbour Road
Lower Dicker, Hailsham
01323 844268
Strawberries & other soft fruit.

GARDENS

45/16 CHARLESTON
Small garden associated with the Bloomsbury Group.

45/17 MICHELHAM PRIORY
Upper Dicker
Hailsham
East Sussex
BN27 3QS
01323 844224
Remains of 13th century priory incorporated into Tudor mansion surrounded by moat & 7 acres, incl. physic, herb and cloister gardens.
Open: Mid-Mar–Oct: Wed–Sun & BH Mons; 11–4 (March & Oct), 11–5 (April–July & Sept), also daily 10.30–5.30 in Aug.
Wheelchairs: Good access, wheelchairs available. Disabled WC.
Toilets: Yes.   **Credit cards:** Yes.
Dogs: Guide dogs only.

45

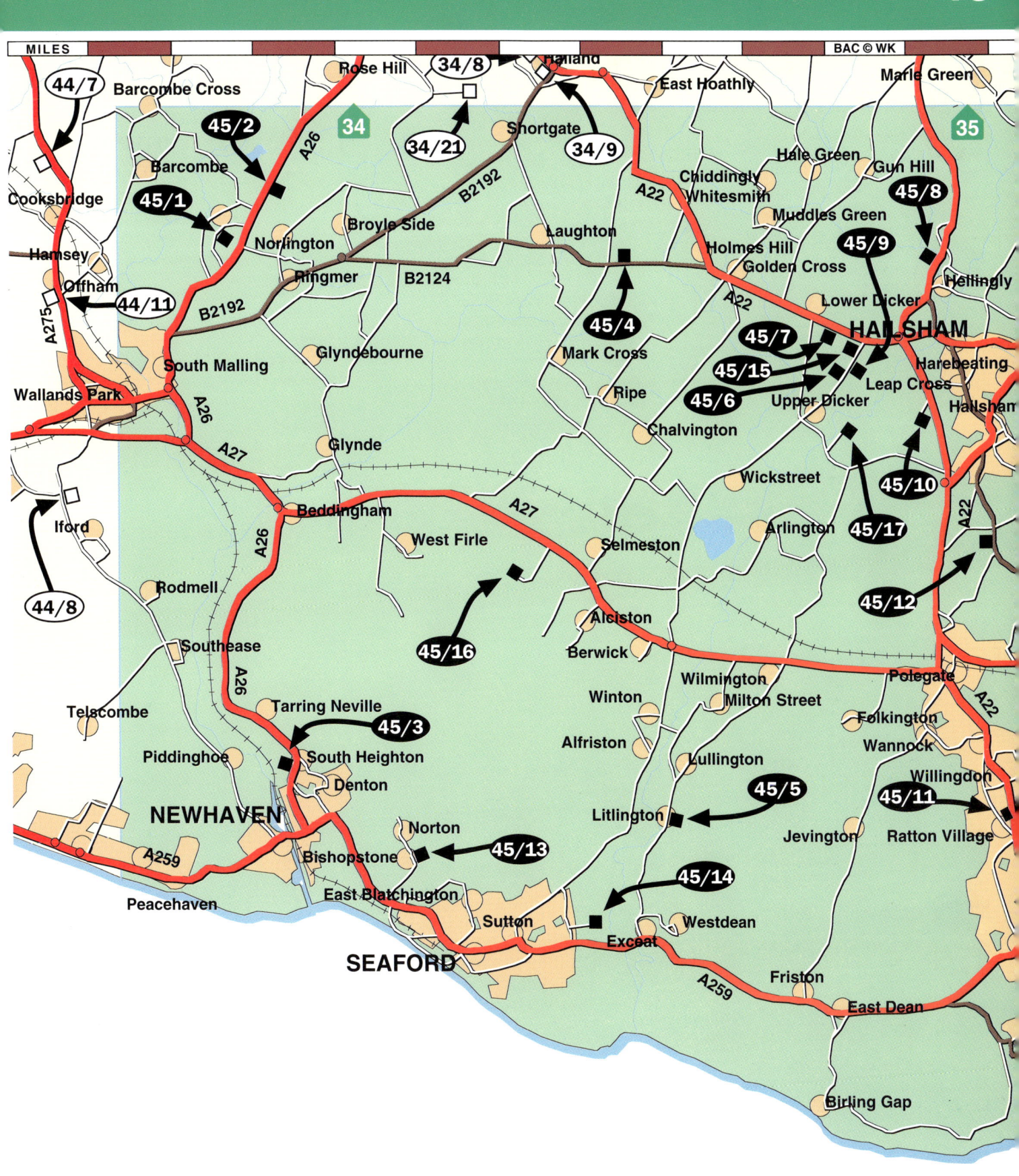

EAST SUSSEX

SPECIALIST & GENERAL NURSERIES, GARDEN AND PLANT CENTRES

46/1 NEW ROAD NURSERIES

46/2 GLYNDLEY GARDEN CENTRE
B2104, Hailsham Road
Stone Cross, Pevensey
East Sussex   BN24 5BS
01323 763240
A large, well established garden centre with quality products; aquatic section, pet shop. Friendly staff.
Open: All year except Xmas & Boxing Days; 7 days a week, Mon–Sat 9–5, Sun 10–4.
Wheelchairs: Easy access. WC.
Toilets: Yes.
Dogs: No.   **Credit cards:** Yes.

WATER GARDEN SPECIALISTS

46/3 CROFT WATER GARDENS & AQUATICS
Glyndley Garden Centre,
Hailsham Road
Stone Cross, Pevensey
East Sussex   BN24 5BS
01323 847868
Specialist water garden centre stocking everything needed for a small pond or a large lake. Experienced advice available.
Open: All year except Xmas & Boxing Days; 7 days a week, Mon–Sat 9–5, Sun 10–4.
Wheelchairs: Good access.
Toilets: Yes.
Dogs: On lead.   **Credit cards:** Yes.

SPECIALIST & GENERAL NURSERIES, GARDEN AND PLANT CENTRES

46/4 DITTONS NURSERY

46/5 USUAL & UNUSUAL PLANTS
Onslow House
Magham Down
Hailsham
East Sussex   BN27 1PL
01323 840967
*A small nursery growing a large range of **unusual perennials**, including, grasses, erysiniums, hardy geraniums & salvias.*
Open: Feb–Oct, 6 days a week (CLOSED TUES), 9.30–5.30.
Wheelchairs: Difficult.
Toilets: Ask if desperate.
Dogs: On lead.   **Credit cards:** No.

46/6 COOPERS CROFT NURSERIES
New Road, Herstmonceux,
BN27 1PX   01323 832151
Country nursery. New owners.

46/7 TUTTS BARN NURSERIES

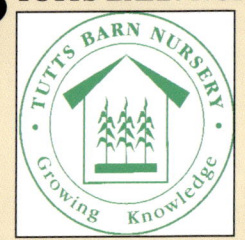

Tutts Barn Lane
Eastbourne
East Sussex   BN22 8XR
01323 734064
Wide range of shrubs, perennials, heathers, trees & roses. 126 varieties of summer & freshly-dug autumn bedding.
Open: All year except Xmas Day; 7 days a week, 8–dusk.
Wheelchairs: Mostly paved.
Toilets: No.
Dogs: On lead.   **Credit cards:** No.

46/8 STONE CROSS NURSERIES

46/9 LIME CROSS NURSERY
Herstmonceux
Hailsham
East Sussex   BN27 4RS
01323 833229
*Well stocked plant centre. Also a specialist grower of over 300 varieties of **ornamental conifers**.*
Open: All year except Xmas–New Year's Days; 7 days a week, Mon–Sat 8.30–5, Sun 9.30–5.
Toilets: Ask if desperate.
Dogs: On lead.   **Credit cards:** Yes.

46/10 UPLANDS FUCHSIA NURSERY
Hooe, Battle
01424 844846
Fuchsias *& stone ornaments.*

PICK-YOUR-OWN FARM

46/11 SHARNFOLD FARM

ARTEFACT SUPPLIERS

46/12 THE TRUGGERY
Coopers Croft, Herstmonceux
BN27 1QL   01323 832314
Genuine Sussex trug baskets.

46/13 SUSSEX TRUGS

GARDEN

46/14 HERSTMONCEUX CASTLE GARDENS

46

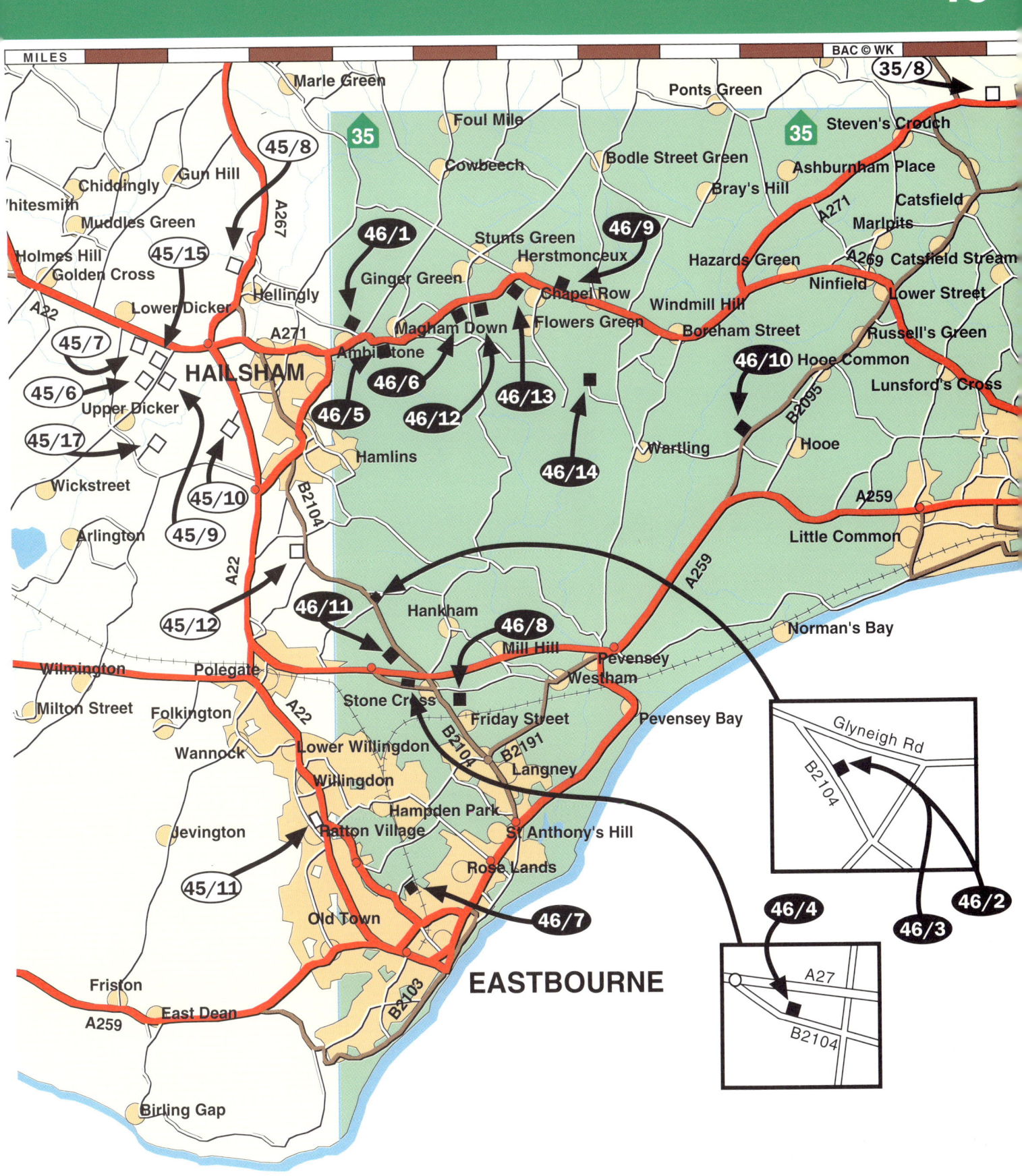

EAST SUSSEX 47

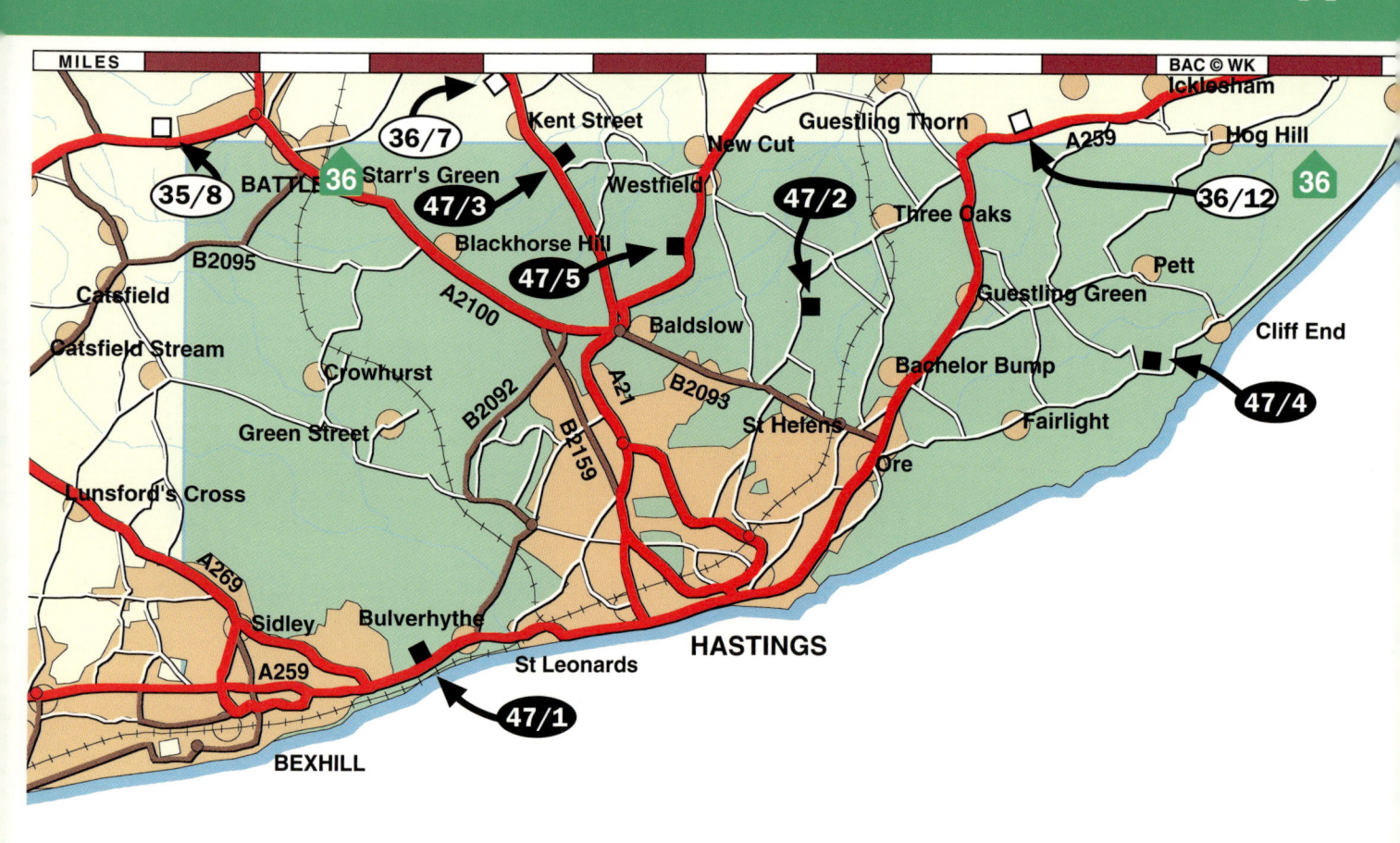

SPECIALIST & GENERAL NURSERIES, GARDEN AND PLANT CENTRES

47/1 COUNTRY GARDENS HASTINGS
Bexhill Road
St. Leonards-on-Sea
East Sussex TN38 8AR
01424 443414
'Good value garden centre with very wide plant selection. Free local delivery. Buildings, seeds, pots. Coffee shop.'
Open: All year; Mon–Sat 9–6. Sunday 10.30–4.30. Extended spring hours – phone for information.
Wheelchairs: Easy access.
Toilets: Yes.
Dogs: On lead. **Credit cards:** Yes.

47/2 COGHURST NURSERY
Ivy House Lane, Hastings
TN35 4NP   01424 756228
Camellia, azalea *specialists.*

47/3 KENT STREET NURSERIES
Kent Street
Sedlescombe, Battle
East Sussex   TN33 0SF
01424 751134
A family nursery specialising in growing **geraniums & fuchsias.** *Also bedding, shrubs, conifers, roses & herbaceous plants.*
Open: All year except Xmas & Boxing Days; 7 days a week, 9–6 or dusk if earlier.
Wheelchairs: Partial access.
Toilets: No.
Dogs: No.   **Credit cards:** No.

PICK-YOUR-OWN FARMS

47/4 WAKEHAMS PYO & FARM SHOP
Pett Level Road, Fairlight
Hastings   01424 814898
Soft fruit and vegetables.

47/5 FRESHFIELDS PYO

PRIORY FARM

21/21

NUTFIELD REDHILL SURREY

A GARDENER'S DAY OUT

Plant Centre: Enjoy the wide range of exceptional quality bedding, pot and perennial plants available throughout spring, summer and autumn.

Farm Shop: Enjoy our up-market country food shop situated in the restored Victorian stone-built farm buildings. There are many mouth-watering products and interesting gifts.

Pick-Your-Own: Enjoy our parkland setting with large car parks, lakes and many crops including asparagus, raspberries, strawberries and cherries.

Coffee Shop: Enjoy a relaxing cup of tea with home made cakes or have a light lunch in picturesque surroundings.

**OPEN EVERY DAY
9am to 5pm**
Summer extension to 6pm during June, July, August

Plant Centre closed Jan, Feb
Coffee Shop closed 1 Nov – 31 March

Tel: (01737) 823 304

5/21

Enjoy the peace, beauty and tranquillity of this outstanding 35-acre woodland garden

The Savill Garden
in Windsor Great Park

Spring brings a wealth of daffodils, rhododendrons, azaleas, camellias, magnolias and much more.
Summer features the extensive rose gardens, herbaceous borders and alpine plantings.
Autumn offers a breath-taking array of foliage colour and fruit.
Winter is far from dull, particularly for the discerning gardener.

THE NEW QUEEN ELIZABETH TEMPERATE HOUSE NOW OPEN

OPEN DAILY: 10am–6pm March–Oct; 10am–4pm Nov–Feb
Licensed Restaurant • Gift Shop • Plant Centre
Admission: Adults £3.50; Senior Citizens £3.00;
Parties 20+ £3.00; Accompanied children free.

A GARDEN FOR ALL SEASONS

Situated in Wick Lane, Englefield Green, Surrey (off A30)
Signposted from Ascot, Egham (M25) & Windsor (M4)

Free car / coach parking

Enquiries: (01753) 860222

26/5

VICTORIANA
Nursery Gardens

Challock, Kent, TN25 4DG ☎ 01233–740480

Situated on the A251

Our family owned and managed traditional production nursery is currently under construction, though visitors are welcome whilst construction continues! Definitely **not** a garden centre - and never will be! Specialist growers of fuchsias (over 350 varieties), bonsai, citrus fruits, conifers, trees & shrubs, Victorian vegetable seeds & plants, aquatics and exotics and other unusual plants. Friendly, knowledgeable staff – expert advice.

NATIONWIDE MAIL ORDER SERVICE

Request our lists of all we produce

Currently we are open Monday-Friday 9-5. As construction progresses, opening times will be increased, so please telephone.

33/15

TULLEYS FARM
Turners Hill

Our *PYO farm* is set in beautiful Sussex countryside and during the season we have over 25 crops available including Strawberries, Raspberries, Runner Beans and Asparagus.

Visit our award-winning *Farm Shop* and feast your eyes on the wide range of quality produce. Home-made cakes, speciality food, daily baked bread and plenty of ideas for gifts. 
The recently opened *Farmhouse Kitchen* offers a relaxing atmosphere for tea or coffee, cold drinks and home-made country food that depicts the seasons.

Opening times: **Farm Shop**: 9.00am–6.00pm every day
Winter: 9.00am–5.00pm every day except Friday
9.00am–6.00pm and Sunday 10.00am–5.00pm
Farmhouse Kitchen: 10.00am–5.00pm Tues–Sun
(closed Monday except Bank Holidays)
PYO *Soft fruit season*: 9.30am–8.00pm weekdays
9.30am–6.00pm weekends. *Vegetable season*: 9.30am–6.00pm

01342 718472   01342 715365
Farm Shop   Pick-your-own

We are clearly signposted on the Turners Hill to Crawley road.

WHELAN'S
Sheerness, Isle of Sheppey

Birdbaths from £5, planters from £2, benches from £19.50 PLUS ANOTHER 1000 DIFFERENT ITEMS IN STOCK AT FACTORY PRICES

Meon Valley Nurseries

SOBERTON HEATH, SOUTHAMPTON
HAMPSHIRE, SO32 3QF

Telephone: 01329 832266   Fax: 01329 832289

Wholesale growers of quality bedding plants and cyclamen specialists, happy to welcome the public Monday–Friday 8.30–4.30.

Growers for council authorities.
Visits arranged for horticultural societies.
Enquiries welcome.

Where plants come first

Conveniently situated on the Eridge Road Coblands continues to major on top quality plants in an ever increasing diversity. The recently revamped centre now gives outside walkways clearly guiding you to specific areas. Each area offers a superb range of products from Terracotta & stone pots, ornamental stoneware, tools, sheds, fertilisers to green houses and myriad gardening products.

6 MONTHS GUARANTEE ON ALL HARDY PLANTS

NURSERY FRESH PLANTS — MOST GROWN ON OUR OWN NURSERIES

EXPERT ADVICE ALWAYS FREELY AVAILABLE

COBLANDS GARDENING CLUB — Information, talks, visits & discounts.

Access · Visa · Mastercard · National Garden Gift Tokens

MON–SAT 8.30–5.30
SUN 10–4.00

COBLANDS
The Gardeners' Garden Centres

ERIDGE ROAD · TUNBRIDGE WELLS · TEL: 01892 515234

ALSO PLANT CENTRE: SEVENOAKS ROAD · IGHTHAM · TEL: 01732 780816

6/7

"For all your garden needs"

Established over 30 years

A full and unique selection of plants and garden requisites for every season. Specialist suppliers of garden construction materials, with display garden showing over 50 different paving styles. Also planting containers, statuary and water features.

Adrian Hall LTD

ADRIAN HALL LTD
THE GARDEN CENTRE
FELTHAM HILL ROAD, FELTHAM, MIDDX
(0181) 890 5057

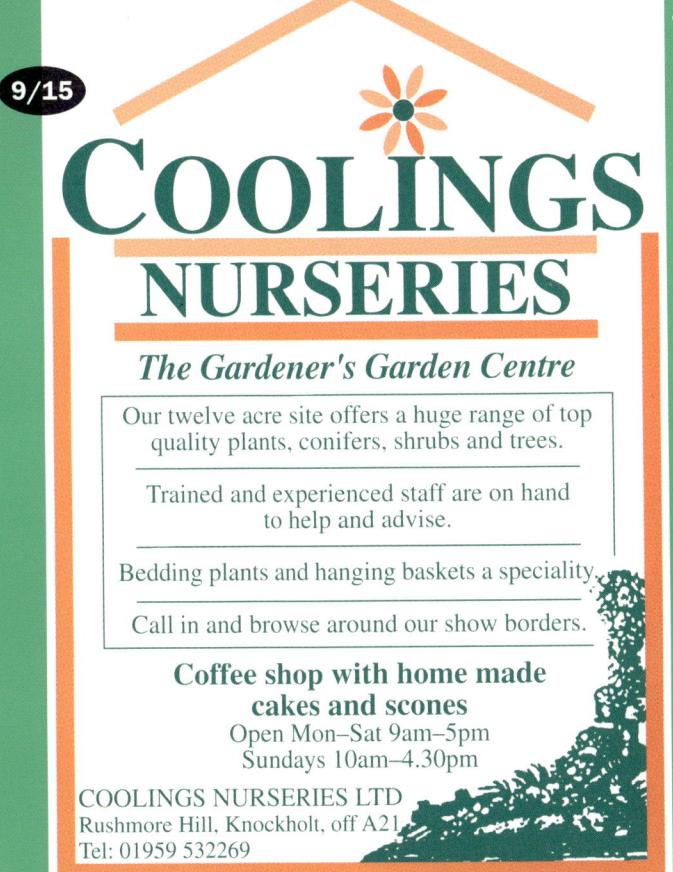

9/15

COOLINGS NURSERIES

The Gardener's Garden Centre

Our twelve acre site offers a huge range of top quality plants, conifers, shrubs and trees.

Trained and experienced staff are on hand to help and advise.

Bedding plants and hanging baskets a speciality.

Call in and browse around our show borders.

Coffee shop with home made cakes and scones
Open Mon–Sat 9am–5pm
Sundays 10am–4.30pm

COOLINGS NURSERIES LTD
Rushmore Hill, Knockholt, off A21
Tel: 01959 532269

39/5

MEDINA NURSERIES

46 Brook Lane
Warsash, Southampton
Hampshire
SO31 9FG
Tel: 01489 584476

A family nursery with friendly, helpful staff, specialising in hanging baskets, tubs and pick-and-mix basket plants. Seasonal bedding plants, shrubs, heathers and stoneware. Special varieties of zonal geraniums.

Open from Mother's day in mid-March to the end of July, then from mid-September to the end of November, 7 days a week:
- Weekdays 9–5 (later in summer, earlier in winter)
- Sunday 10 – 4

ARE YOU OVER 60?
Come and join our 60's 10% discount club every Wednesday.

Our own gift vouchers available.

ROAD ATLAS for GARDENERS

Have you a garden-loving friend or relative?

The Road Atlas for Gardeners
makes the ideal present!

Available from
- good bookshops
- garden shops
- garden & plant centres
- water garden centres
- farm shops

… or order direct from the publisher. You are welcome to send us a greetings card with your own personal message and we will post it with an atlas direct to your friend.

Write to, phone or fax The Road Atlas for Gardeners
phone 0181 678 0593   fax 0181 674 1594
1 Rosebery Mews, Rosebery Road, London SW2 4DQ

£6.95 plus £1 p+p

*Quote your MasterCard or Visa number
or send a cheque payable to G. Cutress*

From the same publisher …

The Factory Shop Guides

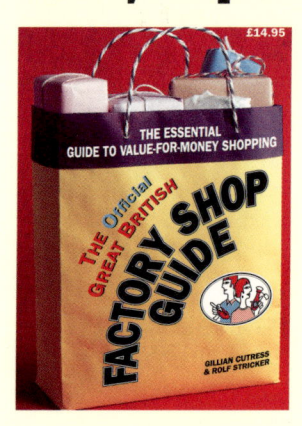

*tell the discerning shopper
how, where and when to find excellent value
for money by buying direct
from the manufacturer.
From designer wear to duvets, from
cashmere to carpets and cutlery,
from tiles to towels …*

*Packed with comprehensive information and
detailed directions to each shop, these
invaluable guides lead you to hundreds of
factory shops throughout the UK.*

Free details about the 11 books in this unique series
from The Factory Shop Guide.

phone 0181 678 0593   fax 0181 674 1594
e-mail factshop@macline.co.uk
1 Rosebery Mews, Rosebery Road, London SW2 4DQ

*Available by mail from the publisher,
or from bookshops, WH Smith, Waterstone's, Dillons etc.*

To Horticultural, Garden & Plant Society Secretaries

The Road Atlas for Gardeners welcomes group purchases from members.
Please phone 0181 678 0593 for details.

Fleurs sans Frontières

The first annual
European Gardens Festival
May–July 1998

A programme of special events at the beautiful gardens
of southern England, northern France and Belgium.

Information and full festival programme from:

78 Leeside Crescent, London NW11 0LA   Phone 00 44 (0)181 731 6106   Fax 00 44 (0)181 731 6103

INDEX

SPECIALIST & GENERAL NURSERIES, GARDEN AND PLANT CENTRES

A
A P NURSERY, Bines Cross 35/10
A P NURSERY, Laughton 45/4
ABBEY CROFT, Titchfield............. 39/14
ABBEY G.C., Cadnam 38/8
ABBEY G.C., Titchfield 39/9
ADRIAN HALL G.C., Feltham ... page 50 & 6/7
ADRIAN HALL G.C., Putney 8/1
AGAR'S NURSERY, Lymington 38/6
ALDERWOOD, Badshot Lea........... 17/7
ALDINGBOURNE, Chichester.......... 42/6
ALKHAM VALLEY G.C., S.Alkham 27/9
ALLINGTON NURSERY, Eastleigh 29/12
APPLE COURT NURSERY, Lymington .. 38/7
APULDRAM CENTRE, Chichester 41/17
APULDRAM ROSES, Chichester 41/15
ARBORTECTURE, Hungerford......... 1/1
ARCHERS LOW, Sandwich............ 27/4
ARCHITECTURAL PLANTS, Horsham ... 32/11
ARTURI'S G.C., Eastleigh 29/11
ARUNDEL ARBORETUM, Arundel 42/13
ASHDOWN FOREST G.C., Uckfield 34/3
ASTOLAT, Peasmarsh 18/14
AVALON NURSERIES, Churt 17/15
AVENUE NURSERIES, Alton........... 15/9
AXLETREE NURSERY, Peasmarsh 36/13
AYLINGS OF TROTTON, Trotton 30/10

B
B & W NURSERIES, Romsey 28/1
BADSHOT LEA G.C., Farnham......... 17/5
BAILEYS G.C., Hook 15/4
BAKERS FARM NURSERY, Bordon 16/8
BARN FARM NURSERIES, Hurst 4/7
BARNES NURSERY, Wallington 8/14
BARNHAWK, Fordingbridge........... 38/2
BARRALETS G.C., Pirbright 18/1
BARROW HILL NURSERY, Henfield... 44/2
BARRY'S BASKETS, Emsworth 41/3
BARTRAM'S G.C., Broad Oak 35/6
BARTRAM, W & SON, Carshalton 8/13
BEACHLANDS, West Ashling.......... 41/6
BEADLE, G.J., Wallington............ 8/12
BEAUREPAIRE, Bramley 15/3
BEECH COURT, Ashford.............. 26/13
BEECHCROFT NURSERY, Epsom 7/15
BELLFIELD NURSERY, Birdham 41/7
BENNETT'S NURSERY, Aldershot 17/4
BERENGRAVE, Gillingham 11/6
BERKSHIRE G.C., Slough............. 5/1
BEXHILL FARM, Benenden............ 36/8
BIDDENDEN NURSERIES 25/13
BIJOU NURSERIES, Maidstone 24/2
BLACKBOYS NURSERY, Uckfield 34/7
BLACKBROOKS G.C., Battle 36/7
BLACKGATE LANE, Pulborough 31/7
BLOSSOMS NURSERY, Ashford 25/4
BODIAM BONSAI, Bodiam 36/4
BODIAM NURSERY, Bodiam.......... 36/3
BOLNEY NURSERY, Bolney 33/4
BOTANY BARNS, Woking............. 5/14
BOURNE HILL, Southwater 32/9
BOURNE VALLEY G.C., Weybridge 5/10
BOWDENSIDE FARM, Pangbourne ... 2/5
BOYER'S, Windsor 4/14
BRADSHAW, J & SON, Herne Bay 13/5
BRAMBER, West Wittering........... 41/8

BRAMBRIDGE PARK G.C., Eastleigh 29/5
BREDHURST, Gillingham 11/4
BRIAN HILEY, Wallington 8/10
BRIARWOOD NURSERY, Mayford 18/6
BRICK KILN NURSERY, Chichester..... 42/2
BRIDGE ROAD, Southampton 39/6
BRINKMANS G.C., Bosham 41/5
BROAD OAK G.C., Broad Oak 35/5
BROGDALE TRUST, Faversham 12/10
BROOK NURSERY, South Godstone .. 21/8
BROOKSIDE CACTUS, Horsham 32/6
BROOKSIDE G.C., East Peckham 24/4
BROOKSIDE, Swallowfield 3/7
BRYAN'S G.C., Tooting Bec 8/5
BUCKLAND NURSERIES 20/6
BUMBLE'S NURSERY, Cranbrook 25/11

C
CAMELIA BOTNAR, West Grinstead 32/3
CARE IDE HILL, Ide Hill............... 22/4
CASTLE NURSERY, Beckenham 9/5
CASTLE NURSERY, Bramber 43/12
CEDAR NURSERIES, Romsey 28/8
CEDAR NURSERY, Cobham 19/8
CHALCROFT, Bognor 42/15
CHANDLERS FARM, Reading......... 3/2
CHEALS G.C., Crawley 33/1
CHERYLDENE NURSERY, Titchfield ... 39/18
CHESSINGTON G.C. 7/14
CHOBHAM NURSERIES, Chobham... 5/16
CHOICE PLANTS, Romsey 28/6
CHUBBS NURSERY, Cooksbridge 34/10
CHURCH HILL COTTAGE, Ashford 25/6
CINDERS LANE NURSERY, Yapton ... 42/11
CITRUS CENTRE, Pulborough 31/8
CLANDON PARK G.C., Guildford 19/2
CLARKE, S.G., Banstead............. 8/16
CLAY LANE NURSERY, Redhill 20/10
CLAYHILL NURSERIES, Lewes 45/2
COACH HOUSE G.C., Hartley Wintney ... 16/1
COBHAM PARK NURSERY, Cobham .. 6/17
COBLANDS G.C., Dartford 10/7
COBLANDS G.C, Tun. Wells ..... page 49 & 23/8
COBLANDS PLANT CENTRE, Ightham ... 23/2
COGHURST NURSERY, Hastings..... 47/2
COLDHARBOUR NURSERY, Halisham ... 45/9
COMPTON NURSERY, Compton...... 18/11
CONIGER NURSERIES, Eastleigh 29/10
CONKERS G.C., Basingstoke......... 15/8
COOLINGS NURSERIES, Knockholt page 50, 9/15
COOMBLAND NURSERY, Coneyhurst... 32/17
COOPERS CROFT, Herstmonceux..... 46/6
COPPED HALL, Camberley 4/22
COPTON ASH, Faversham 12/2
COTTAGE GARDEN, Staplehurst...... 25/12
COTTISMORE G.C., Kingsclere 2/9
COULSDON MARKET, Addiscombe.... 8/17
COUNTRY FAYRE, Ferring 43/7
COUNTRY GARDENS, Alford 31/1
COUNTRY GARDENS, Andover 14/1
COUNTRY GARDENS, Ashford 26/10
COUNTRY GARDENS, Basingstoke.... 15/2
COUNTRY GARDENS, Brighton........ 44/9
COUNTRY GARDENS, Chichester 42/5
COUNTRY GARDENS, Croydon 9/2
COUNTRY GARDENS, Dorking 20/4
COUNTRY GARDENS, Fair Oak 29/7

COUNTRY GARDENS, Faversham..... 12/1
COUNTRY GARDENS, Handcross 33/2
COUNTRY GARDENS, Hastings....... 47/1
COUNTRY GARDENS, Hungerford 1/2
COUNTRY GARDENS, Knockholt 9/14
COUNTRY GARDENS, Osterley 7/4
COUNTRY GARDENS, Pulborough 31/6
COUNTRY GARDENS, Ramsgate...... 13/7
COUNTRY GARDENS, Staines........ 5/3
COUNTRY GARDENS, Thatcham 2/4
COUNTRY GARDENS, Windlesham ... 4/24
COUNTRY GARDENS, Windsor 4/24
COUNTRY GARDENS, Worthing...... 43/8
COUNTRY MARKET, Borden 16/7
CROCKFORD PARK G.C., Addlestone ... 6/14
CROFTERS NURSERY, Ashford, Kent.... 25/7
CROFTWAY NURSERY, Barnham...... 42/9
CROMAR NURSERY, Maidstone...... 24/3
CUCKOO'S NEST NURSERY, Birdham .. 41/13

D
D & S NURSERY, Winnersh............ 3/4
DENMEAD GERANIUMS, Waterlooville... 40/6
DITTONS NURSERY, Pevensey 46/4
DOBBE'S NURSERY, Great Bookham .. 19/5
DOBBE, A.J. AND SONS, Ashtead...... 20/1
DOVES BARN NURSERY, Felbridge ... 21/12
DRYSDALE NURSERY, Fordingbridge ... 38/1

E
EAST ASHLING NURSERIES 41/11
EAST NORTHDOWN FARM, Margate..... 13/6
EASTFIELD PLANT CENTRE, Alton..... 29/14
EDEN PARK, Beckenham 9/7
EGHAM G.C......................... 5/4
ELM NURSERY, Sutton Green 18/12
ELM PARK G.C., Basingstoke 15/6
ENGLEFIELD G.C..................... 3/1
EVERTON NURSERIES, Lymington ... 39/20
EXBURY GARDENS................... 39/1
EYNSFORD NURSERY, Eynsford...... 10/5

F
FAIRHAVEN NURSERY, Littlehampton .. 42/14
FAIRWEATHER G.C., Beaulieu......... 38/15
FALSTON NURSERIES, Gravesend..... 10/13
FANNY'S FARM SHOP, Merstham 20/12
FARM LANE NURSERIES, Ashtead..... 20/2
FARTHING COMMON, Folkestone 26/11
FERRING NURSERY, Ferring 43/13
FIELDFARE OF FAIR OAK, Fair Oak ... 29/8
FLITTONS NURSERY, Wallington...... 8/15
FLOWER POWER, Tunbridge Wells..... 35/1
FOLIAGE, HERB, SCENTED, Ranmore ... 19/6
FONTLEY NURSERY, Titchfield 39/12
FOREST LODGE G.C., Farnham....... 16/6
FOUR SEASONS BONSAI NURSERY ... 24/8
FOXGROVE PLANTS, Newbury 1/3
FOXHILL NURSERY, Canterbury 13/3
FRANK FAIRHEAD, Staines 6/5
FRANK FAIRHEAD, Staines 6/8
FRENCH STREET, Westerham 22/3
FRENSHAM G.C., Frensham......... 17/12
FUCHSIA WORLD, Birdham 41/16

G
G & S SMALLHOLDINGS, Maidstone..... 24/6
GALES NURSERY, Monkfield 30/2
GARDEN CARE, Worcester Park 7/12
GARDEN COTTAGE, New Milton 38/4

INDEX

SPECIALIST & GENERAL NURSERIES, GARDEN AND PLANT CENTRES

GARDEN MARKET, Addiscombe 9/4
GARDEN PRIDE G.C., Ditchling 33/11
GARDEN STYLE, Farnham 16/5
GARSON FARM, Esher 6/19
GARTHOWEN G.C., Alton 30/1
GATE HOUSE FARM, Hildenborough ... 23/7
GEMA NURSERY, Crowborough 34/1
GEORGE BECKETT, Winchester 29/4
GLEN AND NURSERY, Farnham 16/4
GLENVALE NURSERIES, Reading 2/6
GLYNDLEY G.C., Eastbourne 46/2
GOLDCLIFF NURSERIES, Lewes 45/1
GORE HOUSE, Sittingbourne 11/9
GRAFTY G.C., Maidstone 25/8
GREAT DIXTER, Rye 36/14
GREATHAM MILL, Greatham 30/15
GREENACRE NURSERY, Chidham 41/4
GREENACRES, Basingstoke 3/10
GREENGOLD TREE FARM, Ferring 43/9
GREENWAYS, Wisborough Green 31/4
GROVELANDS, Shinfield 3/5

H

HADLOW COLLEGE, Tonbridge 23/6
HAMBROOKS G.C., Titchfield 39/8
HAMPTONS NURSERIES, Tonbridge ... 23/5
HARBOROUGH, Guestling 36/12
HARDY'S COTTAGE GARDEN 15/1
HARE HATCH, Twyford 4/30
HARRINGTON'S NURSERY, Swanley ... 10/3
HASKINS G.C., Southampton 39/2
HAWLEY G.C., Dartford 10/4
HAYDEN NURSERIES, Aston 0/2
HAYWARDS CARNATIONS 40/7
HAZELBANK NURSERY, Tilford 17/11
HEADCORN FLOWER CENTRE 25/9
HEATH NURSERY, Albury 19/7
HEATHFIELD, Reigate Heath 20/8
HEATHROW G.C., West Drayton 6/3
HEMPSTEAD NURSERIES, Halisham ... 45/10
HENRY STREET G.C., Arborfield 3/9
HERONS BONSAI, Lingfield 21/15
HIDDEN GARDEN, Shepperton 6/10
HIGH BEECHES, Handcross 33/6
HIGH TREES, Buckland 20/7
HIGHBANKS NURSERY, Guildford 19/9
HILL BROOK NURSERY, Henfield 44/3
HILL PARK ROSES, Long Ditton 7/10
HILLIER G.C., Ampfield 28/9
HILLIER G.C., Botley 39/3
HILLIER G.C., Hermitage 2/2
HILLIER G.C., Horsham 32/13
HILLIER G.C., Liss 30/8
HILLIER G.C., Romsey 28/7
HILLIER G.C., Winchester 29/2
HILLIER G.C., Windlesham 4/25
HILLSIDE NURSERIES, Pulborough ... 42/12
HILLSIDE NURSERY, Redhill 20/11
HOLE STREET, Ashington 43/11
HOLLAM NURSERIES, Titchfield 39/15
HOLLINGTON HERB, Newbury 1/6
HOLLINS NURSERY, Lymington 38/10
HOLLY BUSH G.C., Brockenhurst 38/12
HOLLY GATE CACTUS, Ashington 32/4
HOMELEIGH NURSERY, Cranleigh ... 19/10
HOMELEIGH NURSERY, Rochester ... 11/1
HOOK G.C., Hook 15/7

HOOKER'S G.C., Winchester 29/1
HOWARDS, Horsham 32/12
HYDE, H.W. & SON, Ruscombe 4/6
HYDON NURSERIES, Godalming 18/17

I

IDEN CROFT HERBS, Staplehurst 25/10
IGHTHAM PLANT CENTRE, Ightham ... 23/1
IMBERHORNE LANE, East Grinstead .. 34/12
INGWERSEN, W.E.Th., East Grinstead .. 33/10

J

JACKMAN'S G.C., Woking 18/3
JAQUES CANN OF WEYBRIDGE 6/16
JOHN GUNNER G.C., Guildford 18/10
JOHN TRAIN PLANTS, West Drayton .. 6/1
JOHNSONS NURSERY, Whitstable 13/1
JUNGLE G.C., Sunbury 6/12
JUNIPER NURSERIES, Guildford 18/8
JUST ROSES, Rye 36/11

K

KEILEEN NURSERIES, Warsash 39/4
KELLY'S NURSERY, Birdham 41/9
KENNEDYS G.C., Bracknell 37/7
KENNEDYS G.C., Claygate 7/2
KENNEDYS G.C., Croydon 9/1
KENNEDYS G.C., Farnham Royal 0/1
KENNEDYS G.C., Hailsham 45/7
KENNEDYS G.C., Twyford 4/1
KENT STREET NURSERIES, Hastings .. 47/3
KEYDELL, Waterlooville 40/10
KINGFISHER PLANTS, Soberton 40/4
KINGS G.C., Hassocks 44/6
KINGS TOLL NURSERY, Tonbridge ... 23/10
KINGSFOLD NURSERY, Kingsfold 32/7
KINGSGATE & KENVER, Broadstairs .. 13/4
KNIGHTS G.C., Chelsham 21/1
KNIGHTS G.C., Godstone 21/4
KNIGHTS G.C., Godstone 21/6
KNIGHTS G.C., Woldingham 21/2
KNOWLE GRANGE, Frant 35/9
KNOWLER NURSERY, Gillingham 11/7
LAKESIDE G.C., Feltham 6/6

L

LAKESIDE G.C., Tadley 2/8
LALEHAM NURSERIES, Shepperton .. 6/9
LANGLEY BOXWOOD, Rake 30/6
LAURELS NURSERY, Benenden 36/10
LAURELS PLANT CENTRE, Reading .. 3/6
LAURENCE HOBBS ORCHIDS 21/14
LAWMANS G.C., Croydon 8/7
LAYHAM G.C., Staple 27/2
LEONARDSLEE PLANTS, Horsham ... 32/19
LEYDENE GARDENS, Titchfield 39/11
LILLIES NURSERY, Barnham 42/7
LIME CROSS NURSERY, Hailsham .. 46/9
LINCLUDEN NURSERY, Bisley 5/13
LINDUM, Eversley Cross 4/18
LITLINGTON NURSERY, Alfriston ... 45/5
LITTLE ACRES, Badshot Lea 17/6
LITTLE BROOK FUCHSIAS, Ash Green .. 17/9
LODGE HILL NURSERY, Wickham ... 40/3
LONGACRE NURSERIES, Hythe 37/5
LONGACRE NURSERY, Faversham ... 26/1
LONGACRES NURSERY, Bagshot 4/23
LONGSTOCK PARK, Longstock 14/2
LOWER ROAD, Effingham 19/12
LOWERTREES, Angmering 43/6

LOXWOOD NURSERIES 31/2
LYMINGTON PLANT CENTRE 38/11

M

MACFARLANES, Folkestone 27/10
MacGREGORS PLANTS, Romsey 28/3
MACNADE G.C., Faversham 12/4
MACPENNYS, Christchurch 38/3
MADRONA NURSERY, Ashford 25/14
MANOR NURSERY, Angmering 43/1
MANOR NURSERY, Barnham 42/10
MANOR NURSERY, Chichester 42/3
MARLE PLACE GARDENS, Brenchley .. 24/10
MARSDEN, Ashtead 20/5
MARTINS NURSERY, Sandwich 27/7
MARYLANDS NURSERY, Bolney 33/5
MATHEWS NURSERY, Halland 34/9
MAUDLIN NURSERY, Chichester 42/1
MAYFIELD NURSERY, Billingshurst .. 32/2
MAYFLOWER NURSERIES, Egham .. 5/5
McBEAN'S ORCHIDS, Cooksbridge .. 44/7
MEADOW FARM, Hayling Island 40/11
MEADOW GRANGE, Whitstable 12/5
MEDINA NURSERY, Southam'n . page 50 &39/5
MELBOURNE NURSERY, Wallington .. 8/18
MENDIP COTTAGE, Beckenham 9/6
MEON VALLEY, Soberton ..... page 49 & 40/5
MERESBOROUGH, Gillingham 11/5
MERRIMENTS, Hurst Green 35/11
MERRIST WOOD, Worplesdon 18/9
MERRYFIELD, Canterbury 26/4
MICHAEL SEYMOUR, Betchworth ... 20/5
MILLAIS NURSERIES, Churt 17/13
MILLBROOK G.C., Crowborough 34/6
MILLBROOK G.C., Gravesend 10/14
MIMBRIDGE G.C., Woking 5/17
MJS G.C., Basingstoke 15/5
MJS G.C., Reading 4/3
MOOR GROWERS, Maidenhead 0/3
MORDEN HALL G.C., Morden 8/4
MOSS END G.C., Warfield 4/10
MOTTINGHAM PLANT CENTRE 9/3
MOUNT FOLLY, Wickham 40/2
MOYSES NURSERIES, Mayfield 35/3
MUD ISLAND NURSERY, Wickham .. 40/1
MURRELLS NURSERY, Pulborough .. 31/9

N

NABOTH'S NURSERY, Faversham ... 12/3
NETTLETON'S NURSERY, Godstone .. 21/5
NEW FOREST WINE, Brockenhurst .. 38/13
NEW ROAD NURSERIES, Hailsham .. 46/1
NEWBRIDGE NURSERIES, Horsham .. 32/8
NEWINGREEN NURSERIES, Hythe .. 37/4
NEWLANDS NURSERY, Sevenoaks .. 22/5
NONSUCH NURSERIES, Windsor ... 4/15
NORTHFIELD NURSERY, Lymington .. 38/14
NOTCUTTS G.C., Bagshot 4/21
NOTCUTTS G.C., Cranleigh 19/11
NOTCUTTS G.C., Laleham 5/6
NOTCUTTS G.C., Maidstone 24/5
NOTCUTTS G.C., Pembury 23/9
NURSERY COURT, Windlesham 5/11
NUTFIELD NURSERIES, Nutfield 21/3
NUTLIN NURSERY, Uckfield 34/11

O

OAKDEAN NURSERY, Horsham 32/10
OAKLEIGH NURSERIES, Alresford ... 30/3

INDEX

SPECIALIST & GENERAL NURSERIES, GARDEN AND PLANT CENTRES

OAKS NURSERY, Ash 17/1
OAKTREE NURSERIES, Warfield 4/11
OCCASIONALLY YOURS, Lingfield 21/10
OLANTIGH GARDEN, Wye 26/6
OLD BARN NURSERIES, Dial Post 32/5
OLDBURY NURSERIES, Ashford 26/12
ORCHARD NURSERIES, Canterbury 26/8
ORCHARD NURSERY, East Grinstead . . . 22/9
ORCHARDLEIGH, Bishops Waltham 29/9
OTTER NURSERY, Ottershaw 5/9
P
PALM CENTRE, East Sheen 7/7
PANNELLS G.C., Heston 7/1
PANTILES NURSERIES, Chertsey 5/7
PARADISE LEISURE, Newhaven 45/3
PARK PLACE FARM, Wickham 39/13
PENWOOD NURSERIES, Newbury 1/5
PERRYHILL NURSERIES, Hartfield 22/10
PETER J. GODDARD LANDSCAPES 37/6
PETER TRENEAR, Eversley Cross 4/20
PETERSHAM NURSERIES, Richmond 7/9
PHOENIX NURSERY, Hastings 36/5
PICKARD'S MAGNOLIA, Canterbury 26/3
PINECOVE NURSERIES, Tenterden 37/1
PLANT CENTRE, Chobham 5/12
PLANTS 'N' GARDENS, Worth 33/7
PLAXTOL NURSERIES, Plaxtol 23/4
PLEASANT VIEW G.C., Maidstone 25/2
POCOCK'S ROSE CENTRE, Romsey 28/2
POLHILL G.C., Sevenoaks 10/11
POTTED GARDEN, Maidstone 25/1
PRIMROSE NURSERY, Twyford 4/2
PRINCES G.C., Rake 30/7
PRIORY FARM, Redhill . . . . . . page 48 & 21/21
PUDDING LANE NURSERY, Reading 3/8
PUMPKIN COTTAGE, Slindon 42/8
R
RALPH'S, Maidstone 24/7
RANDLES, Knockholt 9/16
REDCLIFFE G.C., New Milton 38/5
REDFIELDS G.C., Fleet 16/3
REGGIES PLANTS, Uckfield 34/4
REIGATE G.C., Reigate 20/9
REUTHE, G. LTD, Ightman 23/3
RHS PLANT CENTRE, Wisley 19/19
RICHARD G. BAKER, Canterbury 26/9
RICHARDSON'S NURSERY, Birdham . . . 41/14
RING LODGE NURSERY, Edenbridge . . . 22/2
RINGWOULD ALPINES, Deal 27/8
RIPLEY NURSERIES, Ripley 19/1
RIVERSIDE FUCHSIAS, Sutton 10/6
RIVERSIDE NURSERIES, Chobham 5/18
RIVERSIDE NURSERY, Ower 28/5
ROBINS NURSERY, Lower Dicker 45/6
ROCKHAM NURSERY, Ewell 8/9
ROCKINGHAMS G.C., East Sheen 7/8
ROCKINGTON, Crowborough 34/5
ROGER PLATTS, Edenbridge 22/8
ROMNEY MARSH G.C., Ashford 37/3
ROSSLOW ROSES, Hellingly 45/8
ROTHERHILL, Midhurst 30/11
ROUNDSTONE G.C., Angmering 43/2
ROUNDSTONE PYO, Ferring 43/18
ROYAL MIRES, Crowborough 34/2
RUMSEY GARDENS, Waterlooville 30/4
RUMWOOD, Maidstone 25/3

RURAL CRAFTS, Winnersh 3/3
RUSHFIELDS, Poynings 44/4
RUSKIN ROAD G.C., Carshalton 8/6
RUSSELL'S G.C., Birdham 41/10
RUSSELL, W & SON LTD, Hassocks 44/5
RUSTLINGS, Horndean 40/8
RUXLEY MANOR G.C., Sidcup 9/13
RUXLEY NURSERIES, Sidcup 9/12
RYEHURST COTTAGE, Binfield 4/9
S
SANDYFIELDS, Winchester 29/6
SAUNDERS HOUSE NURSERY, Ash 27/3
SAVILL GARDEN, Windsor . . . . page 48 & 5/21
SCAYNES HILL, Haywards Heath 33/9
SEALE NURSERIES (OAK LODGE) 17/10
SECRETTS G.C., Milford 18/15
SEYMOURS, Stoke D'Abernon 19/4
SHANKS, K.R., Burwash 35/7
SHEFFIELD PARK, Uckfield 34/14
SHILLINGHURST, Sittingbourne 11/10
SHOPWHYKE, Chichester 42/4
SHRUBLANDS, Rake 30/5
SILVER SPRING, Fareham 39/17
SMARTS G.C., Sevenoaks 22/6
SNOW HILL G.C., Copthorne 21/16
SOLENT NURSERIES, Titchfield 39/16
SOUTH HOUSE G.C., Meophan 10/10
SOUTHVIEW, Eversley Cross 4/19
SPINNERS GARDEN, Lymington 38/17
SPITHANDLE NURSERY, Ashurst 43/17
SPRINGHEAD, Gravesend 10/8
SQUIRE'S G.C., Chertsey 5/8
SQUIRE'S G.C., Hersham 6/15
SQUIRE'S G.C., Shepperton 6/11
SQUIRE'S G.C., Twickenham 7/5
SQUIRE'S G.C., West Horsley 19/3
SQUIRE'S G.C., Windsor 4/12
SQUIRE'S G.C., Woking 5/15
ST. DENYS NURSERY, Angmering 43/5
ST. MARGARET'S FUCHSIAS, Fareham . . 39/7
ST. MARY'S NURSERY, Dartford 10/2
STANBRIDGE VIEW, Handcross 33/3
STAPLECROSS, Robertsbridge 36/6
STARBOROUGH, Edenbridge 22/7
STAVERTON NURSERY, Halland 34/8
STEVEN BAILEY LTD, Sway 38/9
STONE CROSS, Pevensey 46/8
STONEHURST, Ardingly 33/8
STUART'S NURSERIES, Sidcup 10/1
SUMMERFIELD NURSERIES, Staple 27/1
SUNNY RISE NURSERIES, Battle 35/8
SUSSEX COUNTRY GARDEN, Mark Cross 35/2
SUTTON GREEN, Guildford 18/7
SWAINS FARM, Henfield 44/1
SYON PARK G.C., Brentford 7/3
T
TANGLEWOOD, Wisborough Green 31/3
TANGLEY GARDENS, Guildford 18/13
TAWNY NURSERIES, Birdham 41/12
TEDDINGTON STATION G.C. 7/6
TENTERDEN G.C. 37/2
THOMMO'S FLOWERS, Sutton 8/3
THOMPSON'S NURSERY, Welling 9/9
THOMPSON'S, Chislehurst 9/10
THOMPSONS G.C., Canterbury 26/7

THORPE G.C., Horam 35/4
THREE ACRES G.C., Littlehampton 43/3
TILE BARN NURSERY, Iden Green 36/9
TITCHFIELD MILLS, Titchfield 39/10
TOOBEES EXOTICS, Woking 18/2
TORRENS G.C., Ashford 25/15
TORRENS G.C., Rochester 11/2
TREVORS NURSERY, Sandwich 27/5
TUTTS BARN, Eastbourne 46/7
U
UCKHAM LANE NURSERY, Battle 36/1
UPLANDS FUCHSIA NURSERY, Battle . . 46/10
USUAL & UNUSUAL PLANTS, Hailsham . . 46/5
V
VALLEY NURSERIES, Alton 15/10
VERMEULEN'S G.C., Staines 5/2
VERNON GERANIUMS, Cheam 8/8
VICARAGE HILL, Hartley Wintey 16/2
VICTORIANA NURSERY, Challock page 48 & 26/5
VILLAGE NURSERIES, Chiltington 32/1
VINCENT NURSERIES, Herne Bay 13/2
W
WALKERS, South Godstone 21/9
WALLABIES, Wisborough Green 31/5
WALNUT HILL NURSERY, Gravesend . . . 10/9
WARMLAKE NURSERY, Maidstone 25/5
WARRENORTH, North Chailey 34/13
WASHFIELD NURSERY, Hawkhurst 36/2
WASHINGTON G.C., Washington 43/14
WATER MEADOW, Alresford 29/13
WAVERLEY NURSERIES, Gillingham 11/8
WEATHERLEY, Sidcup 9/11
WESTERHAM HEIGHTS NURSERY 22/1
WESTMOOR FARM, Rainham 11/11
WHEELER STREET NURSERY, Witley . . 18/16
WHITE TOWER, Aldermaston 2/7
WHITEWATER NURSERY, Hook 3/11
WILLINGDON G.C., Eastbourne 45/11
WILLOUGHBY'S NURSERIES, Oxshott . . . 7/13
WILLOW TREE NURSERY, Lingfield 21/13
WINDMILL NURSERY, Mereworth 24/1
WOBURN HILL NURSERY, Weybridge . . . 6/13
WOKING NURSERY, Woking 18/4
WOKING NURSERY, Woking 18/5
WOKINGHAM G.C., Wokingham 4/16
WONDER NURSERIES, Wallington 8/19
WOODCOTE GREEN, Wallington 8/11
WOODHAM, South Godstone 21/7
WOODLAND, Sevenoaks 10/12
WOODSIDE FARM, Hermitage 2/1
WOODSTOCK G.C., Long Ditton 7/11
WYEVALE G.C., Bracknell 4/8
WYEVALE G.C., Bromley 9/8
WYEVALE G.C., Canterbury 26/2
WYEVALE G.C., Crawley 21/11
WYEVALE G.C., Findon 43/10
WYEVALE G.C., Gillingham 11/3
WYEVALE G.C., Lewes 44/8
WYEVALE G.C., Morden 8/2
WYEVALE G.C., Tonbridge 24/9
WYEVALE G.C., West Drayton 6/2
WYEVALE G.C., Wokingham 4/17
WYLD COURT RAINFOREST, Newbury . . 2/11
Y
YEW TREE FARM G.C., Newbury 1/4

INDEX

WATER GARDEN SPECIALISTS

AIRPORT AQUARIA, West Drayton 6/4
AQUARIUM & POND CENTRE, Copthorne 21/17
AQUARIUM & POND CENTRE, Hounslow . 6/21
AQUASCAPE, Hermitage 2/3
ARCHER-WILLS, West Chiltington 32/15
CROFT WATER GARDENS, Pevensey. . . . 46/3
D.H.WATER GARDENS, Sherfield-on-Loddon 4/4
EGMONT W.G.C., Tolworth 7/16
ENGLISH W.G.C., Washington 43/14
EVERTON W.G.C., Lymington 39/21
HORSHAM W.G.C., Horsham 32/14
JUNGLE AQUATICS, Sunbury 6/22
KOI WATER BARN, Chelsfield 9/19

LISS PET & AQUATIC CENTRE, Liss 30/9
LOCKSACRE AQUATICS, Birdham 41/18
MILL WATER GARDENS, Romsey 28/11
MOSS END W.G.C., Warfield. 4/5
NEWLAKE GARDENS, Copthorne 21/18
NISHIKIGOI CENTRE, Hawkhurst. 36/16
SOUTH EAST W.G.C., Sandwich 27/6
SUNNINGDALE W.G.C., Windlesham 4/26
SWALLOW AQUATICS, Gravesend 10/15
TROPIKOI, Bognor 42/16
WATER MEADOW, Alresford 29/13
WATERLIFE, West Drayton. 5/19
WATERSIDE AQUATICS, Lingfield 21/19

WINCHESTER W.G.C., Winchester 29/3
WORLD OF KOI, Bromley 9/18
WORLD OF WATER, Angwering. 43/4
WORLD OF WATER, Chertsey 5/20
WORLD OF WATER, Croydon 9/17
WORLD OF WATER, Halisham 45/12
WORLD OF WATER, Reading. 3/12
WORLD OF WATER, Rolvenden. 36/15
WORLD OF WATER, Romsey 28/10
WORLD OF WATER, Worth. 33/12
WYCHWOOD WATERLILIES, Odiham 16/9

GARDEN ARTEFACT SUPPLIERS

BOURNE BUILDINGS, Farnham. 17/3
DOMA FARM, Uckfield. 34/15
GARDEN CRAFTS, Biddenden. 25/16
I VASI TERRACOTTA, Bickley 9/21
JARDINIQUE, Grateham 30/12
NEW DAWN FURNITURE, Emsworth. . . . 41/1

POTS AND PITHOI, Turners Hill 33/13
PRIMA POTS, Tonbridge. 23/15
RUNFOLD LANDSCAPES, Runfold 17/2
STUDIO FORGE, Lewes 44/11
SUSSEX TRUGS, Herstmonceux 46/13
THE TRUGGERY, Herstmonceux 46/12

VILLAGE POTTERY, Dulwich 9/20
WHELANS, Sheerness . . . . page 49 & 12/9
WILDERNESS WOOD, Uckfield 34/20
WOODLANDS NURSERY, Guildford . . . 18/18

PICK-YOUR-OWN FARMS

A
ALBOURNE FARM PYO, Hassocks 44/10
ALDERS FIELD, Mereworth 24/11
ARTURI'S G.C., Eastleigh 29/11
AVALON NURSERIES, Churt 17/15
B
BARTRAM. W & SON, Carshalton 8/13
BEECHINWOOD FARM, St Mary's Platt. . 23/12
BOURNE VALLEY PYO, Andover. 14/4
BREDGAR PYO & FARM SHOP 12/6
BROOKFIELD FARM, Petworth 31/10
BUCKHOLDHILL FARM, Pangbourne 2/10
C
CHERRY GARDENS, Groombridge 34/16
CHURCH FARM, Hersham 6/20
CHURCHFIELD FARM, West Chiltington. 32/16
COUNTRY MARKET, Borden 16/7
CROCKFORD BRIDGE, Addlestone. 6/18
D
DOWNINGBURY PYO FARM, Pembury . . 23/13
DURLEIGHMARSH PYO, Petersfield 30/13
F
FLOWER FARM, Godstone. 21/20
FOUR OAKS FIELD PYO, Faversham. . . . 12/7
FRESHFIELDS PYO, Hastings 47/5
G
GANGER FARM PYO, Romsey. 28/12
GARSON FARM, Esher 6/19

GORE FARM PYO, Sittingbourne. 11/12
GRAYS PYO FARM, Wokingham 4/28
H
HAMSTEAD GROWERS, Newbury. 1/8
HAZELCOPSE FARM , Beaulieu. 38/16
HEATHFIELD FARM , Selsdon 9/22
HEATHLANDS FARM, Wokingham. 4/29
HEWITTS FARM, Orpington 9/23
HIGHCLOSE PYO, Hungerford. 1/7
HOLLAM NURSERIES, Titchfield 39/15
HOW LANE FARM, Maidenhead. 4/27
HYDE ORCHARDS, Churt 17/14
L
LITTLE CROCKSHARD, Canterbury 27/11
LOWER HOCKENDEN PYO, Swanley . . . 10/16
LOWER MOUNT FARM, Maidenhead. 0/4
M
MACNADE PYO, Faversham. 12/8
MANOR FARM, Farnham. 17/8
MEADOW FARM PYO, Lower Dicker 45/15
MORTIMER HILL FRUIT, Reading. 3/13
N
NORTH LOOE FRUIT FARM, Ewell. 8/20
NUTBERRY FRUIT FARM, Ripley 19/13
NUTHILL FRUIT FARM, Guilford 19/14
O
OAST FARM, Buxted 34/17
OCKLEY COURT FARM, Ockley 20/13

P
PARK HOUSE PYO, Old Arlesford 29/15
PATERNOSTERS FRUIT, Warninglid . . . 33/14
PERRYHILL ORCHARD, Hartfield. 22/11
PIPPINS FRUIT, Tunbridge Wells 23/14
PRIORY FARM, Redhill . . . . . . page 48 & 21/21
R
ROCK FARM, Washington 43/20
ROOKERY WOOD FRUIT, Seaford 45/13
ROUNDSTONE PYO, Ferring 43/18
RUNCTON FARM PYO, Runcton 42/17
S
SECRETTS PYO, Milford. 18/15
SEPHAM FARM, Shoreham, Kent 10/17
SHARNFOLD FARM, Pevensey 46/11
SILVERHILL COBNUTS, Tonbridge 23/11
SPRING GARDENS PYO, Washington. . . 43/19
SUTTON GREEN, Guildford 18/7
T
TESTON FARM STALL, Maidstone. 24/12
TULLENS FRUIT FARM, Pulborough 31/11
TULLEYS FARM, Turners Hill   page 48 & 33/15
TUTTI FRUTTI PYO, Seaford. 45/14
W
WAKEHAMS PYO, Hastings 47/4
WESTMOOR FARM, Rainham. 11/11
WESTON APPLE FARM, Nutbourne. 41/2
WHERWELL FARM PYO, Andover. 14/5
WILLOW FARM PYO, Andover 14/3